# Readings in the Economics of the Division of Labor: The Classical Tradition

## Increasing Returns and Inframarginal Economics

**Series Editors:** James Buchanan, Yew-Kwang Ng, (Xiaokai Yang)
**Associate Editor:** Guang-Zhen Sun

---

*Published*

Vol. 1 *An Inframarginal Approach to Trade Theory*
Edited by Xiaokai Yang, Wenli Cheng, Heling Shi & Christis G. Tombazos

Vol. 2 *Readings in the Economics of the Division of Labor: The Classical Tradition*
Edited by Guang-Zhen Sun

Increasing Returns and Inframarginal Economics - Vol. 2

# Readings in the Economics of the Division of Labor:

## The Classical Tradition

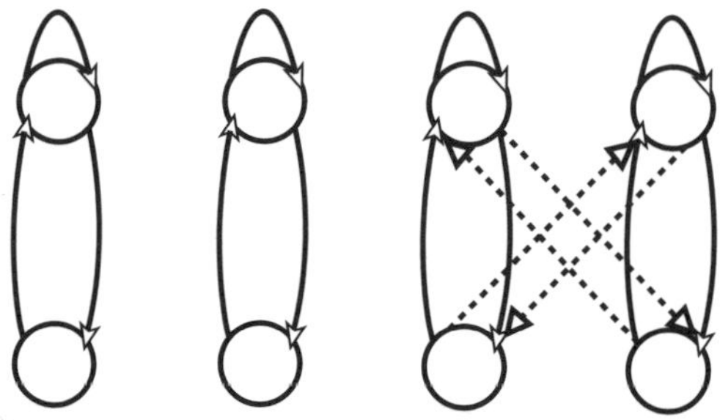


edited by

Guang-Zhen Sun

Monash University, Australia



World Scientific

NEW JERSEY • LONDON • SINGAPORE • BEIJING • SHANGHAI • HONG KONG • TAIPEI • CHENNAI

*Published by*

World Scientific Publishing Co. Pte. Ltd.
5 Toh Tuck Link, Singapore 596224
*USA office:* 27 Warren Street, Suite 401-402, Hackensack, NJ 07601
*UK office:* 57 Shelton Street, Covent Garden, London WC2H 9HE

**British Library Cataloguing-in-Publication Data**
A catalogue record for this book is available from the British Library.

**READINGS IN THE ECONOMICS OF THE DIVISION OF LABOR: THE CLASSICAL TRADITION**



ISBN 981-256-124-2

Printed in Singapore.

# Preface

Since the late 1970s ---- about half a century after Sraffa's (1926, *The Economic Journal*) devastating analysis of the notorious difficulty in accommodating increasing returns into a competitive equilibrium framework ---- there has been an increasing interest in economics of specialization and the division of labor, which is deservedly referred to as "Return to Increasing Returns" (James Buchanan and Yong J. Yoon (Eds.), *The Return to Increasing Returns*. University of Michigan Press 1994). That may be not surprising, for the division of labor is necessarily associated with increasing returns. Only quite recently did economic theorists successfully demonstrate the comparability between generalized increasing returns to the division of labor and competitive equilibrium. Some authors even simply discard the general equilibrium framework altogether in studying the progressive division of labor by instead working with alternative evolutionary models.

Regardless of the difference and/or disagreement in methodology and emphasis among students of the division of labor, the profound implications of the emergent order of the division of labor from within the economic system for economic progress in general has been recognized and explored by more and more economists in the recent two decades (see, e.g., Buchanan and Yoon 1994; Kenneth Arrow etc. (eds.) *Increasing Returns and Economic Analysis*. Macmillan 1998; and Geoffrey Heal (ed.), *The Economics of Increasing Returns,* Edward Elgar 1999). Yet, much more remains to be understood, and it may be fair to say that the study of the (progressive) division of labor is still a burgeoning industry. In fact, some authors (e.g., George Stigler 1976,

*Journal of Political Economy*) go as far as to predict that topics related to the division of labor may keep economists busy for many decades to come.

On the other hand, classical authors, even dating back as early as 500 BC have indeed made insightful analyses on the determinants and implications of the division of labor, which unfortunately are rather scattered and not readily accessible to many economists who have great interest in the economics of specialization. The project of *Readings of Economics of the Division of Labor*, of which this book is the first volume, aims to fill this void in the book market, serving as a reference for scholars interested in the division of labor. Under this *Readings* project, three volumes will be edited. Volume One, the current one, covers the Classical Tradition, dating from Xenophon and Plato till the modern Austrian economics represented by F. A. Hayek in 1930s-1940s. Volume Two puts together selected modern economic analyses largely since post WWII till the early 2000s. Volume Three focuses on theories and insights contributed from neighboring disciplines including sociology, philosophy, anthropology, etc. The three volumes, complementary though as they stand, are largely independent from one another, and each can therefore be used independently for its own interest.

This volume begins with the precursors of political economy including the ancient Greeks, medieval Islamic scholastics and mercantilists, continues with the classical political economists and the neoclassicists, and concludes with Hayek's economics of dispersed knowledge well into 1940s. It covers major themes and perspectives about the division of labor that have emerged in the discipline of the economic science till WWII. As such, it is intended that this volume can well serve as a handy reference book for economists of the division of labor, as well as a supplementary text on courses in history of economic thought, labor economics, development economics, etc. for both the graduate and undergraduate levels.

No "Readings" book can claim to be comprehensive. This book is no exception. Indeed, bearing in mind that a book on the classical tradition in economics of the division of labor can never be exhaustive in coverage due to the very nature of the topic, we intentionally make this book rather selective and short, in the hope that the reader can thereby readily grasp the main themes in classical studies of division of labor. We must apologize for omission of any pieces that appear important to some readers.

Minor alternations, exclusively in style, have been made in several chapters from their original sources, dating centuries back, not only for purpose of consistency but also for convenience in modern readership.

*G.-Z. Sun*
Dec. 2004

# Acknowledgement

The editor should like to thank the following for permission to reproduce copyright material:

Xenophon, *Oeconomicus*, Translated by Sarah B. Pomeroy, Clarendon Press. Oxford, 1994, pp.141, 143, 145 and 147.

Plato, *Complete Works*, Edited by John M. Cooper and D. S. Hutchinson, Hackett Publishing Company, Inc., 1997, book II, p1008–13.

Aristotle, *The Works of Aristotle*, Vol. X, Edited by W. D. Ross, Benjamin Jowett, E. S. Forster and Frederic G. Kenyon, Clarendon Press. Oxford, 1921, book I, p1257a–1257b

Ibn Khald n, *The Muqaddimah: An Introduction to History, 3 Volumes,* Translated by Franz Rosenthal. Bollingen Series XLIII, Pantheon Books, New York, 1958, Vol.1, pp. 89-90; and Vol.2, pp. 271-2, 276-8, 313-4, 346-7 and 351.

Bernard Mandeville, *The Fable of The Bees*: *or, Private Vices, Publick Benefits*, With a Commentary Critical, Historical, and Explanatory by F. B. Kaye, Clarendon Press. Oxford, 1957, VOL. 1, pp356-8; VOL. 2, pp.141–7, p284

Adam Ferguson, *An Essay on the History of Civil Society,* Edited by Fania OZ-Salzberger, Cambridge University Press, 1995, pp172–5.

Adam Smith, *An Inquiry into the Nature and Causes of the Wealth of Nations*, Edited by R. H. Campbell, A. S. Skinner and W. B. Todd, Clarendon Press, Oxford, 1976, Vol. 1, pp. 13-44, 277, 377-8, 446-8; and Vol. 2, pp.781-4 (text only, without notes).

Charles Babbage, *The Economy of Machinery and Manufactures*, Edited by Martin Campbell-Kelly, William Pickering, London, 1989, Volume 8, pp121–5, 130-40 and 143.

Karl Marx, *Capital*, Translated by Ben Fowkes, Penguin Books in association with New Left Review (Edition and Notes copyright holder), 1976, Volume One, pp. 470–80.

Alfred Marshall, *Principles of Economics*, Alfred Marshall, Ninth Edition, Macmillan and Co Limited, New York, 1961, pp.240–1, 250-66 and 318–22.

Piero Sraffa, "The Laws of returns under Competitive Conditions", *The Economic Journal* (Blackwell Publishing), No. 144(Vol. XXXVI December 1926), pp. 535–50.

Allyn Young, "Increasing Returns and Economic Progress", *The Economic Journal* (Blackwell Publishing), No.152(Vol. XXXVIII 1928), pp.527–42.

Carl Menger, "*On the Origin of Money*", *The Economic Journal* (Blackwell Publishing), No.6 (Vol. II 1892), pp. 239–55.

Friedrich A. Hayek, "The Use of Knowledge in Society", *American Economic Review (*the American Economic Association), No.4 (Vol. XXXV September 1945), pp. 519–30.

Every effort has been made to contact copyright holders but if any have been inadvertently overlooked the editor will be grateful to be informed and thereby to make the necessary arrangement at the first opportunity.

Excellent research assistance from Miss Ye Deng and Mr. Dean Liu, especially in preparing the camera-ready manuscript copy of the book, is greatly appreciated. My thanks also go to Chean Chian Cheong and Yubing Zhai of the World Scientific Publishing Co. for their support and assistance with this project. Of course, neither of them holds responsibility for any remaining errors. The editor should also like to gratefully acknowledge the support from the Logan Fellowship and the Research Committee of Department of Economics, both at Monash University.

# Contents

Emergence of Political Economy of the Division of Labor



## Part III. Classical Political Economy

# Part I. Introduction

## Chapter 1

# The Economics of Division of Labor from Xenophon to Hayek (1945): A Review of Selected Literature*

**Guang-Zhen Sun**

**By means of the old, we come to know the new. ----- Confucius**

This introductory chapter is not intended to be comprehensive in its coverage. Rather, partially due to the space constraint, imposed on an introduction of a *Readings* book of such a modest size as the present volume, it focuses on a deliberately selected body of studies on the division of labor ranging from Xenophon to Hayek (1945) as represented by those reproduced in this volume, with particular attention paid to what I believe has been relatively unknown among economists of specialization. A more systematic examination, covering hundreds of studies on the division of labor by ancient Greeks, ancient Chinese, medieval Islamic scholars, medieval Latin scholasticists and Anglo-Europeans of recent centuries is found in Sun (2005).

But what is the (commonly accepted definition of) division of labor? The one that Peter Groenewegen uses for the entry "division of labor" in *New Palgrave's Dictionary of Economics* (1987, p.901) may be accepted

* The author thanks James Buchanan, Yew-Kwang Ng and Russell Smyth for helpful comments on an earlier draft of this article. The usual caveat applies.

by overwhelmingly most, if not all, economists: "The division of labor may be defined as the division of a process or employment into parts, each of which is carried out by a separate person." That is, individuals cooperate, consciously or not, to undertake a divisible process or employment. As such, there naturally emerge two fundamental questions: Why, and how does the separation of employment among persons bear upon important economic and social consequences? In fact, the studies to be surveyed below that emerged over twenty-five centuries or so up to WWII basically centre round the above questions.

We will first of all map out the evolution of ideas about division of labor up to the classical political economy in Sections I and II. For the body of economic analysis was considerably enriched since then, with different schools/perspectives simultaneously developing and sometimes competing with one another, we will focus on three themes, explored respectively by three most influential schools that have made contributions of lasting value to the economics of the division of labor. Section III examines the idea of mutual interdependence between increasing returns to the division of labor and the extent of the market originating from Smith, substantiated by Wakefield, Mill, Marshall and culminating in Young (1928). Section IV focuses on the division of labor in society and the division of labor in manufacture, on which Marx offers important insights, foreshadowing some modern theories of the firm well into 1990s. Analyses of unfavorable sociological consequences of the division of labor are also briefly surveyed in this section. Finally, Section V examines literature on the overarching theme of the spontaneous order, which can be traced back to Mandeville and was later on elaborated by the Scottish Enlightenment men, and the Austrians especially Hayek. Indeed, the Austrians not only developed a general theory of the spontaneous order but also applied it to analyses of many issues that are concomitant with the division of labor, in particularly the origin of money and the socio-economics of dispersed knowledge.

## I. Greek Origins, Medieval Islamic Wisdom and Schumpeter's "Great Gap" Thesis

The idea of increasing returns to specialization is old. At the latest, ancient Greek philosophers, dated from Democritus (460BC - 370BC), had already brought it to the fore in their socio-economic discourses.[1] In the writings of Xenophon and Plato in particular, two most important insights of the division of labor that Adam Smith (1776) famously articulated about two millennium later, namely increasing returns to labor specialization and the division of labor being limited by the extent of the market, figured prominently. Xenophon clearly perceived the association of the size of the city in terms of inhabitants with the division of labor in illustrating why a larger city, compared to a smaller one, allows for greater division of occupations and thus renders products of both a finer quality and a larger quantity (Cyropaedia, pp 244-5, reproduced in Ch 2 of the present volume; all the chapter numbers mentioned hereafter refer to those in this volume unless specified otherwise). In particular, gains from the division of labor are exemplified by cooking for the king in Xenophon (Ch 2). Furthermore, Xenophon discussed in somewhat details the sexual division of labor within a family, a topic that was to be picked up by Thomas Hodgskin (1827) and Marxists in the 19th century and nicely integrated into a neoclassical theory of human capital in the 20th century (e.g., Becker 1985).

Similar to Xenophon, Plato (Ch 3) also based his theory of the emergence and development of the city on the notion of increasing returns to the division of labor. Indeed, Plato developed, quite consciously, a theory of how a city emerges and then grows by exploiting the gains from the division of labor and saving on trading costs.[2] Perhaps more remarkably, in Plato's model growth of a city leads

---

[1] It may be fair to say that Democritus is the first among the Greeks to recognize the intrinsic connection between the division of labor and the division of resources as well as the efficiency implications of private ownership (refer to, e.g., Gordon (1975), p.4, and Landreth and Colander (1994), pp 21-35.)

[2] The idea of agglomeration economies originating from the division of labor still plays a key role in the urban economics literature of the 1990s based on increasing returns, which is prominently represented by the so-called New Economic Geography (see, e.g., Yang and Rice 1994, Fujita et al 1999).

to emergence of professional merchants, *a legal system and army* among other new occupations, thus anticipating what Rosenberg (1976) refers to as "another advantage of the division of labor" in Smith's economic system. As a matter of fact, Plato's conception of social division of labor in some important aspects bears resemblance to what were to be powerfully developed by Smith among other classical economists. In a very intriguing study of the possible influence the Greek philosophers had on Smith's theory of the division of labor, Foley (1974) has gone so far as to suggest "that Smith could have gotten his original inspiration from the division of labor principle, not from the sources usually cited in this connection --- the Encyclopédie, Harris, Locke, Mun, or Mandeville – but from the ancient Greeks" (pp.221-2), notably from Plato who "provides Smith with important initial inspirations" (p.235) to Smith's theory of progressive division of labor in connection with his four-stage societal evolution. For a discussion on the fundamental difference between the two men, however, see McNulty (1975).

Although it is already rightly pointed out in Plato (Ch 3) that the double coincidence problem of wants between buyers and sellers in the marketplace gives rise to currency, it is Aristotle (Ch 4) who offered a vivid illustration of the origin of barter money and its evolution into fiat money. Aristotle articulated the necessity of money in maintaining the network of social (inter-household) exchange of commodities. It may be worth emphasizing that Aristotle's analysis of the function of money is rooted in his focus on the trade between households in his city-state setting, rather than the genuine market exchange between a good number of sellers and buyers.[1]

Perhaps not surprisingly, the Greeks are not the only ones, even at their time, to observe the phenomenon of increasing returns to labor specialization. For instance, in ancient China at roughly the same time of Plato, Mencius (390BC-305BC), and a bit later on, Hsün Tsu (Xun Kuang), both argued for the necessity and significance of the social division of labor, and the division between mental labor and manual labor. (refer to, e.g., Hu 1988, pp. 65-66 and pp 167-8).

---

[1] For a cogently presented analysis of how the philosopher significantly influenced, and was on occasions misinterpreted by, the medieval Latin Scholastics, see Gordon (1993).

Schumpeter's (1954) "Great Gap" thesis, stating that very little if any was achieved in economic analysis during the several centuries before the rise of Latin Scholastics in the 13th century, has been challenged in recent decades by Essid (1987), Ghazanfar (2000) and Hosseini (1998) among others. It is widely known among students of medieval cultures that medieval Islam played a crucial role in the intellectual movement originating from the Greeks and eventually resulting in the rise of European Scholastics. As documented in Philip Hitti's (1970/2002) monumental volume, the "rediscovery" of Aristotlian scholarship and the renaissance of Europe would have been simply unimaginable but for the intellectual contribution by medieval Islamic scholarship which had a definitive influence on St Albert the Great and St Thomas Aquinas (and thereby on later generations of scholars including political economists, see below): when "Europe was almost totally ignorant of Greek thought and science", the Islamic scholars during "the great epoch of translation" (mid 8th century to mid 9th century) had already got well acquainted with, and further developed, Aristotlian scholarship (2002, p. 315).

As far as the economics of the division of labor is concerned, it seems that medieval Islamic scholarship was absorbed by the Latin Scholastics, without due acknowledgement though, thereby exerting influence on Mercantilists and classical political economists including Adam Smith (see, e.g., Essid 1987 and Hosseini 1998). As is nicely demonstrated in Hosseini (1988, pp 667-673), social division of labor was discussed by Fārābi (875-50), sexual division of labor by Ibn Sīna (Avicenna 980-1037) and Tusi (1201-1274), and most prominently, a more general treatment by al-Ghazali (1058-1111), "unquestionably the greatest theologian of Islam and one of its noblest and most original thinkers" (Hitti 2002, p.431). Al-Ghazali appears to have well understood the interrelation between market exchange and the division of labor. More impressively, al-Ghazali's theory of vertical division of labor strikingly resembles Adam Smith's in an interesting manner. In his most important book, *Ihya Ulum al-Din* (Revivification of the Sciences of Religion), paralleling to, and constituting an influence on, St Thomas Aquinas' *Summa Theologica* (Ghazanfar 2000, pp.863-4), al-Ghazali wrote explicitly on the division of labor,

> "For a bread, for example, first the farmer prepares and cultivates the land, then the bullock and tools are needed to plough the land. Then the land is irrigated. It is cleared from weeds, then the crop is harvested and grains are cleaned and separated. Then there is milling into flour before baking. Just imagine – how many tasks are involved; and we here mention just only some. And imagine the number of people performing these various tasks, and the number of various kinds of tools, made from iron, wood, stone, etc. If one inquires, one will find that perhaps a single loaf of bread takes its final shape with the help of perhaps more than a thousand workers" (*Ihya*, 4:118; quoted in Ghazanfar and Islahi 1990, p. 390).

In further articulating the gains from, and necessary coordination in, the manufacture division of labor, al-Ghazali took needle production as an example, "even the small needle becomes useful only after passing through the hands of needle-makers about twenty-five times, each time going through a different process" (*Ihya*, 4:119; quoted in Ghazanfar and Islahi 1990, p. 390). As it happened, al-Ghazanfar's needle example well resembles the French Encyclopédie's "Epingle" (1750s) production (consisting of eighteen separate processes), from which Smith's famous pin-factory story is taken (see below).

We now turn to another towering figure of Islamic thought, Ibn Khaldūn (1332-1406), whose *The Muqaddimah: An Introduction to History* (1402) firmly established himself as "the greatest historical philosopher Islam produced and one of the greatest of all time" (Hitti 2002, p.568). This man is perhaps one of the most original minds in social sciences in general and in economic sciences in particular across all human civilizations. His deep insights into the socio-economic dynamics, that the driving forces of historical change come from within the present social structures, long anticipated the Scots, Karl Marx, Joseph Schumpeter and Mancur Olson (see, e.g., Kuran 1987, pp108-110) and he has been deservedly claimed as one forerunner of a great number of European thinkers in socio-politics and historical philosophy. In the field of economics at large, his contributions have nonetheless been considerably under-estimated relative to what they deserve. As demonstrated in Boulakia (1971) and Soofi (1995), Ibn Khaldūn can be well claimed in economics as a forerunner of Ricardo and Marx in labor theory of value, of Malthus in population theory, of Keynes in the theory of the expenditure multiplier, and most relevant to our purpose here, of Smith in the theory of the division of labor. We reproduce in Ch 5 of this volume only a number of deliberately selected paragraphs from his masterpiece *The Muqaddimah*, from which emerges a coherent division of labor theory of production. Anticipating Turgot (1769-70) and Smith (1776), Ibn Khaldūn (1402) starts with analysis of the prerequisite and formation of civilization in his opening sentences of chapter one in *The Muqaddimah* by emphasizing the necessity of, and gains from, the division of labor. Later on, in chapters V and VI, which are largely about what centuries later was referred to as political economy, he cogently demonstrated that the division of labor facilitated by a larger market leads to higher productivity and renders products cheaper. Effectively developing a labor theory of value, he further argued that capital has to be understood essentially as a realized value from previous labor, and that capital, as intermediate products in the linkage of vertical production, in turn enhances further labor productivity. As such, his capital theory resembles Smith, Ricardo, and more strikingly, Marx. Nonetheless, Ibn Khaldūn, not trapped in the labor theory of value, on a number of occasions, as shown in Ch 5, explicitly talked about both demand and supply sides in the price determination. His observation of the enormous, positive impact of production and consumption of luxury goods on the division of labor and social civilization anticipated Mandeville and French Encyclopédists.[1] He also illustrated why the wage of the skilled laborer is higher in a larger city than otherwise.[2]

## II. Emergence of Political Economy of the Division of Labor

More direct precursors of Smith on doctrines of the division of labor of course are Petty, Mandeville, Hutcheson and the French Encyclopédists

---

1 See, e.g., Goldsmith (1988) for an analysis of Mandeville's thesis on luxury consumption. On the debate between Diderot and his fellow encyclopedists on the good or bad effects of luxury goods, see, e.g., Lough (1989, pp.350-4).

2 To reflect on the development of the modern literature of human capital, note that Gary Becker complains as late as the mid-1960s that "surprisingly little attention has been paid to ... the influence of market size on the incentives to invest in skills" (1964, p.52).

among others. William Petty used the production of clothes, watches and ships as telling examples to illustrate gains from specialization of labor (Ch 6). Henry Martyn (the mysterious "anonymous" author of the well known pamphlet *Considerations on the East-India Trade* 1701)[1], taking his cue from Petty and the brilliant mercantilist Dudley North (1691), also used examples of making cloth, ships and watches to show the productivity implication of the division of labor. Incidentally, both also touch upon the issue of specialization of machinery, while Martyn (1701) seems to be much more aware of its far-reaching consequences, especially in bringing "more order and regularity into manufactures" (Ch 7), which is more often referred to as "standardization (of products)" in the literature nowadays. This theme was later further explored by Charles Babbage, Andrew Ure and John S. Mill among others (see below). As is widely known, Mandeville (Ch 8) coined the very term "division of labor" and exemplified its significance by taking, once again, the instance of cloth-making.[2] Hutcheson (1755; Ch 10) articulated the necessity of the division of labor and cooperation for civilized society.

The extent to which Smith's celebrated division of labor principle was directly inspired by the French Encyclopédie has long been a focus of controversy. It cannot be denied after all that the three major advantages of labor specialization Smith (1776; reproduced in Ch 13) famously identified --- namely, increase in dexterity in every particular workman, saving of time in passing from one job to another, and invention of machines (technical progress) --- have figured out clearly in Encyclopédie (1971; Ch 9). In particular, as to the well known example of pin-making that Smith used to illustrate the efficiency implication of the division of labor, Edwin Cannan remarked that,

> "In Adam Smith's *Lecture*, p. 164, the business is, as here, divided into eighteen operations. This number is doubtless taken from the *Encyclopédie*, tom.v (published in 1755), s.v. Épingle. The article is ascribed to M. Delaire, 'qui décrivait la fabrication de l'épingle dans les ateliers même des

---

[1] MacLeod (1983) cogently presents an identification of the authorship of the widely read pamphlet as Henry Martyn.

[2] For an interesting analysis of the extent to which Mandeville might derive his division of labor principle from Plato, see pp 235-8 in Foley (1974).

> ouvriers,' p.807. In some factories the division was carried further. E. Chambers, *Cyclopedia*, vol. ii, 2nd ed., 1738, and 4th ed., 1741, s.v., Pin., makes the number of separate operations twenty-five." (The Wealth of Nations, edited by E. Cannan, Methuen, 1950, p.8, footnote 4).

As Lough (1970, p.17) rightly points out, it is an extremely tricky business to figure out what source and how much Diderot and his colleagues drew on from the English encyclopaedias, and so is the matter as to how much the English encyclopaedia in turn derived from the non-English sources. But Chambers'(1941) *Cyclopaedia* may most likely be credited as one source for the French Encyclopédia. Note, however, as mentioned above, in al-Ghazali's needle-factory example, the number of separate operations is also twenty-five, an interesting coincidence to Chambers' story. Another interesting facet of the pin-factory episode is that the French Encyclopédia's pin example, as well as the derived principle of the division of labor, finds its original source decades earlier, in the brilliant German scholar Ernst Ludwig Carl's (1682-1743) three-volume *Treatise* (1722-3), an overlooked original theorist in the history of economic thought, who seems to be well aware of the gains from labor specialization as well as the profound implication of market size for the division of labor in manufacture. Incidentally, Carl mentioned both needle and pin factories when exemplifying the effect of manufacture division of labor (Hutchison 1988, pp 160-3 and footnote 2 on p.396).

Both Ferguson (1767; Ch11) and Turgot (1769-70; Ch12) contain important insights into the crucial role played by the division of labor in social civilization and socio-economic development, thus giving rise to two much debated controversies over priority of the division of labor principle, namely the "Turgot-Smith myth" (termed by Edwin Cannan, see Groenewegen 1969, p.271, footnote 3) and the "Ferguson-Smith controversy". The opening chapters of Turgot (1769-70) focus on economies of the division of labor, strikingly resembling Smith's *magnum opus* published a few years later. There also exists similarity in the theoretical frameworks between the two books. These, in addition to personal acquaintance and correspondence between the two men, give rise, naturally, to speculations and controversies over the priority of Smith (1776). We do not intend to delve into this controversy and related literature here. Interested readers may refer to, for instance, Groenewegen's (1969) nice treatment and references therein. Groenewegen's scrutiny of the two authors' writings and historical evidence of contact between the two men suggests that the charge against Smith is not well grounded despite the similarity between their books, for they appear to be inspired by the same group of scholars' writings, namely, Locke, Cantillon, Hume and Quesnay (Groenewegen 1969, p.287). As to the Ferguson-Smith controversy over the priority of the division of labor doctrine, see, e.g., Hamowy (1968), which demonstrates that Smith's charge of plagiarism against Ferguson's (1767; Ch 11) analysis of the division of labor can not hold. Nor does the opposite suggestion, made by Karl Marx among others, that Smith borrowed Ferguson's theory of the division of labor without giving due credit. I can only concur with Hamowy that it is Ferguson who had developed a penetrating analysis of the far-reaching *sociological* consequences of the division of labor, which afterwards, interestingly, served as a major inspiration to two fundamentally different figures: Marx and Hayek.

As Smith's celebrated economics of the division of labor is well known, we make only a few points below. Firstly, it cannot be denied that it is Smith who made the greatest contribution to the economics of the division of labor even in the light of penetrating insights of forerunners including Plato, Ibn Khaldūn and Mandeville as mentioned earlier, for only in Smith's hand was the division of labor assigned *the* central role in the system of economic analysis and did economic science *per se* emerge as a systematic scientific enterprise under such an overarching theme. Schumpeter's (1954, p.187) oft-cited remarks contain elements of truth of particular relevance, at a certain measure of exaggeration, as to the treatment of the division of labor in Smith (1776), "there is nothing original about it, one feature must be mentioned that has not received the attention it deserves: nobody, either before or after A. Smith, ever thought of putting such a burden upon division of labor. With A. Smith, it is practically the only factor in economic progress". As is widely known among students of history of ideas in social sciences, it is often both tedious and less fruitful than one would initially expect to trace *the* original source of virtually any idea, testified by the commonsense contained in the proverb, "nothing is new under the sun", which we deliberately take as the title of Part II of this book. To put many old ideas into a well framed, novel scientific superstructure itself is a most important achievement and deserves the highest credit. Secondly, Smith does differ from his forerunners in an important way. The intellectual powerfulness of his mind well allows for a *coherently* and *systematically* presented scientific theory of labor specialization that contains many brilliant ideas, which perhaps were well known to a good number of his contemporaries and earlier authors, but whose importance remains to be illustrated and more fully appreciated. For instance, in Smith's theory of the division of labor, differences between individuals of different occupations, "is not upon many occasions so much the cause, as the effect of the division of labor" (Ch 13). As such, the Smithian endogenous comparative advantage sharply differs from many, including notions attributed to Plato and other Greeks, before him as well as many influential ones like the Ricardian exogenous comparative advantage as the cause of division of labor (Ch14) after him. This difference, subtle as it is, has been already noticed, but perhaps more needs to be drawn on its far-reaching implications for understanding politico-philosophy, economic development, international trade, government intervention, etc. (Cf. McNulty 1975, Foley 1975, Yang 1994, Buchanan and Yoon 2000 and Buchanan 2005). The last point we should like to make here is that in elaborating on "old" ideas Smith realized some deep, hitherto often overlooked, connection among different aspects of potential gains from the division of labor. A case in point is his clear perception of the inter-dependence between the division of labor and the extent of the market, to which we shall immediately turn in the next section.

## III. Extent of the Market, Increasing Returns and the Division of Labor: From Adam Smith to Allyn Young

The idea that the division of labor is limited by the extent of the market, as mentioned above, has long before Smith figured in the writings of Xenophon, Plato and Ibn Khaldūn. Incidentally, the authors, as well as Smith and quite a few other classical political economists, all relate the population size, in the city in particular, to the extent to which the employment may be divided. In addition, Plato (Ch 3), North (1691), Mandeville (1714/1729; Ch 8), Ferguson (1767; Ch11), all have realized the importance of (foreign) trade to the division of labor in (domestic) production, and hence to economic development.

But Smith appears to be the first author to be well aware of the other side of the coin: division of labor plays a crucial role in determining the extent of the market, as revealed by Wakefield's (1835) perusal of Smith's *Wealth of Nations* (Ch 17). As a matter of fact, Wakefield (1835), drawing upon the work of Richard Whately (1831), who insightfully saw political economy as a science of exchange and whom Wakefield highly regarded as "a profound thinker and a powerful reasoner", considerably substantiated the theory of mutual reinforcement between the two things (Ch 17). His reasoning, a fairly interesting one indeed, can be summarized as the following. The division of labor is, as has been widely understood, depends on the extent of the market, that is, "the power of exchanging". But the latter, Wakefield argues, "depends on the productiveness of labor employment which relate to the means of subsistence", especially the productiveness of agriculture, which in turn depends on fertility of soil and climate, which are "beyond the control of man", and labor's skill. We are thus lead to an important proposition, "that while division of employments is limited by the extent of the market, the extent of the market is, in great measure, at least, limited by the division of employments." Wakefield nonetheless sees in no way his treatment on this issue as completion of a promising scientific inquiry. Rather, he calls for a more systematic undertaking,

> "(T)he division of employments and the power of exchanging are mutually dependent means of increasing human enjoyments. At the same time, however, it must be confessed, that the power of exchanging has not been thoroughly analyzed by any writer on the subject. Of what elements that complex power is composed, and by what circumstances it is apt to be increased or diminished; these are questions which would occupy much space in a complete treatise on the principles of political economy." (Wakefield 1835; Ch 17)

It is worth noting that Wakefield seriously took issue with Smith, charging the term "division of labor", which is taken from Mandeville and used throughout in Smith's writings, as misleading. He submitted that it should be referred to instead as "division of employment" or "division of operations", which necessarily implies another important aspect of the social phenomenon of what Smith refers to as "the division of labor": "union of labor", or more generally yet, "cooperation".[1] Remarkably, Wakefield applied his "cooperation principle" into practice in his well known social experiments in the American colony, an achievement John S. Mill (1848; Ch 18) admired with great passion in his further elaboration of the "cooperation principle" underlying the division of labor.

Marshall (1890; Ch 21) draws on biological analogies in his articulation on the "two sides of the same coin", emphasizing, one the one hand, the increased specialization of labor skill, knowledge, machinery ("differentiation") and, on the other, the more intimate and firm connection facilitated by markets between separate parts ("integration") of what he famously refers to as "the industrial organism".[2]

This naturally brings us to a topic of importance to later advancement in theories of increasing returns, namely the productivity implication of such an industrial organism (especially for the particular individual firm), for which Marshall introduced the notion of "external economies" (to what Marshall referred to as "the representative firm" within the industry). As Sraffa (1926; reproduced as Ch 22) cogently demonstrates with his characteristic precision, increasing returns, as originating from

---

[1] For a defence of the long used term "division of labor" by William S. Jevons, see Jevons (1875-6/1977), p.27. Concurring with Wakefield's concern about, as well as his insights into, the integration due to increasingly dense market exchanging, we shall interchangeably use terms "division of labor" and "division of employment" below.

[2] The notion that the economic system can be seen as one part of, and hence embedded in, the social organism, or as an independently working organism, is of course an old tradition in economics, which was later on lamentably associated with social Darwinism and racism. For instance, see Michael Hutter (1994) for an informative historical survey of the German literature on the organism as a metaphor in economics. Moreover, the potential powerfulness of the organism analogy which serves as an important inspiration for Marshall's economic analysis of the division of labor network, does not fully play out in his economic system, due to his having to resort to the pre-Darwin mechanistic analyses of economic equilibrium (see, e.g., Limoges and Ménard 1994).

the division of labor in the classical political economy literature, cannot be accommodated within a Marshallian competitive framework.[1]

Partially in response to, and in defense of Marshall's concept of external economies against, attacks initialized in Sraffa's (1926), Allyn Young, in his presidential address before the section of Economic Sciences and Statistics of the British Association for the Advancement of Science at Glasgow, on Sept 10, 1928, drew heavily upon the ideas of the best known man the city has ever produced,

> "I shall venture to put further stress upon two points ... The first point is that the principal economies which manifest themselves in increasing returns are the economies of capitalistic or roundabout methods of production ... largely identical with the economies of the division of labor in its most important modern forms. ... The second point is that the economies of roundabout methods, even more than the economies of other forms of the division of labor, depend upon the extent of the market — and that, of course, is why we discuss them under the head of increasing returns." (Ch 23).

To Young, Marshall's external economies to an individual firm arise from the whole industrial organism, that is, the network of exchanges and connections among separate parts of the division of labor. He explicitly points out that Marshall's external economies "show themselves only in changes of the organization of the industry as a whole". As such, to focus on the scale of operation by the individual firm, or even the individual industry, is misleading. The promising direction to pursue, Young contends, is to investigate the interdependence between the complicated network of *exchange* with a great number of nexus and dense linkages among them on the one hand,

---

[1] For the heated debate initialized by Sraffa's devastating analysis, see the *"Increasing Returns and the Representative Firm"* symposium, *The Economic Journal*, March 1930 issue. The literature emerging on this issue before the mid-1930s, as well as that after the mid-1980s due to the revival of interest in increasing returns, is too vast to permit consideration in this Introduction. But I would avail myself to mention that one way out of the incomparability of increasing returns and perfect competition is, as suggested by Stigler (1941, pp. 72-3), to discard Marshallian partial equilibrium and resort instead to a general equilibrium analysis, on which a modern treatment is found in Sun and Lio (2003).

and on the other the progressive division of labor in *production*, which often manifests itself in roundabout methods of production in its modern forms.[1] He thus concludes his address as,

> "(T)he division of labor depends upon the extent of the market, but the extent of the market also depends upon the division of labor. In this circumstance lies the possibility of economic progress, apart from the progress which comes as a result of the new knowledge which men are able to gain, whether in the pursuit of their economic or of their non-economic interests." (Ch 23)

It is interesting to notice that while Wakefield established the interdependence between the extent of the market and the division of employment by largely drawing upon the productiveness of labor employed in agriculture, Young focused on the market for intermediate products in manufacturing industries, partially due to the American's overriding of UK in manufacturing industries, a topic receiving much attention at Young's time. Another, indeed more important, reason, however, lies in his appreciation of insights contained in Marshall's industrial organism theory, which was under attack or/and being misunderstood by Sraffa and Knight among others, and which Young decisively and powerfully defended as *one important tradition older than the Marshallian economics per se.*

## IV. Division of Labor in Society and Division of Labor in Manufacture

As indicated earlier, the division of labor in manufacture has on many occasions been discussed before the rise of the factory-system: e.g., the needle production in Ibn Khaldūn (1402) and Carl (1722-3), the pin production in Carl, Chambers's Cyclopedia (1741), the French

---

[1] Young once remarked rather plainly on the manuscript of Frank Knight's book to be published as *Risk, Uncertainty and Profit (*Houghton Mifflin, Boston, 1921), which was based on Knight's PhD thesis under the supervision of Young, "You miss the point, I fear, of Marshall's external economies. They are the economies (in general) of greater specialization and div. of labor" (Quoted from Blitch 1983, p. 362).

Encyclopédie (1751) and Smith (1763, 1776), etc. Despite that Smith (1776) unquestionably contains many insights of enormous influence to later economic theories, especially of the division of labor, Smith did fail to grasp some important points. As criticized rightly by Dugald Stewart, Babbage, Ure, and Cannan among a few others (Cf. Cannan 1964, pp. 96-8), and recently by Rashid (1986), Smith's treatment is rather too narrowly focused on the primitive production of the pin and its like, largely ignorant of the role played by other factors, including machinery and economic organization. Smith established convincingly the relation between the extent of the market and the division of labor exploiting the pin-factory example, which is nonetheless misleading as far as the crucial distinction between social division of labor and manufacture division of labor is concerned. The reason is fairly simple: the pin-factory model cannot be meaningfully interpreted as a theory of *social* division of labor *coordinated* by an (often complicated) network of market exchange (Cf., e.g., Buchanan 1994). Of course, as it happened, and as has been hopefully demonstrated above, inadequacy in Smith's analysis left great room for Young to considerably elaborate on such an important topic in his brilliant presidential address (1928).

Unsatisfied with, as well as inspired by, Smith's treatment of the division of labor, Babbage (1835; Ch 15), Ure (1835; Ch 16) and John Mill (1848; Ch 18), before Marx (1867; Ch19), to whom we shall shortly devote more detailed discussion, emphasized the fundamental change in the landscape of manufacturing and industrial organizations caused by the factory-system thriving at their time, and investigated the underlying division of labor principles. Babbage pointed to fixed learning costs, in terms of "time" and "waste of material" in apprenticeship, as another important factor of increasing returns to scale, which indeed would play the central role in the literature of human capital and labor specialization represented by Rosen (1983) and Barzel and Yu (1984) in the 1980s. Babbage's major contribution, however, lies in his "new principle" of standardization in manufacturing, on which the principal forerunner of modern computer science offers a nice illustration of how the principle can be practically applied to produce an extremely spectacular effect even in the division of *mental* labor (refer to Ch 15 for the fascinating story of how the French mathematician, de Prony, inspired by a random read of Adam Smith's (1776) opening chapters on the division of labor, organized the making of logarithematical and trigonometric functions based on elementary difference calculations).[1] Ure (1835) further argues that a definitive feature of the standardized production due to extensive employment of manufacturing machines is that the machinery supercedes skillful labors. John S. Mill (1848) highlights the organizational change and large-scale manufacturing, which allow for a greater degree of the division of labor within the factory.

Notwithstanding the above authors' important observations, it appears fair to say that the analysis on the connection and distinction between the division of labor in society and division of labor in manufacturing finds it culmination in Karl Marx (1867; Ch 19), which provide stimulating intellectual source even to theorists of economic organizations today. Marx firstly pointed out, rightly, that the manufacture division of labor originated historically from the development in social division of labor but exerts feedback on, and indeed further promotes, the latter. Moving on to their fundamental difference, Marx wrote,

> "in spite of the numerous analogies and links connecting them, the division of labor in the interior of a society, and that in the interior of a workshop, differ not only in degree, but also in kind. .... But what is it that forms the bond between the independent labors of the cattle-breeder, the tanner and the shoemaker? It is the fact that their respective products are commodities. What, on the other hand, characterizes the division of labor in manufacture? The fact that the specialized worker produces no commodities. It is only the common product of all the specialized workers that becomes a commodity. The division of labor within society is mediated through *the purchase and sale of the products* of different branches of industry, while the connection between the various partial operations in a workshop is mediated through *the sale of the labor-power* of several workers to one capitalist, who applies it as combined labor-power. ... Division of labor within the workshop implies the undisputed authority of the capitalist over men, who are merely the members of a total mechanism which belongs to him. The division of labor within

[1] For a short bibliography and contribution to economics by Babbage, see Stigler (1991).

> society brings into contact independent producers of commodities, who acknowledge no authority other than that of competition, of the coercion exerted by the pressure of their reciprocal interests." (Ch 19; my emphasis).

For Marx, the definitive distinction between social division of labor and manufacture division of labor is rooted in mechanisms by which they are respectively coordinated. In the former, it is the decentralized market exchange of commodities, while in the latter the centralized mediation of labor allocation characterized by the employment relationship. Marx's observation on the sale of labor (within factory) *or* commodities (in society) essentially grasps one major aspect of modern transaction cost theories of the firm. (see, e.g., Coase 1937, Pitelis 1994, Yang and Ng 1995, Holmstrom 1999). The distinction made by Marx between the two major mechanisms by which the division of labor is coordinated, i.e., authority in the employment relation associated with the firm and decentralized exchange without central authority in the market, must have a familiar ring to a Coasian economist, for it is precisely this distinction that plays *the* crucial role in Coase's (1937) celebrated theory of the firm. Yet, Coase did not seem to be aware of Marx's pioneering insights when developing his path-breaking transaction cost theory of the firm (Cf. Putterman and Kroszner 1996, p.17).

As to organization of production within a factory, Amasa Walker (1874; Ch 20) made some fairly interesting points on coordination (supervision) costs, which he presciently realized impose limitations to "prevent aggregation of capital ... (that) would (otherwise) swallow up the whole industry of a state".[1] Coordination costs, or essentially the same thing put in different terms, of course has received a great deal of attention in the modern literature as a limiting factor of the division of labor, especially of the scale of operations of the firm, (see, e.g., Williamson 1967, Becker and Murphy 1992 among many others).

One major detrimental *sociological* consequence of the division f labor, namely, alienation, has occurred virtually throughout the history of

---

[1] Another observation by Amasa Walker that may be worthy a mention is on the division of *mental* labor. He, drawing attention to increasing specialization in the fields of law and medicine, offers an interesting illustration (see Ch 20).

ideas of the division of labor, ranging from Plato (Apology; see Plato 1997, pp22-23) and Aristotle (Cf. e.g., Gordon 1993, p.3) to Ferguson (1767; Ch 11), Smith (1776; Ch 13), Ure (1835; Ch 16), Marx (1867; Ch 19), let alone to mention philosophical critique by Rousseau, Herder, Schiller, Hegel, etc. No attempt, however, is made here to consider the voluminous literature, mostly sociological, philosophical or political, centred around such a topic of undoubted importance. Instead, I content myself with referring only to some particularly interesting conceptual clarifications. The seeming contradiction contained in Smith's (1776; Ch 13) writings on the positive and negative effects of the division of labor could be largely resolved by drawing a distinction between its *economic* (favorable) and *sociological* (partly unfavorable) consequences. (see, e.g., Groenewegen 1977 and an exchange of views between West 1964 and Rosenberg 1965). Although Ferguson (1767) and Smith (1776) both explicitly discuss harmful effects on specialized laborers, as already mentioned, Ferguson (1767) appears of deeper insight to its far-reaching sociological consequences, having served as a more important inspiration on this crucial point to both Marx and Hayek.[1] Marx's (1844, 1867) "alienation" thesis of the capitalist division of labor is more complicated in several dimensions than Smith and Ferguson's. West (1969) contends, by drawing upon sociologists' approach to studies of alienation of which a survey is found in Seeman (1959), that Marx's alienation indeed includes "powerlessness", "isolation", and the most philosophically rich notion of "self-estrangement" (dehumanized, and alienated from the laborer's "inner self") and that the similarity between Smith and Marx's understanding of the harmful sociological effect of the division of labor largely lies in the third aspect: self-estrangement alienation. It should go without saying that the sociological consequences, both favorable aspects (social cohesion, for instance) and unfavorable ones, have been extensively explored in sociology (see, for instance, Durkheim's (1893/1933) classical study of social division of labor).

[1] See, e.g., Hamowy (1968), and Rosenberg (1965, esp. footnote 2 on p.135).

## V. Spontaneous Order, Money and Knowledge: Mandeville, Ferguson and the Austrian Insights

As shown above, it seems legitimate to claim that Ibn Khaldūn deserves to be seen as one pioneering theorist of the self-generating socio-economic dynamics. The very thesis of the spontaneous order, was nonetheless fully developed only in the hands of Mandeville, the Scots and Austrians. It is Mandeville, as Hayek (1978, p.250) points out, who made the "definitive breakthrough in modern thought of the twin ideas of evolution and of the spontaneous formation of an order". It appears that Hayek (1960) coined the term "spontaneous order". That which emerged from Mandeville's writings is nicely summarized by Hayek as,

> "His main contention became simply that in the complex order of society the results of men's actions were very different from what they had intended, and that the individuals, in pursuing their own ends, whether selfish or altruistic, produced useful results for others which they did not anticipate or perhaps even know; and finally, that the whole order of society, and even all that we call culture, was the result of individual strivings which had no such end in view, but which were channelled to serve such ends by institutions, practices, and rules which also had never been deliberately invented but had grown up by the survival of what proved successful." (1978, p.253)

It is worth noticing that the theme of spontaneously generated order is an overarching one, of which the spontaneous market order coordinated by the decentralized price system stands only as one special case, and so do the language, morals, money, property rights, etc.[1]

The Scottish moral philosophers, noticeably David Hume, Adam Smith and Adam Ferguson, significantly further developed Mandeville's thesis of the spontaneously formed order, especially its vast importance to understanding the self-regulating nature of the market in coordinating

[1] There has recently emerged a literature coming to grips with the origins of social conventions by exploiting evolutionary game theory. For instance, Sugden (1989), drawing on the replicator model in evolutionary games, analyses the spontaneously evolving conventions, especially property rights. We shall turn to the modern literature of the origin of money that was inspired by Menger (1892; Ch 24) below.

the division of labor and exchange.[1] Largely through Hume and Savigny, Mandeville's thesis was also an important inspiration to Carl Menger's theory of the formation of law, morals, market order, and money (Hayek 1978, pp.264-5).

One remarkable feature of Ferguson's theory of spontaneously formed social orders including the division of labor and civil laws is its emphasis on unintended consequences of actions of numerous *ordinary* human individuals (1867; Ch 11). He wrote,

> "Mankind, in following the present sense of their minds, in striving to remove inconveniencies, or to gain apparent and contiguous advantages, arrive at ends which even their imagination could not anticipate, and pass on, like other animals, in the track of their nature, without perceiving its end. He who first said, "I will appropriate this field: I will leave it to my heirs", did not perceive, that he was laying the foundation of civil laws and political establishments." (1767/1995, p.119).

It may deserve notice that the last point above spells out what later on appears as a promising research agenda on the origin and evolution of property rights (see, e.g., Sugden 1989).

Ferguson's emphasis on the unintended long-term consequence of interplay of actions, rather than of designs, which individuals undertake in pursuing myopically their own ends, was highly regarded and significantly advanced by Hayek (see, Ferguson 1767/1995, p.119, Hayek 1967), who, unquestionably the most original and the most important thinker in the 20th century of the spontaneous order theory without which theories of liberalism would be unimaginable, pioneered some important theses to be "rediscovered" by complexity scientists during 1980-1990s.[2] Indeed, Hayek's theory of the spontaneously generated social order has become one thriving industry since the fall of

---

[1] The intellectual influence of Mandeville on the Scots (with measurable reservations on some of Mandeville's views) has been extensively studied. See, e.g., Campbell and Skinner (1982), Hont and Ignatieff (1983), Hamowy (1987) and Goldsmith (1988).

[2] Cf. Tucker 1996; for refutations of the "rediscovery" allegation, refer to, e.g., Kilpatrick 2001.

the Berlin Wall (see, e.g., Birner and van Zijp 1994, Vanberg 1994 and Fleetwood 1995).

But in what follows we focus on only his socio-economic theory of (dispersed) knowledge, perhaps *the* most important contribution among many other ones made by Hayek to the economic science.[1] Critically examining the meaning of "economic equilibrium" in his 1937 "*Economics and Knowledge*" paper, a turning point not only for Hayek himself in economic thinking, Hayek identifies what he sees as the "central question of all social sciences: How can the combination of fragments of knowledge existing in different minds bring about results which, if they were to be brought about deliberately, would require a knowledge on the part of the directing mind which no single person can possess?" (Hayek 1948/1937, p.54). As a matter of fact, the question Hayek asks also lies in the very core of the Smithian economics, namely, the economics of how the division of labor (and hence division of knowledge), which Smith believes constitutes *the* source of economic progress, can be coordinated by the "invisible hand". Division of labor necessarily implies division of knowledge, or as Hayek characteristically puts it, dispersion of knowledge among individuals. As such, any scientific theory of the division of labor has to come to grips with a sound understanding of how the knowledge dispersed among individuals of different specializations is utilized by society as a whole (Hayek 1945; Ch 25). Hayek convincingly rules out the feasibility for any imaginable central planning mechanism to undertake this task, for the data of which the central authority can make use to do such a job has to be "given", yet the dispersed knowledge of particular circumstances, which are continuously changing, of time and space, can not be given as such.

It is the decentralized price system, standing as an instance of spontaneous orders, that can effectively convey the local knowledge

---

[1] Upon reflecting on his career as an economic theorist, Hayek himself remarks that, "... the paper on "Economics and Knowledge" which I read in 1936 as the presidential address to the London Economic Club, together with some later related papers reprinted in *Individualism and Economic Order* (1948), ... seems to me in retrospect the most original contribution I have made to the theory of economics." (Kresge and Wenar 1994, p.79)

among the individuals and thus makes efficient utilization of the dispersed knowledge.

> "The price system is just one of those formations which man has learned to use (though he is still very far from having learned to make the best use of it) after he had stumbled upon it without understanding it. Through it not only a division of labor but also a coordinated utilization of resources based on an equally divided knowledge has become possible." (Hayek 1945; Ch 25)

Decades later, in a public lecture, Hayek puts it more succinctly, "We can have a far-reaching division of labor only by relying on the impersonal signals of prices" (Hayek 1983, pp 19-20).

In illustrating the powerfulness of the price system in utilizing division of knowledge and division of labor, Hayek remarkably noticed that, "The most significant fact about this system is the economy of knowledge with which it operates, or how little the individual participants need to know in order to be able to take the right action" (Ch 25). The economy of information required by the price mechanism was rigorously formulated in the later literature of the mechanism design (Cf. e.g., Hurwicz 1973).[1]

As mentioned earlier, the necessity of money as a medium of exchange to support the network of the division of labor was already noticed by Greeks. John Law and Adam Smith further elaborated on this topic, and in fact Smith illustrated in anthropological details the origin of barter money and its historical evolution into fiat money. Despite that, it is only in the hands of Carl Menger (1892; Ch 24) that a theory of the origin of money as a spontaneously generated institution was developed.[2]

---

[1] The informative nature of the price system had indeed been noticed, without explicit reference to dispersed knowledge problem as in Hayek's theory, in earlier generations of the Austrian economists. See, e.g., Streissler (1990) for an illustration of how Wieser's economics topics that emerged during 1880-1890s had inspired Mises and Hayek.

[2] The most influential, and the most widely read, piece by Menger on money is doubtless his 1892 *Economic Journal* publication (translated by Caroline A. Foley; Ch 25), which indeed contains the most important elements of his spontaneous order theory of the origin of money. The original article in German, a much more lengthy one in Menger's verbose and unusually complicated writing style, of which his *Economic Journal* 1892 article is a deliberately shortened, more neatly presented version, was accessible to the English

Menger's central thesis is that the nature of commodity which can be used as the medium of exchange (money) lies in its degree of "Absatzfähigkeit" ("saleableness", as translated by Caroline A. Foley in 1892; Leland B. Yeager and Monika Streissler translate as "marketability" (see Menger 2002)), and that money essentially arises spontaneously from interplay of individuals' pursuit of their own self-interests without government intervention.

It should be noticed that Menger (1892) also indicates the role played "by way of legislation" in establishing the *social* institution of money, but emphasizes that "this is neither the only, nor the primary mode in which money has taken its origin" (Ch 24). He contends that the network effect, a crucial element in the interplay between decentralized actions of heterogeneous agents, suffices for the most marketable commodity to be eventually instituted as money.[1] Despite some controversies centred around Menger's thesis that money as a *social* institution arises without intervention from social organizations,[2] Menger (1892), as it happened, has recently been serving as a major intellectual inspiration to an extensive literature of the origin of money, which indeed is still explosively growing. Schmitz (2002) provides a critical review of neoclassical theories of money, represented by Townsend's (1980) spatial separation model, the overlapping generation dynamics model, and most prominently, the search model originating from Kiyotaki and Wright ( 1989, 1991). Schmitz cogently argues that, compared to Menger's original theory on the genesis of money, a common and major drawback of all the above-mentioned models is their crucial assumption of an exogenously given social institution of money, which effectively begs the very Mengerian question of its emergence.

---

readership only quite recently due to Leland B. Yeager and Monika Streissler's valuable work (see Menger 2002). The original version is "Geld", *Handwoerterbuch der Staatswissenschaften* (3rd edition), J. Conrad et al. (eds.), Vol IV., Fischer, Jena, 1892, pp. 555-610.

[1] For a recent study that incorporates adaptive learning and network effects into the standard search-theoretical model in an attempt to account for the spontaneous evolution from barter money to fiat money, see Selgin (2003).

[2] See, e.g., Goodhart's (2004) book review of Latzer and Schmitz (2002) for a criticism of this aspect of Menger's monetary theory.

## VI. Concluding Remarks

Hopefully we have in the above sketched out, at least one major part of, the intellectual development of the economics of division of labor over twenty-five centuries up to Hayek's (1940s) thesis of the division of knowledge as a by-product of the division of labor. In particular, we emphatically highlight important insights of ancient Greeks, medieval Islam and pre-Smithian political economists, and critically review literature of recent two centuries on three deliberately chosen topics, namely, the interdependence between the division of labor and the extent of the market, distinction as well as connection between social division of labor and manufacturing division of labor, and the spontaneous order theory of division of knowledge and the origins of money. Due to lack in space, there are quite some topics of importance, such as implications of increasing returns to the division of labor for international trade, economic growth, general equilibrium analysis, organizational change, technical progress, income distribution, industrialization, etc., which we either discuss fairly briefly and superficially or leave untouched at all in this article, and which we address elsewhere (Sun 2005). Nonetheless, we hope that this introductory chapter might serve as a mini guide-book to major path-breaking developments in history of the economics of division of labor.

## References

Barzel, Y. and Yu, B. T. (1984). The effect of the utilization rate on the division of labor, *Econ. Inquiry,* 22, pp. 18-27.

Becker, G. (1964). *Human Capital*, Columbia University Press, New York.

Becker, G. (1985). Human capital, effort, and the sexual division of labor, *J Labor Econ.*, 3, pp. 533-58.

Becker, G. and Murphy, K. (1992). The division of labor, coordination costs, and knowledge, *Quart. J Econ.*, 107, pp. 1137-60.

Birner, J. and van Zijp, R. (1994). (Eds.) Hayek, Co-Ordination and Evolution: His Legacy in Philosophy, Politic, Economics, and the History of Ideas. Routledge, London and New York.

Blitch, C. P. (1983). Allyn Young on increasing returns, *J. Post Keynes. Econ.*, 5, pp. 359-72.

Boulakia, J. D. C. (1971). Ibn Khaldūn: A fourteenth-century economist, *J. Politic. Econ.*, 79, pp. 105-18.
Buchanan, J. M. (1994). The return to increasing returns: An introductory summary, in Buchanan, J. and Y. Yoon, eds., *The Return to Increasing Returns*, University of Michigan Press, pp. 3-13.
Buchanan, J. M. (2005). Natural equality, increasing returns, and economic progress: A re-interpretation of Adam Smith's system, *Div. Labor Trans. Costs*, 1(1).
Buchanan, J. M. and Yoon, Y.J. (2000), A Smithian perspective on increasing returns, *J. His. Econ. Thought*, 22, pp. 43-8.
Campbell, R.H. and Skinner, A.S. (1982). (Eds.) *The Origins and Nature of the Scottish Enlightenment,* Edinburgh.
Cannan, E. (1929/1964). A *Review of Economic Theory*, with a New Introduction by BA Corry , Frank Cass and Co. LTD, 1964, 2nd ed. (1st ed. 1929).
Chambers, E. (1741). Cyclopaedia: or, An Universal Dictionary of Arts and Sciences . 4th Edition, London.
Coase, R. (1937). The nature of the firm, *Economica*, 4, pp. 386-405.
Durkheim, E. (1893/ 1933). *The Division of Labor in Society*, Translated by George Simpson. New York: The Free Press.
Essid, M. Y. (1987). Islamic economic thought, in S. Todd Lowry ed. *Pre-Classical Economic Thought: from the Greeks to the Scottish Enlightenment*, pp.77-102.
Ferguson, A. (1767/1995), *An Essay on the History of Civil Society*, with a new introduction by Louis Schneider. Transaction Publishers, London, 1995.
Fleetwood, S. (1995). *Hayek's Political Economy: The Socio-Economics of Order*, Routledge, London and New York.
Foley, V. (1974). The division of labor in Plato and Smith, *His. Politic. Econ.*, 6, pp. 220-242.
Foley, V. (1975). A Reply, *His. Politic. Econ.*, 7, pp. 379-89.
Fujita, M., Krugman, P. and Venables, A.J. (1999). *The Spatial Economy: Cities, Regions and International Trade*, MIT.
Ghazanfar, S. M. (2000). The economic thought of Abu Hamid al-Ghazali and St Thomas Aquinas: some comparative parallels and links, *His. Politic. Econ.*, 32, pp. 857-888.
Ghazanfar, S. M. and A. A. Islahi (1990). Economic thought of an Arab scholastic: Abu Hamid al-Ghazali (1058-1111), *His. Politic. Econ.*, 22, pp. 381-403.
Goldsmith, M.M. (1988), Regulating anew the moral and political sentiments of mankind: Bernard Mandeville and the Scottish Enlightenment, *J. His. Ideas*, pp. 587-606.
Goodhart, C. (2004). Book review of Latzer and Schmitz (2002), *His. Politic. Econ.*, 36, pp. 210-2.
Gordon, B. (1975). Economic Analysis before Adam Smith: Hesiod to Lesius. London, Macmillan.
Gordon, B. (1993). Aristotelian economic analysis and the medieval schoolmen, *His. Econ. Rev.*, 20, pp. 1-12.
Groenewegen, P. D. (1969). Turgot and Adam Smith, *Scottish J .Politic. Econ.*, 16, pp. 271-287.

Groenewegen, P. D. (1977). Adam Smith and the division of labor: a bicentenary estimate, *Australian Econ. Papers*, 16, pp. 161-74.

Groenewegen, P. D. (1987). Division of labor, in J. Eatwell, M. Milgate and P. Newman, eds., *The New Palgrave: A Dictionary of Economics*, Macmillan, London, pp. 901-7.

Hamowy, R. (1968), Adam Smith, Adam Ferguson, the division of labor, *Economica*, 35, pp. 249-259.

Hamowy, R. (1987). The Scottish Enlightenment and the Theory of Spontaneous Order. Southern Illinois University Press.

Hayek (1948/1937). Economics and knowledge, in *Individualism and Economic Order*, University of Chicago Press, 1948, pp. 33-56.

Hayek, F. A.(1960), *The Constitution of Liberty*. Chicago: University of Chicago Press.

Hayek, F. A. (1967). The results of human action but not of human design, in *Studies in Philosophy, Politics and Economics,* Routledge and Kegan Paul, London, pp. 96-105.

Hayek, F.A.(1978). Dr Bernard Mandeville (1670-1733), in *New Studies in Philosophy, Politics, Economics and the History of Ideas*, Routledge and Kegan Paul, pp. 249-266.

Hayek, F.A.(1983). Coping with ignorance, in *Knowledge, Evolution and Society*, Adam Smith Institute, UK, pp 17-27.

Hitti, P.K. (2002), *History of the Arabs*. $10^{th}$ edition, Palgrave Macmillan, New York.

Hodgskin, T. (1827), *Popular Political Economy*. London.

Holmstrom, B. (1999). The firm as a subeconomy. *J. Law Econ. Org.* 15, pp. 74-102.

Hont, I. and Ignatieff, M. (1983) (Eds.) Wealth and Virtue: the Shaping of Political Economy in the Scottish Enlightenment, Cambridge University Press.

Hosseini, H. (1998). Seeking the roots of Adam Smith's division of labor in medieval Persia, *His. Politic. Econ.*, 30, pp. 653-681.

Hu, J. (1988), *A Concise History of Chinese Economic Thought*, Foreign Languages Press, Beijing.

Hurwicz, L. (1973). The design of mechanisms for resource allocation, *Amer. Econ. Rev.*, 63, pp. 1-30.

Hutchison, T.W. (1988), Before Adam Smith: the Emergence of Political Economy, 1662-1776. Basic Blackwell, Oxford.

Hutter, M. (1994). Organism as a metaphor in German economic thought, in P. Mirowski (ed.) *Natural Imagines in Economic Thought*, Cambridge University Press, New York, pp. 289-321.

Jevons, W.S., (1977) Papers and Correspondence of William Stanley Jevons, Vol VI, *Lectures on Political Economy 1875-1876*, edited by R. D. Collison Black, Macmillan.

Kilpatrick, H. E. (2001). Complexity, spontaneous order and Friedrich Hayek: Are spontaneous order and complexity essentially the same thing? *Complexity*, 6, pp. 16-20.

Kiyotaki, N. and Wright, R. (1989). On money as a medium of exchange, *J. Politic. Econ.*, 97, pp. 927-954.

Kiyotaki, N. and Wright, R. (1991). A contribution to the pure theory of money, *J. Econ. Theory* 53, pp. 215-235.

Kresge, S. and Wenar, L. (1994). (Eds.) *Hayek on Hayek: An Autobiographical Dialogue*, Routledge, London.

Kuran, T. (1987). Commentary on "Islamic Economic Thought" by M. Y. Essid, in S. Todd Lowry ed. *Pre-Classical Economic Thought: from the Greeks to the Scottish Enlightenment*, pp. 103-113.

Landreth, H. and Colander, D.C. (1994) *History of Economic Thought*. Third edition, Houghton Mifflin Company, Boston.

Latzer, M. and Schmitz, S. W. (2002). (Eds.) Carl Menger and the Evolution of Payment Systems: From Barter to Electronic Money. Edward Elgar US.

Limoges, C. and Ménard, C. (1994). Organization and the division of labor: biological metaphors at work in Alfred Marshall's Principles of Economics, in P. Mirowski (ed.) *Natural Imagines in Economic Thought*, Cambridge University Press, New York, pp. 336-59.

Lough, J. (1970). *The Encyclopédie in Eighteenth-Century England and Other Studies*. Oriel Press Limited, Newcastle upon Tyne, UK.

Lough, J. (1971/1989), *The Encyclopédie*. Slatkine Reprints, Genève.

MacLeod, C. (1983). Henry Martyn and the authorship of the Consideration upon the East-India Trade, *Bull. Inst. His. Res.*, 56, pp. 222-9.

Marx, K. (1844) Economic and Philosophic Manuscripts.

McNulty, P.J. (1975). A Note on the division of labor in Plato and Smith, *His. Politic. Econ.*, 7, pp. 372-8.

Menger, C. (2002). Money, translated by L. B. Yeager with M. Streissler, in M. Latzer and S. W. Schmitz (Eds.), pp. 25-107.

North, D. (1691/1907). *Discourses upon Trade*, edited by Jacob H. Hollander, Lord Baltimore Press, 1907.

Pitelis, C. (1994). On transaction costs economics and the nature of the firm, *Economie Appliquée*, XLVI, pp. 109-130.

Plato (1997). *Completed Works*, edited with Introduction and Notes by John M Cooper, Hackett, Indianapolis.

Putterman, L. and Kroszner, R.S. (1996). The economic nature of the firm: A new introduction, in Putterman, L. and R. S. Kroszner (eds.) *The Economic Nature of the Firm: A Reader*. 2nd edition, Cambridge University Press, New York, pp. 1-31.

Rashid, S. (1986). Adam Smith and the division of labor: a historical view, *Scot. J. Politic. Econ.*, 33, pp. 292-7.

Rosen, S. (1983). Specialization and human capital, J. *Labor Econ.*, 1, 43-9.

Rosenberg, N. (1965). Adam Smith on the division of labor: two views or one, *Economica*, Feb 1965, pp. 127-39.

Rosenberg, N. (1976). Another advantage of the division of labor, *J. Politic. Econ.*, 84, pp. 861-8.

Schmitz, S. W. (2002). Carl Menger's "Money" and the current neoclassical models of money, in Latzer and Schmitz (Eds.), pp. 111-132.

Schumpeter, J. A. (1954). *History of Economic Analysis*, Oxford University Press, New York.

Seeman, M. (1959). On the meaning of alienation, *Amer. Socio. Rev.*, 24, pp. 783-791.

Selgin, G. (2003). Adaptive leaning and the transition to fiat money, *Econ. J.*, 113, pp. 147-165.

Smith, A. (1896/1763). *Lectures on Justice, Police, Revenue and Arms*, ed. By E Cannan, Oxford University Press, 1896.

Soofi, A. (1995). Economics of Ibn Khaldūn revisited, *His. Politic. Econ.*, 27, pp. 385-404.

Stigler, G. (1941). Production and Distribution Theories, Macmillan, New York.

Stigler, G. (1991). Charles Babbage, *J. Econ. Lit.* , XXIX, pp. 1149-52.

Streissler, E. (1990). Arma virumque cano: Friedrich von Wieser, the bard as economist", in Stephen Littlechild (ed.), *Austrian Economics*, Vol I, Edward Elgar, pp.72-95.

Sugden, R. (1989). Spontaneous order, *J. Econ. Perspectives*, 3, pp. 85-97.

Sun, G.-Z. (2005), *A Study of History of the Economics of the Division of Labor*, mimeo, Department of Economics, Monash University.

Sun, G.-Z. and Lio, M. (2003). The division of labor and roundabout production: Allyn Yioung revisited, *Pacific Econ. Rev.*, 8, pp. 219-38.

Townsend, R. M. (1980). Models of money with spatially separated agents, in J. H. Kareken and N. Wallace, eds., *Models of Monetary Economics* (Federal Reserve Bank of Minneapolis), pp. 169—210.

Tucker, W. (1996). Complex questions: the new science of spontaneous order, *Reason*, January 1996 Issue, pp. 34-8.

Vanberg, V. (1994). *Rules and Choices in Economics*, Routledge, London.

West, E.G. (1964). Adam Smith's two views on the division of labor, *Economica*, 31, pp. 23-32.

West, E.G. (1969). Then political economy of alienation: Karl Marx and Adam Smith, *Oxford Econ. Papers*, 21, pp. 1-23.

Whately, R. (1831). Introductory Lectures on Political Economy, London.

Williamson, O. E. (1967). Hierarchical control and optimum firm size, *J. Politic. Econ.*, 75, pp. 123-138.

Yang X. (1994). Endogenous vs. exogenous comparative advantage and economies of specialization vs. economies of scale, *J. Econ.*, 60, pp. 29-54.

Yang, X. and Ng, Y.-K.(1995). Theory of the firm and structure of residual rights, *J. Econ. Behavior Org.*, 26, pp. 107-128.

Yang, X. and Rice, R. (1994). An equilibrium model endogenizing the emergence of a dual structure between the urban and rural sectors, *J. Urban Econ.*, 35, pp. 346-68.

# Part II. Nothing New under the Sun?
# Pieces up to Adam Smith

# Ancient Greek Wisdoms

## Chapter 2*

# From *Cyropædia* and *Oeconomicus*

**Xenophon**

### From *Cyropædia*

Nor is it on, these accounts only, that have been mentioned, that the things sent from the king are pleasing, but dishes that come from the king's table are in reality superior in flavour; and it is not at all wonderful that such is the case; for as other arts, in great cities, are brought to a high degree of excellence, so the meats on the king's table are dressed in the best possible manner. In small towns, the same man makes a couch, a door, a plough, and a table; and frequently the same person is a builder too, and is very well content if he can thus find customers enough to maintain him; and it is impossible for a man who works at many things to do them all well; but, in great cities, because there are numbers that want each particular thing, one art alone suffices for the maintenance of each individual; and frequently indeed, not an entire art, but one man makes shoes for men, and another for women; sometimes it happens, that one gets a maintenance merely by stitching shoes, another by cutting them out, another by cutting out upper-leathers only, and another by doing none of these things, but simply putting together the pieces. He, therefore, that is employed in a work of the smallest compass, must, of

* Taken from *Cyropædia*, Translated by J. S. Watson and Henry Dale, George and Sons,1886, book VIII, p244-245; and *Oeconomicus*, Translated by Sarah B. Pomeroy, Clarendon Press. Oxford, 1994, Chapter VII , pp. 141, 143, 145, and 147.

necessity, do it best. Matters relating to the table are in the very same case; for he that has the same man to spread the couches, to set out the table, to knead the dough, to dress sometimes one dish, and sometimes another, must necessarily, I think, fare in each particular as it may happen; but where there is employment enough for one man to boil meat, for another to roast it, for one to boil fish, for another to broil it, and for another to make bread, (and that not of every sort either, but it is enough for him to furnish one sort good,) each man, in my opinion, must of necessity bring the things that are thus made to very great perfection. Cyrus therefore, by such means, greatly exceeded all other people in making presents of dishes from his table.

## From *Oeconomicus*

Ischomachus replied, 'Well, Socrates, as soon as she was sufficiently tamed and domesticated so as to be able to carry on a conversation, I questioned her more or less as follows: "Tell me, wife, have you ever thought about why I married you and why your parents gave you to me? It must be quite obvious to you, I am sure, that there was no shortage of partners with whom we might sleep. I, on my part, and your parents, on your behalf, considered who was the best partner we could choose for managing an estate and for children. And I chose you, and your parents, apparently, chose me, out of those who were eligible. Now if some day the god grants us children, then we shall consider how to train them in the best way possible. For this will be a blessing to us both, to obtain the best allies and support in old age. But at present we two share this estate. I go on paying everything I have into the common fund; and you deposited into it everything you brought with you. There is no need to calculate precisely which of us has contributed more, but to be well aware of this: that the better partner is the one who makes the more valuable contribution."

'In reply to this, Socrates, my wife answered, "What should I be able to do to help you? What ability have I got? Everything depends on you. My mother told me that my duty is to practise self-control."

"'By Zeus, wife," I said, "my father said the same to me. But self-control for both man and woman means behaving so that their property will be in the very best condition and that the greatest possible increase will be made to it by just and honourable means."

"And what do you envisage that I might do to help improve our estate?", asked my wife.

"'By Zeus," I said, "try to do as well as possible what the gods have given you the natural ability to do, and which the law encourages, as well."

"And what is that?", she asked.

"'I suppose," I said, "that they are not trivial matters, unless, of course, the activities that the queen bee presides over in the hive are trivial. Wife, the gods seem to have shown much discernment in yoking together female and male, as we call them, so that the couple might constitute a partnership that is most beneficial to each of them. First of all, so that the various species of living creatures may not become extinct, this pair sleeps together for the purpose of procreation. Then this pairing provides offspring to support the partners in their old age, at least in the case of human beings. And finally, human beings do not live outdoors like cattle, but obviously have need of shelter.

"'Those who intend to obtain produce to bring into the shelter need someone to work at the outdoor jobs. For ploughing, sowing, planting, and herding is all work performed outdoors, and it is from these that our essential provisions are obtained. As soon as these are brought into the shelter, then someone else is needed to look after them and to perform the work that requires shelters. The nursing of newborn children requires shelters, and so does the preparation of bread from grain, and likewise, making clothing out of wool. Because both the indoor and the outdoor tasks require work and concern, I think the god, from the very beginning, designed the nature of woman for the indoor work and concerns and the nature of man for the outdoor work. For he prepared man's body and mind to be more capable of enduring cold and heat and travelling and military campaigns, and so he assigned the outdoor work to him. Because the woman was physically less capable of endurance, I think the god has evidently assigned the indoor work to her. And because the god was aware that he had both implanted in the woman and assigned to her the nurture of newborn children, he had measured out to her a greater share of affection for newborn babies than he gave to the man. And because the god had also assigned to the woman the duty of guarding what had been brought into the house, realizing that a tendency to be afraid is not at all disadvantageous for guarding things, he measured out a greater portion of fear to the woman than to the man. And knowing that the person responsible for the outdoor work would have to serve as defender against any wrong doer, he measured out to him a greater share of courage.

"'Because it is necessary for both of them to give and to take, he gave both of them equal powers of memory and concern. So you would not be able to distinguish whether the female or male sex has the larger share of these. And he gave them both equally the ability to practise self-control too, when it is needed. And the god granted the privilege to whichever one is superior in this to gain a larger share of the benefit accruing from it, whether man or woman. So, because they are not equally well endowed with all the same natural aptitudes, they are consequently more in need of each other, and the bond is more beneficial to the couple, since one is capable where the other is deficient.

"'Well, wife, because we know what has been assigned to each of us by the god, we must each try to perform our respective duties as well as possible. The law encourages this, for it yokes together husband and wife, and just as the god made them partners in children, so the law has appointed them partners in the estate. And the law declares honourable those duties for which the god has made each of them more naturally capable. For the woman it is more honourable to remain indoors than to be outside; for the man it is more disgraceful to remain indoors than to attend to business outside. If someone behaves in a way contrary to the nature the god has given him, perhaps his disobedience will not escape the notice of the gods, and he will pay a penalty for neglecting his proper business or for performing his wife's work. It seems to me", I added, "that the queen bee toils constantly at such work appointed by the god."

'My wife asked, "How does the work of the queen bee resemble that which I must perform?"

'I replied, "She remains in the hive and does not allow the bees to be idle, but those who ought to work outside she dispatches to their job, and she knows and receives what each brings in, and keeps it until it is necessary to use it. And when the time comes to use it, she distributes a fair share to each. She supervises the construction of the combs inside the hive, so that they are woven beautifully and quickly, and she is concerned that the offspring shall be reared to maturity. When the little ones have been reared and are capable of working, she sends them out to found a colony with someone to lead the new generation."

'My wife asked, "Shall I have to do this too?"

"'Certainly," I replied, "you will have to stay indoors and send forth the group of slaves whose work is outdoors, and personally supervise those whose work is indoors. Moreover, you must receive what is brought inside and dispense as much as should be spent. And you must plan ahead and guard whatever must remain in reserve, so that the provisions stored up for a year are not spent in a month. And when wool is brought in to you, you must see that clothes are produced for those who need them. And you must also be concerned that the dry grain is in good condition for eating. However," I said, "one of your proper concerns, perhaps, may seem to you rather thankless: you will certainly have to be concerned about nursing any of the slaves who becomes ill."

"'Oh, no," exclaimed my wife, "it will be most gratifying if those who are well cared for will prove to be thankful and more loyal than before.'"

Ischomachus went on: 'I was delighted with her response and said, "Wife, because of such thoughtful actions on the part of the queen bee, isn't the relationship of the bees to her, too, of such a kind that when she deserts the hive, not one of the bees considers staying behind, but all follow her?"

'My wife replied, "It would surprise me if the leader's activities did not apply more to you than to me. For if you were not concerned that supplies were brought in from outside, surely my guarding the things indoors and my budgeting would seem pretty ridiculous."

'And I replied: "Yes, but my bringing in supplies would appear just as ridiculous if there were not someone to look after what has been brought in. Don't you see how people pity those who draw water in a leaky jar, as the saying goes, because they seem to labor in vain?"

"'Yes, by Zeus," said my wife, "they are truly miserable if they do that."

"'But, wife, your other special concerns turn out to be pleasant: whenever you take a slave who has no knowledge of spinning, and teach her that skill so that you double her value to you: and whenever you take one who does not know how to manage a house or serve, and turn her into one who is a skilled and faithful servant and make her invaluable; and whenever it is in your power to reward the helpful and reasonable members of your household and to punish any of them who appears to be vicious. But the sweetest experience of all will be this: if you prove to be better than I am and make me your servant. Then you will have no need to fear that as your years increase you will be less honoured in the household; but you may be confident that when you become older, the better partner you have been to me, and the better guardian of the estate for the children, the greater the respect you will enjoy in the household. For it is not because of youthful grace that beautiful and good things increase for human beings, but rather because of their virtues," I said. As far as I can recall, those are the kind of subjects, Socrates, that I believe I discussed with her first.'

## Chapter 3[*]

# From *The Republic*

**Plato**

I think a city comes to be because none of us is self-sufficient, but we all need many things. Do you think that a city is founded on any other principle?

No.

And because people need many things, and because one person calls on a second out of one need and on a third out of a different need, many people gather in a single place to live together as partners and helpers. And such a settlement is called a city. Isn't that so?

It is.

And if they share things with one another, giving and taking, they do so because each believes that this is better for himself?

That's right.

Come, then, let's create a city in theory from its beginnings. And it's our needs, it seems, that will create it.

It is, indeed.

Surely our first and greatest need is to provide food to sustain life.

Certainly.

Our second is for shelter, and our third for clothes and such. That's right.

---

[*] Taken from *Complete Works*, ed, John M. Cooper and D. S. Hutchinson, Hackett Publishing Company, Inc., 1997, Book II, pp. 1008–1013.

How, then, will a city be able to provide all this? Won't one person have to be a farmer, another a builder, and another a weaver? And shouldn't we add a cobbler and someone else to provide medical care?

All right.

So the essential minimum for a city is four or five men?

Apparently.

And what about this? Must each of them contribute his own work for the common use of all? For example, will a farmer provide food for everyone, spending quadruple the time and labor to provide food to be shared by them all? Or will he not bother about that, producing one quarter the food in one quarter the time, and spending the other three quarters, one in building a house, one in the production of clothes, and one in making shoes, not troubling to associate with the others, but minding his own business on his own?

Perhaps, Socrates, Adeimantus replied, the way you suggested first would be easier than the other.

That certainly wouldn't be surprising, for, even as you were speaking it occurred to me that, in the first place, we aren't all born alike, but each of us differs somewhat in nature from the others, one being suited to one task, another to another. Or don't you think so?

I do.

Second, does one person do a better job if he practices many crafts or—since he's one person himself-if he practices one?

If he practices one.

It's clear, at any rate, I think, that if one misses the right moment in anything, the work is spoiled.

It is.

That's because the thing to be done won't wait on the leisure of the doer, but the doer must of necessity pay close attention to his work rather than treating it as a secondary occupation.

Yes, he must.

The result, then, is that more plentiful and better-quality goods are more easily produced if each person does one thing for which he is naturally suited, does it at the right time, and is released from having to do any of the others.

Absolutely.

Then, Adeimantus, we're going to need more than four citizens to provide the things we've mentioned, for a farmer won't make his own plough, not if it's to be a good one, nor his hoe, nor any of his other farming tools. Neither will a builder — and he, too, needs lots of things. And the same is true of a weaver and a cobbler, isn't it?

It is.

Hence, carpenters, metal workers, and many other craftsmen of that sort will share our little city and make it bigger.

That's right.

Yet it won't be a huge settlement even if we add cowherds, shepherds, and other herdsmen in order that the farmers have cows to do their ploughing, the builders have oxen to share with the farmers in hauling their materials, and the weavers and cobblers have hides and fleeces to use.

It won't be a small one either, if it has to hold all those.

Moreover, it's almost impossible to establish a city in a place where nothing has to be imported.

Indeed it is.

So we'll need yet further people to import from other cities whatever is needed.

Yes.

And if an importer goes empty-handed to another city, without a cargo of the things needed by the city from which he's to bring back what his own city needs, he'll come away empty-handed, won't he?

So it seems.

Therefore our citizens must not only produce enough for themselves at home but also goods of the right quality and quantity to satisfy the requirements of others.

They must.

So we'll need more farmers and other craftsmen in our city.

Yes.

And others to take care of imports and exports. And they're called merchants, aren't they?

Yes.

So we'll need merchants, too.

Certainly.

And if the trade is by sea, we'll need a good many others who know how to sail.

A good many, indeed.

And how will those in the city itself share the things that each produces? It was for the sake of this that we made their partnership and founded their city.

Clearly, they must do it by buying and selling.

Then we'll need a marketplace and a currency for such exchange.

Certainly.

If a farmer or any other craftsman brings some of his products to market, and he doesn't arrive at the same time as those who want to exchange things with him, is he to sit idly in the marketplace, away from his own work?

Not at all. There'll be people who'll notice this and provide the requisite service — in well-organized cities they'll usually be those whose bodies are weakest and who aren't fit to do any other work. They'll stay around the market exchanging money for the goods of those who have something to sell and then exchanging those goods for the money of those who want them.

Then, to fill this need there will have to be retailers in our city, for aren't those who establish themselves in the marketplace to provide this service of buying and selling called retailers, while those who travel between cities are called merchants?

That's right.

There are other servants, I think, whose minds alone wouldn't qualify them for membership in our society but whose bodies are strong enough for labor. These sell the use of their strength for a price called a wage and hence are themselves called wage-earners. Isn't that so?

Certainly.

So wage-earners complete our city?

I think so.

Well, Adeimantus, has our city grown to completeness, then?

Perhaps it has.

Then where are justice and injustice to be found in it? With which of the things we examined did they come in?

I've no idea, Socrates, unless it was somewhere in some need that these people have of one another.

You may be right, but we must look into it and not grow weary. First, then, let's see what sort of life our citizens will lead when they've been provided for in the way we have been describing. They'll produce bread, wine, clothes, and shoes, won't they? They'll build houses, work naked and barefoot in the summer, and wear adequate clothing and shoes in the winter. For food, they'll knead and cook the flour and meal they've made from wheat and barley. They'll put their honest cakes and loaves on reeds or clean leaves, and, reclining on beds strewn with yew and myrtle, they'll feast with their children, drink their wine, and, crowned with wreaths, hymn the gods. They'll enjoy sex with one another but bear no more children than their resources allow, lest they fall into either poverty or war.

It seem that you make your people feast without any delicacies, Glaucon interrupted.

True enough, I said, I was forgetting that they'll obviously need salt, olives, cheese, boiled roots, and vegetables of the sort they cook in the country. We'll give them desserts, too, of course, consisting of figs, chick-peas, and beans, and they'll roast myrtle and acorns before the fire, drinking moderately. And so they'll live in peace and good health, and when they die at a ripe old age, they'll bequeath a similar life to their children.

If you were founding a city for pigs, Socrates, he replied, wouldn't you fatten *them* on the same diet?

Then how should I feed these people, Glaucon? I asked.

In the conventional way. If they aren't to suffer hardship, they should recline on proper couches, dine at a table, and have the delicacies and desserts that people have nowadays.

All right, I understand. It isn't merely the origin of a city that we're considering, it seems, but the origin of a *luxurious* city. And that may not be a bad idea, for by examining it, we might very well see how justice and injustice grow up in cities. Yet the true city, in my opinion, is the one we've described, the healthy one, as it were. But let's study a city with a fever, if that's what you want. There's nothing to stop us. The things I mentioned earlier and the way of life I described won't satisfy some people, it seems, but couches, tables, and other furniture will have to be added, and, of course, all sorts of delicacies, perfumed oils, incense, prostitutes, and pastries. We mustn't provide them only with the necessities we mentioned at first, such as houses, clothes, and shoes, but painting and embroidery must be begun, and gold, ivory, and the like acquired. Isn't that so?

Yes.

Then we must enlarge our city, for the healthy one is no longer adequate. We must increase it in size and fill it with a multitude of things that go beyond on what is necessary for a city—hunters, for example, and artists or imitators, many of whom work with shapes and colours, many with music. And there'll be poets and their assistants, actors, choral dancers, contractors, and makers of all kinds of devices, including, among other things, those needed for the adornment of women. And so we'll need more servants, too. Or don't you think that we'll need tutors, wet nurses, nannies, beauticians, barbers, chefs, cooks, and swineherds? We didn't need any of these in our earlier city, but we'll need them in this one. And we'll also need many more cattle, won't we, if the people are going to eat meat?

Of course.

And if we live that, we'll have a far greater need for doctors than we did before?

Much greater.

And the land, I suppose, that used to be adequate to feed the population we had then, will cease to be adequate and become too small. What do you think?

The same.

Then we'll have to seize some of our neighbours' land if we're to have enough pasture and plough-land. And won't our neighbours want to seize part of ours as well, if they too have surrendered themselves to the endless acquisition of money and have overstepped the limit of their necessities?

That's completely inevitable, Socrates.

Then our next step will be war, Glaucon, won't it?

It will.

We won't say yet whether the effects of war are good or bad but only that we've now found the original of war. It comes from those same desires that are most of all responsible for the bad things that happen to cities and the individuals in them.

That's right.

Then the city must be further enlarged, and not just by a small number, either, but by a whole army, which will do battle with the invaders in defence of the city's substantial wealth and all the other things we mentioned.

Why aren't the citizens themselves adequate for that purpose?

They won't be, if the agreement you and the rest of us made when we were founding the city was a good one, for surely we agreed, if you remember, that it's impossible for a single person to practice many crafts or professions well.

That's true.

Well, then, don't you think that warfare is a profession?

Of course.

Then should we be more concerned about cobbling than about warfare?

Not at all.

But we prevented a cobbler from trying to be a farmer, weaver, or builder at the same time and said that he must remain a cobbler in order to produce fine work. And each of the others, too, was to work all his life at a single trade for which he had a natural aptitude and keep away from all the others, so as not to miss the right moment to practice his own work well. Now, isn't it of the greatest importance that warfare be practiced well? And is fighting a war so easy that a farmer or a cobbler or any other craftsman can be a soldier at the same time? Though no one can become so much as a good player of checkers or dice if he considers it only as a sideline and doesn't practice it from childhood. Or can someone pick up a shield or any other weapon or tool of war and immediately perform adequately in an infantry battle or any other kind? No other tool makes anyone who picks it up a craftsman or champion unless he has acquired the requisite knowledge and has had sufficient practice.

# Chapter 4*

# From *Politica*

**Aristotle**

Let us begin our discussion of the question with the following considerations:

Of everything which we possess there are two uses: both belong to the thing as such, but not in the same manner for one is the proper, and the other the improper or secondary use of it. For example, a shoe is used for wear, and is used for exchange; both are uses of the shoe. He who gives a shoe in exchange for money or food to him who wants one, does indeed use the shoe as a shoe, but this is not its proper or primary purpose, for a shoe is not made to be an object of barter. The same may be said of all possessions, for the art of exchange extends to all of them, and it arises at first from what is natural, from the circumstance that some have too little, others too much. Hence we may infer that retail trade is not a natural part of the art of getting wealth; had it been so, men would have ceased to exchange when they had enough. In the first community, indeed, which is the family, this art is obviously of no use, but it begins to be useful when the society increases. For the members of the family originally had all things in common; later, when the family divided into parts, the parts shared in many things, and different parts in different things, which they had to give in exchange for what they

---

* Taken from *The Works of Aristotle*, Vol. X, ed. W. D. Ross, M.A., Benjamin Jowett, E. S. Forster and Frederic G. Kenyon, Clarendon Press. Oxford, 1921, Book I Chapter 9, pp. 1257a–1257b.

wanted, a kind of barter which is still practised among barbarous nations who exchange with one another the necessaries of life and nothing more; giving and receiving wine, for example, in exchange for corn, and the like. This sort of barter is not part of the wealth-getting art and is not contrary to nature, but is needed for the satisfaction of men's natural wants. The other or more complex form of exchange grew, as might have been inferred, out of the simpler. When the inhabitants of one country became more dependent on those of another, and they imported what they needed, and exported what they had too much of, money necessarily came into use. For the various necessaries of life are not easily carried about, and hence men agreed to employ in their dealings with each other something which was intrinsically useful and easily applicable to the purposes of life, for example, iron, silver, and the like. Of this the value was at first measured simply by size and weight, but in process of time they put a stamp upon it, to save the trouble of weighing and to mark the value. When the use of coin had once been discovered, out of the barter of necessary articles arose the other art of wealth-getting, namely, retail trade; which was at first probably a simple matter, but became more complicated as soon as men learned by experience whence and by what exchanges the greatest profit might be made.

# Medieval Islamic Insights

# Chapter 5*

# From *The Muqaddimah*

**Ibn Khaldūn**

## Human Civilization in General

Human social organization is something necessary. The philosophers expressed this fact by saying, "Man is 'political' by nature". That is, he cannot do without the social organization for which the philosophers use the technical tem "town" (*polis*).

That is what civilization means. The necessary character of human social organization or civilization is explained by the fact that God created and fashioned man in a form that can live and subsist only with the help of food. He guided man to a natural desire for food and instilled in him the power that enables him to obtain it.

However, the power of the individual human being is not sufficient for him to obtain the food he needs, and does not provide him with as much food as he requires to live. Even if we assume an absolute minimum of food – that is, food enough for one day, a little wheat, for instance – that amount of food could be obtained only after much preparation such as grinding, kneading and baking. Each of these three operations requires utensils and tools that can be provided only with the

---

* Taken from *The Muqaddimah: An Introduction to History, 3 Volumes,* Trans. By Franz Rosenthal. Bollingen Series XLIII, Pantheon Books, New York, 1958, Vol.1, Chapter I, First Prefatory Discussion; and Vol.2, Chapter IV, Sections 11, 12, Chapter V, Sections 1, 15, 16, 18. Most parentheses in Rosenthal's translation inserted by the translator to indicate words added that are not *literally* in the original Arabic text are removed.

help of several crafts, such as the crafts of the blacksmith, the carpenter, and the potter. Assuming that a man could eat unprepared grain, an even greater number of operations would be necessary in order to obtain the grain: sowing and reaping, and threshing to separate it from the husks of the ear. Each of these operations requires a number of tools and many more crafts than those just mentioned. It is beyond the power of one man alone to do all that, or even part of it, by himself. Thus, he cannot do without a combination of many powers from among his fellow beings, if he is to obtain food for himself and for them. Through cooperation, the needs of a number of persons, many times greater than their own number, can be satisfied.

### With Regard to the Amount of Prosperity and Business Activity in Them, Cities and Towns Differ in Accordance with the Different Size of Their Civilization (Population)

The reason for this is that, as is known and well established, the individual human being cannot by himself obtain all the necessities of life. All human beings must co-operate to that end in their civilization. But what is obtained through the cooperation of a group of human beings satisfies the need of a number of many times greater than themselves. For instance, no one, by himself, can obtain the share of the wheat he needs for food. But when six or ten persons, including a smith and a carpenter to make the tools, and others who are in charge of the oxen, the plowing of the soil, the harvesting of the ripe grain, and all the other agricultural activities, undertake to obtain their food and work toward that purpose either separately or collectively and thus obtain through their labor a certain amount of food, that amount will be food for a number of people many times their own. The combined labor produces more than the needs and necessities of the workers.

If the labor of the inhabitants of a town or city is distributed in accordance with the necessities and needs of those inhabitants, a minimum of that labor will suffice. The labor available is more than is needed. Consequently, it is spent to provide the conditions and customs of luxury and to satisfy the needs of the inhabitants of other cities. They import the things they need from people who have a surplus through exchange or purchase. Thus, the people who have a surplus get a good deal of wealth.

## Prices in Towns

It should be known that all markets cater to the needs of people. Some of these needs are necessities, foodstuffs, for instance, such as wheat and barley; corresponding foods, such as beans, chick-peas, peas, and other edible grains; and wholesome foods such as onions, garlic, and the like. Other things are conveniences or luxuries, such as seasonings, fruits, clothes, utensils, mounts, and all the crafts, and buildings. When a city is highly developed and has many inhabitants, the prices of necessary foodstuffs and corresponding items are low, and the prices for luxuries, such as seasonings, fruits, and the things that go with them, are high. When the inhabitants of a city are few and its civilization weak, the opposite is the case.

The reason for this is that the different kinds of grains belong among the necessary foodstuffs. The demand for them, therefore, is very large. Nobody would neglect to provide for his own food or that of his establishment for a month or a year. Thus, the procurement of grain concerns the entire population of a city, or the largest of them, both in the city itself and in its environs. This is inevitable. Everyone who procures food for himself has a great surplus beyond his own and his family's needs. This surplus is able to satisfy the needs of many of the inhabitants of that particular city. No doubt, then, the inhabitants of a city have more food than they need. Consequently, the price of food is low, as a rule, except when misfortunes occur due to celestial conditions that may affect the supply of food in certain years. If people did not have to store food against such possible misfortunes, it would be given away entirely gratis, since it would be plentiful because of the large civilization (population of the city).

All other conveniences, such as seasonings, fruits, and whatever else belongs to them, are not matters of general concern. Their procurement does not engage the labor of all the inhabitants of a city or the largest part of them. Then, when a city has a highly developed, abundant civilization and is full of luxuries, there is a very large demand for those conveniences and for having as many of them as a person can expect in view of his situation. This results in a very great shortage of such things. Many will bid for them, but they will be in short supply. They will be needed for many purposes, and prosperous people used to luxuries will pay exorbitant prices for them, because they need them more than others. Thus, as one can see, prices come to be high.

Crafts and labor also are expensive in cities with an abundant civilization. There are three reasons for this. First, there is much need of them, because of the place luxury occupies in the city on account of the city's large civilization. Second, industrial workers place a high value on their services and employment, for they do not have to work since life is easy in a town because of the abundance of food there. Third, the number of people with money to waste is great, and these people have many needs for which they have to employ the services of others and have to use many workers and their skills. Therefore, they pay more for the services of workers than their labor is ordinarily considered worth, because there is competition for their services and the wish to have exclusive use of them. Thus, workers, craftsmen, and professional people become arrogant, their labor becomes expensive, and the expenditures of the inhabitants of the city for these things increase.

Foodstuffs in small cities that have few inhabitants are few, because these cities have a small supply of labor and because, in view of the small size of the city, the people fear food shortages. Therefore, they hold on to the food that comes into their hands and store it. It thus becomes something precious to them, and those who want to buy it have to pay higher prices. On the other hand, they also have no demand for conveniences, because the inhabitants are few and their condition is weak. Little business is done by them, and the prices there, consequently, become particularly low.

## The Real Meaning and Explanation of Sustenance and Profit. Profit Is the Value Realized from Human Labor[1]

Everything comes from God. But human labor is necessary for every profit and capital accumulation. When the source of profit is work as such, as, for instance, the exercise of a craft, this is obvious. When the source of gains is animals, plants, or minerals, this is not quite as obvious, but human labor is still necessary, as one can see. Without human labor, no gain will be obtained, and there will be no useful result.

Furthermore, God created the two mineral "stones", gold and silver, as the measure of value for all capital accumulations. Gold and silver are what the inhabitants of the world, by preference, consider treasure and property to consist of. Even if, under certain circumstances, other things are acquired, it is only for the purpose of ultimately obtaining gold and silver. All other things are subject to market fluctuations, from which gold and silver are exempt. They are the basis of profit, property, and treasure.

If all this has been established, it should be further known that the capital a person earns and acquires, if resulting from a craft, is the value realized from his labor. This is the meaning of "acquired capital". There is nothing here originally except the labor, and the labor is not desired by itself as acquired capital, but the value realized from it.

Some crafts are partly associated with other crafts. Carpentry and weaving, for instance, are associated with wood and yarn (and the respective crafts needed for their production). However, in the two crafts (first mentioned), the labor that goes into them is more important, and its value is greater.

If the profit results from something other than a craft, the value of the resulting profit and acquired capital must also include the value of the labor by which it was obtained. Without labor, it would not have been acquired.

In most such cases, the share of labor in the profit is obvious. A portion of the value, whether large or small, comes from the labor. The

[1] Note the term "profit" used in *The Muqaddimah* refers to total production (Cf., A. Soofi (1995), *History of Political Economy*, Vol. 27, p. 391). – Guang-Zhen Sun.

share of labor may be concealed. This is the case, for instance, with the prices of foodstuffs. The labor and expenditures that have gone into them show themselves in the price of grain, as we have stated before. But they are concealed in regions where farming requires little care and few implements. Thus, only a few farmers are conscious of the costs of labor and expenditures that have gone into their products.

It has thus become clear that grains and profits, in their entirety or for the most part, are value realized from human labor. The meaning of the word "sustenance" has become clear. It is the part of the profit that is utilized. Thus, the meaning of the words "profit" and "sustenance" has become clear. The meaning of both words has been explained.

**The Crafts Require Teachers**

It should be known that a craft is the habit of something concerned with action and thought. In as much as it is concerned with action, it is something corporeal and perceptible by the senses. Things that are corporeal and perceptible by the senses are transmitted through direct practice more comprehensively and more perfectly than otherwise, because direct practice is more useful with regard to them.

A habit is a firmly rooted quality acquired by doing a certain action and repeating it time after time, until the form of that action is firmly fixed. A habit corresponds to the original action after which it was formed. The transmission of things one has observed with one's own eyes is something more comprehensive and complete than the transmission of information and things one has learnt about. A habit that is the result of personal observation is more perfect and more firmly rooted than a habit that is the result of information. The skill a student acquires in a craft, and the habit he attains, correspond to the quality of instruction and the habit of the teacher.

Furthermore, some crafts are simple, and others are composite. The simple ones concern the necessities. The composite ones belong to the luxuries. The simple crafts are the ones to be taught first, firstly because they are simple, and then because they concern the necessities and there is a large demand for having them transmitted. Therefore, they take precedence in instruction. But the instruction in them, as a consequence, is something inferior.

The mind, however, does not cease transforming all kinds of crafts, including the composite ones, from potentiality into actuality through the gradual discovery of one thing after the other, until they are perfect. This is not achieved all at one stroke. It is achieved in the course of time and of generations. Things are not transformed from potentiality into actuality all at one stroke, especially not technical matters. Consequently, a certain amount of time is unavoidable. Therefore, the crafts are found to be inferior in small cities, and only the simple crafts are found there. When sedentary civilization in those cities increases, and luxury conditions there cause the use of the crafts, they are transformed from potentiality into actuality.

## The Crafts Are Perfected Only If There Exists a Large and Perfect Sedentary Civilization

The reason for this is that, as long as sedentary civilization is not complete and the city not fully organized, people are concerned only with the necessities of life, that is with the obtaining of food, such as wheat and other things. Then, when the city is organized and the available labor increases and pays for the necessities and is more than enough for the inhabitants, the surplus is spent on luxuries.

The crafts and sciences are the result of man's ability to think, through which he is distinguished from the animals. His desire for food, on the other hand, is the result of his animal and nutritive power. It is prior to sciences and crafts because of its necessary character. The sciences and crafts come after the necessities. The susceptibility of the crafts to refinement, and the quality of the purposes they are to serve in view of the demands made by luxury and wealth, then correspond to the civilization of a given country.

### Crafts Can Improve and Increase Only When Many People Demand Them

The reason for this is that man cannot afford to give away his labor for nothing, because it is his source of profit and livelihood. Throughout his life, he has no advantage from anything else. Therefore, he must employ his labor only on whatever has value in his city, if it is to be profitable to him.

If a particular craft is in demand and there are buyers for it, that craft, then, corresponds to a type of goods that is in great demand and imported for sale. People in the towns, therefore, are eager to learn that particular craft, in order to make a living though it. On the other hand, if a particular craft is not in demand, there are no buyers for it, and no one is interested in learning it. As a result, the craft is destined to be left alone and disappears because of neglect.

# Emergence of Political Economy of the Division of Labor

# Chapter 6*

# From *Political Aritmetick* and *Another Essay on Political Aritmetick*

**William Petty**

## From *Political Aritmetick*

Those who have the command of the sea trade, may work at easier freight with more profit, than others at greater: for as cloth must be cheaper made, when one cards, another spins, another weaves, another draws, another dresses, another presses and packs; than when all the operations above-mentioned, were clumsily performed by the same hand; so those who command the trade of shipping, can build long slight ships for carrying masts, fir-timber, boards, balks, etc. And short ones for lead, iron, stones, etc. One sort of vessels to trade at ports where they need never lie a ground, others where they must jump upon the sand twice every twelve hours; One sort of vessels, and way of manning in time of peace, and cheap gross goods, another for war and precious commodities; One sort of vessels for the turbulent sea, another for inland waters and rivers; One sort of vessels, and rigging, where haste is requisite for the maidenhead of a market, another where 1/5 or 1/4 part of the time makes no matter. One sort of masting and rigging for long voyages, another for coasting. One sort of vessels for fishing, another for trade. One sort for war for this or that country, another for burthen only.

* Taken from *The Economic Writings of Sir William Petty*, ed. Charles Henry Hull, Augustus M. Kelley, New York, 1963, Vol. I, pp. 260-1; Vol. II, p. 473.

Some for oars, some for poles, some for sails, and some for draught by men or horses, some for the northern navigations amongst ice, and some for the south against worms, etc. And this I take to be the chief of several reasons, why the *Hollanders* can go at less freight than their neighbours, *viz.* because they can afford a particular sort of vessels for each particular trade.

### From *Another Essay on Political Aritmetick*

Whether more would be gained by Foreign Commerce:

The gain which *England* makes by *lead, coals,* the freight of shipping, etc. may be the same, for ought I see, in both cases. But the gain which is made by *manufactures,* will be greater, as the manufacture it self is greater and better. For in so vast a city *manufactures* will beget one another, and each *manufacture* will be divided into as many parts as possible, whereby the work of each *artisan* will be simple and easier; as for example. In the making of a *watch,* if one man shall make the *wheels,* another the *spring,* another shall engrave the *dial-plate,* and another shall make the *cases,* then the *watch* will be better and cheaper, than if the whole work be put upon any one man. And we also see that in *towns,* and in the *streets* of a great *town,* where all the *inhabitants* are almost of one trade, the commodity peculiar to those places is made better and cheaper than elsewhere.

# Chapter 7*

# From *Considerations upon the East-India Trade*

**Henry Martyn**

Arts, and mills, and engines, which save the labor of hands are ways of doing things with less labor, and consequently with labor of less price, though the wages of men employed to do them should not be abated. The *East-India* Trade procures things with less and cheaper labor than would be necessary to make the like in *England;* it is therefore very likely to be the cause of the invention of arts, and mills, and engines, to save the labor of hands in other manufactures. Such things are successively invented to do a great deal of work with little labor of hands; they are the effects of necessity and emulation; every man must be still inventing himself, or be still advancing to farther perfection upon the invention of other men; if my neighbour by doing much with little labor, can sell cheap, I must contrive to sell as cheap as he. So that every art, trade, or engine, doing work with labor of fewer hands, and consequently cheaper, begets in others a kind of necessity and emulation, either of using the fame art, trade, or engine, or of inventing something like it, that every man may be upon the square, that no man may be able to undersell his neighbour. And thus the *East-India* Trade by procuring things with less, and consequently cheaper labor, is a very likely way of forcing men upon the invention of arts and engines, by which other things may be also done

* Taken from *East Indian Trade: Selected Works, 17th Century*, ed. Charles Henry Hull, Green International Publishers Limited, London, 1968, Chapter 5, pp. 66–72.

with less and cheaper labor, and therefore may abate the price of manufactures, though the wages of men should not be abated.

Again the *East-India* Trade is no unlikely way to introduce more artists, more order and regularity into our *English* manufactures, it must put an end to such of them as are most useless and unprofitable; the people employed in there will betake themselves to others, to others the most plain and easier or to the single parts of other manufactures of mort variety; for plain and easier work is soonest learned and men are more perfect and expeditious in it: And thus the *East-India* trade may be the cause of applying proper parts of works of great variety to single and proper artists, of not leaving too much to be performed by the skill of single persons; and this is what is meant by introducing greater order and regularity into our *English* manufactures.

The more variety of artists to every manufacture, the less is left to the skill of single persons; the greater the order and regularity of every work the same must needs be done in less time, the labor must be less, and consequently the price of labor less, though wages should not be abated. Thus a piece of cloth is made by many artists; one cards and spins, another makes the loom, another weaves, another dyes, another dresses the cloth, and thus to proper artists proper parts of the work are still assigned, the weaver must needs be more skilful and expeditious at weaving, if that shall be his constant and whole imployment, than if the same weaver is also to card and spin, and make the loom, and weave, and dress; and dye the cloth. So the spinner, the fuller, the dyer or cloth-worker, must needs be more skilful and expeditious at *his* proper business, which shall be his whole and constant imployment, than any Man can be at the same work, whose skill shall be pusled and confounded with variety of other business.

A watch is a work of great variety, and 'tis possible for one artist: to make all the several parts, and at last to join them all together; but if the demand of watches should become so very great as to find constant imployment for as many persons as there are parts in a watch, if to everyone shall be assigned his proper and constant work, if one shall have nothing else to make but cases, another weels, another pins, another screws, and several others their proper parts; and lastly, if it shall be the constant and only imployment of one to pin there several parts together, this man must needs be more skilful and expeditious in the composition of there several parts, than the same man could be if he were also to be employed in the manufacture of all these parts. And so the maker of the pins, or wheels, or screws, or other parts, must needs be more perfect and expeditious at his proper work, if he shall have nothing else to pusle and confound his skill, than if he is also to be employed in all the variety of a watch.

But of all things to be performed by the labor of man, perhaps there is not more variety in any thing than in a ship: The manufacture of the keel, the ribbs, the planks, the beams, the shrouds, the masts, the sails, almost thousands of other parts, together with the composition of these several parts, require as much variety of skill. And still as the sizes and dimensions of ships differ, the skill in the manufacture of the several parts, and again in the Composition of them, must needs be different; it is one kind of skill to make the keel, or ribbs, or planks, or beams, or rudders, or other parts of a ship of one hundred tons, and another to make the same parts of a ship of five hundred; and in the same manner, the composition of parts of different scantlings and dimensions must needs be different. Wherefore, if the demand of shipping shall be so very great, as to make constant imployment for as many several artists as there are several different parts of ships of different dimensions, if to everyone shall be assigned his proper work, if one man shall be always and only employed in the manufacture of keels of one and the same dimensions, another of ribbs, another of beams, another rudders, and several others of several other parts, certainly the keel, the ribbs, the beams, the rudders, or other parts, must needs be better done and with greater expedition, by any artist whose whole and constant imployment shall be the manufacture of that single part, than if he is also to work upon different parts or different scantlings. Thus the greater the order and regularity of every work, the more any manufacture of much variety shall be distributed and assigned to different artists, the same must needs be better done and with greater expedition, with less loss of time and labor; the labor must be less, and consequently the price of labor less, though wages should continue still as high as ever. And therefore the *East-India* trade, if it is the cause that greater order and regularity is introduced into every work, that manufactures of much variety are distributed and assigned to proper artists, that things are done in less time and consequently with less labor, then without abating the wages of the laborer, it may well abate the price of labor.

# Chapter 8[*]

# From *The Fable of the Bees*

**Bernard Mandeville**

## On the Nature of Society

What a bustle is there to be made in several parts of the world, before a fine scarlet or crimson cloth can be produced, what multiplicity of trades and artificers must be employed! Not only such as are obvious, as wool-combers, spinners, the weaver, the cloth-worker, the scourer, the dyer, the setter, the drawer and the packer; but others that are more remote and might seem foreign to it; as the mill-wright, the pewterer and the chymist, which yet are all necessary as well as a great number of other handicrafts to have the tools, utensils and other implements belonging to the trades already named: But all these things are done at home, and may be performed without extraordinary fatigue or danger; the most frightful prospect is left behind, when we reflect on the toil and hazard that are to be undergone abroad, the vast seas we are to go over, the different climates we are to endure, and the several nations we must be obliged to for their assistance. Spain alone it is true might furnish us with wool to make the finest cloth; but what skill and pains, what experience and ingenuity are required to dye it of those beautiful colours! How widely are the drugs and other ingredients dispersed through the

[*] Taken from *The Fable of The Bees: or, Private Vices, Publick Benefits*, With a Commentary Critical, Historical, and Explanatory by F. B. Kaye, Clarendon Press. Oxford, 1957, Vol. 1, pp. 356-8; Vol. 2, pp. 141–7, p. 284.

universe that are to meet in one kettle! Allum indeed' we have of our own; argol we might have from the Rhine, and vitriol from Hungary; all this is in Europe; but then for saltpetre in quantity we are forced to go as far as the East-Indies. Cochenille, unknown to the ancients, is not much nearer to us, though in a quite different part of the Earth: we buy it 'tis true from the Spaniards; but not being their product they are forced to fetch it for us from the remotest corner of the New World in the West-Indies. While so many sailors are broiling in the sun and sweltered with heat in the East and West of us, another set of them are freezing in the North to fetch pot ashes from Russia.

When we are thoroughly acquainted with all the variety of toil and labor, the hardships and calamities that must be undergone to compass the end I speak of, and we consider the vast risques and perils that are run in those voyages, and that few of them are ever made but at the expence, not only of the health and welfare, but even the lives of many: When we are acquainted with, I say, and duly consider the things I named, it is scarce possible to conceive a tyrant so inhuman and void of shame, that beholding things in the same view, he should exact such terrible services from his innocent slaves; and at the same time dare to own, that he did it for no other reason, than the satisfaction a man receives from having a garment made of scarlet or crimson cloth. But to what height of luxury must a nation be arrived, where not only the king's officers, but likewise his guards, even the private soldiers should have such impudent desires!

But if we turn the prospect, and look on all those labors as so many voluntary actions, belonging to different callings and occupations that men are brought up to for a livelihood, and in which every one works for himself, how much soever he may seem to labor for others: If we consider, that even the sailors who undergo the greatest hardships, as soon as one voyage is ended, even after a ship-wreck,. are looking out and solliciting for employment in another: If we consider, I say, and look on these things in another view, we shall find that the labor of the poor is so far from being a burthen and an imposition upon them; that to have employment is a blessing, which in their addresses to heaven they pray for, and to procure it for the generality of them is the greatest care of every legislature.

**From the Third Dialogue**

Hor. That rational creatures should do all this, without thinking or knowing what they were about, is inconceivable. Bodily motion is one thing, and the exercise of the understanding is another; and therefore agreeable postures, a graceful mein, an easy carriage, and a genteel outward behaviour, in general, may be learned and contracted perhaps without much thought; but good manners are to be observed every where, in speaking, writing, and ordering actions to be performed by others.

Cleo. To men who never turned their thoughts that way, it certainly is almost inconceivable to what prodigious height, from next to nothing, some arts may be and have been raised by human industry and application, by the uninterrupted labor, and joint experience of many ages, though none but men of ordinary capacity should ever be employed in them. What a noble as well as beautiful, what a glorious machine is a first-rate man of war, when she is under sail, well rigged, and well manned! As in bulk and weight it is vastly superior to any other moveable body of human invention, so there is no other that has an equal variety of differently surprising contrivances to boast of. There are many. sets of hands in the nation, that, not wanting proper materials, would be able in less than half a year to produce, fit out, and navigate a first-rate: yet it is certain, that this task would be impracticable, if it was not divided and subdivided into a great variety of different labors;[1] and it is

[1] Allusions to division of labor were common throughout antiquity (see Trever, *History of Greek Economic Thought,* Chicago, 1916), but rarely accompanied with much consciousness of the economic implications of the fact. Plato's *Republic* 369-71 and 433 A and Xenophon's *Cyropaedia* VIII. ii. 5-6 are perhaps the most analytical. In modern times, Petty is the earliest author whom I have found to develop the consequences of this division fully enough to deserve being credited with what we now term the division of labor theory. In his *Political Arithmetick* (published 1690, but written and circulated in manuscript long before) there is a definite statement of the division of labor theory (*Economic Writings,* ed. Hull, 1899, i. 260) ; and an equally clear exposition will be found in his *Another Essay in Political Arithmetick,* 1683 *(Economic Writings* ii. 473). The anonymous *Considerations on the East-India Trade*, 1701, contains a still more

as certain, that none of these labors require any other, than working men of ordinary capacities.

Hor. What would you infer from this?

Cleo. That we often ascribe to the excellency of man's genius, and the depth of his penetration, what is in reality owing to length of time, and the experience of many generations, all of them very little differing from one another in natural parts and sagacity. And to know what it must have cost to bring that art of making ships[1] for different purposes, to the perfection in which it is now, we are only to consider in the first place; that many considerable improvements have been made in it within these fifty years and less; and in the second, that the inhabitants of this island did build and make use of ships eighteen hundred years ago, and that from that time to this, they have never been without.

Hor. Which all together make a strong proof of the slow progress that art has made, to be what it is.

Cleo. The Chevalier Renau has written a book, in which he shows the mechanism of sailing, and accounts mathematically for every thing that belongs to the working and steering of a ship.[2] I am persuaded, that neither the first inventors of ships and sailing, or those, who have made improvements since in any part of them, ever dreamed of those reasons, any more than now the rudest and most illiterate of the vulgar do, when they are made sailors, which time and practice will do in spight of their teeth. We have thousands of them, that were first hauled on board and detained against their wills, and yet in less than three years time knew every rope and every pully in the ship, and without the least scrap of mathematics had learned the management, as well as use of them, much

---

definite statement of the theory, together with a very able elaboration of it (see *Select Collection of Early English Tracts on Commerce,* ed. Political Economy Club, 1856, pp. *591-3).* Compare, also, the slighter anticipation by Locke (*Of Civil Government* II. v. 43) and by Simon Clement *(Discourse of the General Notions of Money,* ed. *1695,* ch. I). For the influence of Mandeville in giving currency to the division of labor theory see above, i. cxxxiv-cxxxv. ------ F. B. Kaye.

[1] The anonymous author of *Considerations on the East-India Trade,* who had anticipated Mandeville in 1701 in the exposition of the division of labor theory, also used ship-construction to illustrate his point (see *Select Collection of Early English Tracts on Commerce,* ed. Political Economy Club, 1856, p. 592) ----- F. B. Kaye.

[2] See the *Théorie de la Manoeuvre des Vaisseaux*, Paris, 1689, by Bernard Renau d'Elicagaray (1652-1719), a leading designer of vessels and naval commander.

better than the greatest mathematician could have done in all his lifetime, if he had never been at sea. The book I mentioned, among other curious things, demonstrates what angle the rudder must make with the keel, to render its influence upon the ship the most powerful. This has its merit; but a lad of fifteen, who has served a year of his time on board of a hoy, knows every thing that is useful in this demonstration practically. Seeing the poop always answering the motion of the helm, he only minds the latter, without making the least reflection on the rudder, 'till in a year or two more his knowledge in sailing, and capacity of steering his vessel become so habitual to him, that he guides her as he does his own body, by instinct, though he is half asleep, or thinking on quite another thing.

Hor. If, as you said, and which I now believe to be true, the people, who first invented, and afterwards improved upon ships and sailing, never dreamed of those reasons of Monsieur Reneau, it is impossible, that they should have acted from them, as motives that induced them a priori, to put their inventions and improvements in practice, with knowledge and design; which, I suppose, is what you intended to prove.

Cleo. It is; and I verily believe, not only that the raw beginners, who made the first essays in either art, good manners as well as sailing, were ignorant of the true cause, the real foundation those arts are built upon in nature; but likewise that, even now both arts are brought to great perfection, the greatest part of those that are most expert, and daily making improvements in them, know as little of the rationale of them, as their predecessors did at first: though I believe at the same time Monsieur Reneau's reasons to be very just, and yours as good as his; that is, I believe, that there is as much truth and solidity in your accounting for the origin of good manners, as there is in his for the management of ships. They are very seldom the same sort of people, those that invent arts, and improvements in them, and those that enquire into the reason of things: this latter is most commonly practised by such, as are idle and indolent, that are fond of retirement, hate business, and take delight in speculation: whereas none succeed oftener in the first, than active, stirring, and laborious men, such as will put their hand to the plough, try experiments, and give all their attention to what they are about.

Hor. It is commonly imagined, that speculative men are best at invention of all sorts.

Cleo. Yet it is a mistake. Soap-boyling, grain-dying, and other trades and mysteries, are from mean beginnings brought to great perfection; but the many improvements, that can be remembered to have been made in them, have for the generality been owing to persons, who either were brought up to, or had long practised and been conversant in those trades, and not to great proficients in chymistry or other parts of philosophy, whom one would naturally expect those things from. In some of these arts, especially grain or scarlet-dying, there are processes really astonishing; and by the mixture of various ingredients, by fire and fermentation, several operations are performed, which the most sagacious naturalist cannot account for by any system yet known; a certain sign, that they were not invented by reasoning *a priori.* When once the generality begin to conceal the high value they have for themselves, men must become more tolerable to one another. Now new improvements must be made every day, 'till some of them grow impudent enough, not only to deny the high value they have for themselves, but likewise to pretend that they have greater value for others, than they have for themselves.[1] This will bring in complaisance, and now flattery will rush in upon them like a torrent. As soon as they are arrived at this pitch of insincerity, they will find the benefit of it, and teach it their children. The passion of shame is so general, and so early discovered in all human creatures, that no nation can be so stupid, as to be long without observing and making use of it accordingly. The same may be said of the credulity of infants, which is very inviting to many good purposes. The knowledge of parents is communicated to their off-spring, and every one's experience in life, being added to what he learned in his youth, every generation after this must be better taught than the preceding; by which means, in two or three centuries, good manners must be brought to great perfection.

Hor. When they are thus far advanced, it is easy to conceive the rest: For improvements, I suppose, are made in good manners, as they are in all other arts and sciences. But to commence from savages, men I believe would make but a small progress in good manners the first three hundred

---

[1] Cf. Esprit, *La Fausseté des Vertus Humaines* (1678) i. 449: '... il [man] a porté sa fausseté au comble de l'impudence lors qu'il a osé dire qu'il est desinteressé ...'

years. The Romans, who had a much better beginning, had been a nation above six centuries, and were almost masters of the world, before they could be said to be a polite people. What I am most astonished at, and which I am now convinced of, is, that the basis of all this machinery is pride. Another thing I wonder at is, that you chose to speak of a nation, that entered upon good manners before they had any notions of virtue or religion, which I believe there never was in the world.

Cleo. Pardon me, Horatio; I have no where insinuated that they had none, but I had no reason to mention them. In the first place, you asked my opinion concerning the use of politeness in this world, abstract from the considerations of a future state: Secondly, the art of good manners has nothing to do with virtue or religion, though it seldom clashes with either. It is a science that is ever built on the same steady principle in our nature, whatever the age or the climate may be, in which it is practised.

Hor. How can any thing be said not to clash with virtue or religion, that has nothing to do with either, and consequently disclaims both?

Cleo. This I confess seems to be a paradox; yet it is true. The doctrine of good manners teaches men to speak well of all virtues, but requires no more of them in any age, or country, than the outward appearance of those in fashion. And as to sacred matters, it is every where satisfied with a seeming conformity in outward worship; for all the religions in the universe are equally agreeable to good manners, where they are national; and pray what opinion must we say a teacher to be of, to whom all opinions are probable alike? All the precepts of good manners throughout the world have the same tendency, and are no more than the various methods of making ourselves acceptable to others, with as little prejudice to ourselves as is possible: by which artifice we assist one another in the enjoyments of life, and refining upon pleasure; and every individual person is rendered more happy by it, in the fruition of all the good things he can purchase, than he could have been without such behaviour. I mean happy, in the sense of the voluptuous. Let us look back on old Greece, the Roman Empire, or the great Eastern nations, that flourished before them, and we shall find, that luxury and politeness ever grew up together, and were never enjoyed asunder: that comfort and delight upon Earth have always employed the wishes of the beau monde; and that, as their chief study and greatest solicitude, to outward appearance, have ever been directed to obtain happiness in this world, so what would become of them in the next seems, to the naked eye, always to have been the least of their concern.

Hor. I thank you for your lecture: you have satisfied me in several things, which I had intended to ask: but you have said some others, that I must have time to consider; after which I am resolved to wait upon you again, for I begin to believe, that concerning the knowledge of ourselves most books are either very defective or very deceitful.

Cleo. There is not a more copious nor a more faithful volume than human nature, to those who will diligently peruse it; and I sincerely believe, that I have discovered nothing to you, which, if you had thought of it with attention, you would not have found out yourself. But I shall never be better pleased with myself, than when I can contribute to any entertainment you shall think diverting.

**From the Sixth Dialogue**

Cleo. No number of men, when once they enjoy quiet, and no man needs to fear his neighbour, will be long without learning to divide and subdivide their labor.

Hor. I don't understand you.

Cleo. Man, as I have hinted before, naturally loves to imitate what he sees others do, which is the reason that savage people all do the same thing: This hinders them from meliorating their condition, though they are always wishing for it: But if one will wholly apply himself to the making of bows and arrows, whilst another provides food, a third builds huts, a fourth makes garments, and a fifth utensils, they not only become useful to one another, but the callings and employments themselves will in the same number of years receive much greater improvements, than if all had been promiscuously followed by everyone of the five.

Hor. I believe you are perfectly right there; and the truth of what you say is in nothing so conspicuous, as it is in watch-making, which is come to a higher degree of perfection, than it would have been arrived at yet, if the whole had always remained the employment of one person; and I am persuaded, that even the plenty we have of clocks and watches, as well as the exactness and beauty they may be made of, are chiefly owing to the division that has been made of that art into many branches.

## Chapter 9*

# From "*Art*" in *Encyclopedia*

**Dennis Diderot and Jean Le Rond d'Alembert**

### Of the Superiority of One Process of Manufacture over Another

But the superiority of one process over another will depend primarily on the quality of the materials used, together with the speed of work and the perfection of workmanship. The quality of the materials must be assured by inspection. As for the speed of work and the perfection of workmanship, they depend only on the number of workers brought together. When a process of manufacture employs many workers, each operation will be the responsibility of a different man. A particular workman will spend his lifetime performing one single operation; hence each operation is carried out quickly and well, and moreover the best-made product is also the cheapest. It is also true that when a great number of workers are assembled, taste and workmanship necessarily improve because there will be some who are able to reflect, put facts together, and discover the only way to surpass their fellow workers: they must economize on materials, make better use of time, or excel in inventiveness. This they can do by introducing either a new machine or a more practical process. If foreign industry does not surpass our manufacture in Lyon, it is not because our processes are unknown elsewhere; everywhere we find the same looms, the same silks, and more

* Taken from *Encyclopedia,* Translated, with an Introduction and Notes by Nelly S. Hoyt and Thomas Cassirer, Bobbs-Merrill Company, Inc. 1965, pp. 17–18.

or less the same practices, but only in Lyon are there thirty thousand workers assembled, all working on the manufacture of the same material.

# Chapter 10*

# From *A System of Moral Philosophy*

**Francis Hutcheson**

## On the Necessity of a Social Life

In the first place, 'tis obvious that for the support of human life, to allay the painful cravings of the appetites, and to afford any of those agreeable external enjoyments which our nature is capable of, a great many external things are requisite; such as food, cloathing, habitations, many utensils, and various furniture, which cannot be obtained without a great deal of art and labor, and the friendly aids of our fellows.

Again, 'tis plaint at a man in absolute solitude though he were of mature strength, and fully instructed in all our arts of life, could scarcely procure to himself the bare necessaries of life, even in the best soils or climates; much less could he procure any graceful conveniencies. One uninstructed in the arts of life, though he had full strength, would be still more incapable of subsisting in solitude: and it would be absolutely impossible, without a miracle, that one could subsist in this condition from his infancy. And suppose that food, raiment, shelter, and the means of sensual pleasure, were supplied by a miracle; yet a life in solitude must be full of fears and dangers. Suppose farther all these dangers removed; yet in solitude there could be no exercise for many of the natural powers and instincts of our species; no love, or social joys, or

* Taken from *A System of Moral Philosophy*, Francis Hutcheson, Augustus M. Kelley. New York, 1968, Vol. 1, pp. 287–90.

communication of pleasure, or esteem, or mirth. The contrary dispositions of soul must grow upon a man in this unnatural state, a sullen melancholy, and discontent, which must make life intolerable. This subject is abundantly explained by almost all authors upon the law of nature.

The mutual aids of a few in a small family, may procure most of the necessaries of life, and diminish dangers, and afford room for some social joys as well as finer pleasures. The same advantages could still be obtained more effectually and copiously by the mutual assistance of a few such families living in one neighbourhood, as they could execute more operose designs for the common good of all; and would furnish more joyful exercises of our social dispositions.

Nay 'tis well known that the produce of the labors of any given number, twenty, for instance, in providing the necessaries or conveniences of life, shall be much greater by assigning to one, a certain sort of work of one kind, in which he will soon acquire skill and dexterity, and to another assigning work of a different kind, than if each one of the twenty were obliged to employ himself, by turns, in all the different sorts of labor requisite for his subsistence, without sufficient dexterity in any. In the former method each procures a great quantity of goods of one kind, and can exchange a part of it for such goods obtained by the labors of others as he shall stand in need of. One grows expert in tillage, another in pasture and breeding cattle, a third in masonry, a fourth in the chace, a fifth in iron-works, a sixth in the arts of the loom, and so on throughout the rest. Thus all are supplied by means of barter with the works of complete artists. In the other method scarce anyone could be dextrous and skilful in anyone sort of labor.

Again some works of the highest use to multitudes can be effectually executed by the joint labors of many, which the separate labors of the same number could never have executed. The joint force of many can repel dangers arising from savage beasts or bands of robbers, which might have been fatal to many individuals were they separately to encounter them. The joint labors of twenty men will cultivate forests or drain marshes, for farms to each one, and provide houses for habitation, and inclosures for their flocks, much sooner than the separate labors of the same number. By concert, and alternate relief, they can keep a perpetual watch, which without concert they could not accomplish.

Larger associations may further enlarge our means of enjoyment, and give more extensive and delightful exercise to our powers of every kind. The inventions, experience, and arts of multitudes are communicated; knowledge is increased, and social affections more diffused. Larger societies have force to execute greater designs of more lasting and extensive advantage.[†] These considerations abundantly show the necessity of living in society, and obtaining the aid of our fellows, for our very subsistence; and the great convenience of larger associations of men for the improvement of life, and the increase of all our enjoyments.

---

[†] See this whole subject beautifully explained in second book of *Cicero de Officiis*.

# Chapter 11[*]

# From *An Essay on the History of Civil Society*

**Adam Ferguson**

## Of the Separation of Arts and Professions

It is evident, that, however urged by a sense of necessity, and a desire of convenience, or favoured by any advantages of situation and policy, a people can make no great progress in cultivating the arts of life, until they have separated, and committed to different persons, the several tasks, which require a peculiar skill and attention. The savage, or the barbarian, who must build and plant, and fabricate for himself, prefers, in the interval of great alarms and fatigues, the enjoyments of sloth to the improvement of his fortune: he is, perhaps, by the diversity of his wants, discouraged from industry; or, by his divided attention, prevented from acquiring skill in the management of any particular subject.

The enjoyment of peace, however, and the prospect of being able to exchange one commodity for another, turns, by degrees, the hunter and the warrior into a tradesman and a merchant. The accidents which distribute the means of subsistence unequally, inclination, and favourable opportunities, assign the different occupations of men; and a sense of utility leads them, without end, to subdivide their professions.

The artist finds, that the more he can confine his attention to a particular part of any work, his productions are the more perfect, and

---

[*] Taken from *An Essay on the History of Civil Society*, ed. Fania OZ-Salzberger, Cambridge University Press, 1995, pp. 172–5.

grow under his hands in the greater quantities. Every undertaker in manufacture finds, that the more he can subdivide the tasks of his workmen, and the more hands he can employ on separate articles, the more are his expences diminished, and his profits increased. The consumer too requires, in every kind of commodity, a workmanship more perfect than hands employed on a variety of subjects can produce; and the progress of commerce is but a continued subdivision of the mechanical arts.

Every craft may ingross the whole of a man's attention, and has a mystery which must be studied or learned by a regular apprenticeship. Nations of tradesmen come to consist of members who, beyond their own particular trade, are ignorant of all human affairs, and who may contribute to the preservation and enlargement of their commonwealth, without making its interest an object of their regard or attention. Every individual is distinguished by his calling, and has a place to which he is fitted. The savage, who knows no distinction but that of his merit, of his sex, or of his species, and to whom his community is the sovereign object of affection, is astonished to find, that in a scene of this nature, his being a man does not qualify him for any station whatever: he flies to the woods with amazement, distaste, and aversion.

By the separation of arts and professions, the sources of wealth are laid open; every species of material is wrought up to the greatest perfection, and every commodity is produced in the greatest abundance. The state may estimate its profits and its revenues by the number of its people. It may procure, by its treasure, that national consideration and power, which the savage maintains at the expence of his blood.

The advantage gained in the inferior branches of manufacture by the separation of their parts, seem to be equalled by those which arise from a similar device in the higher departments of policy and war. The soldier is relieved from every care but that of his service; statesmen divide the business of civil government into shares; and the servants of the public, in every office, without being skilful in the affairs of state, may succeed, by observing forms which are already established on the experience of others. They are made, like the parts of an engine, to concur to a purpose, without any concert of their own: and, equally blind with the trader to any general combination, they unite with him, in furnishing to the state its resources, its conduct, and its force.

The artifices of the beaver, the ant, and the bee, are ascribed to the wisdom of nature. Those of polished nations are ascribed to themselves, and are supposed to indicate a capacity superior to that of rude minds. But the establishments of men, like those of every animal, are suggested by nature, and are the result of instinct, directed by the variety of situations in which mankind are placed. Those establishments arose from successive improvements that were made, without any sense of their general effect; and they bring human affairs to a state of complication, which the greatest reach of capacity with which human nature was ever adorned, could not have projected; nor even when the whole is carried into execution, can it be comprehended in its full extent.

Who could anticipate, or even enumerate, the separate occupations and professions by which the members of any commercial state are distinguished; the variety of devices which are practised in separate cells, and which the artist, attentive to his own affair, has invented, to abridge or to facilitate his separate task? In coming to this mighty end, every generation, compared to its predecessors, may have appeared to be ingenious; compared to its followers, may have appeared to be dull: and human ingenuity, whatever heights it may have gained in a succession of ages, continues to move with an equal pace, and to creep in making the last as well as the first step of commercial or civil improvement.

It may even be doubted, whether the measure of national capacity increases with the advancement of arts. Many mechanical arts, indeed, require no capacity; they succeed best under a total suppression of sentiment and reason; and ignorance is the mother of industry as well as of superstition. Reflection and fancy are subject to err; but a habit of moving the hand, or the foot, is independent of either. Manufactures, accordingly, prosper most, where the mind is least consulted, and where the workshop may, without any great effort of imagination, be considered as an engine, the parts of which are men.

The forest has been felled by the savage without the use of the axe, and weights have been raised without the aid of the mechanical powers. The merit of the inventor, in every branch, probably deserves a preference to that of the performer; and he who invented a tool, or could work without its assistance, deserved the praise of ingenuity in a much higher degree than the mere artist, who, by its assistance, produced a superior work.

But if many parts in the practice of every art, and in the detail of every department, require no abilities, or actually tend to contract and to limit the views of the mind, there are others which lead to general reflections, and to enlargement of thought. Even in manufacture, the genius of the master, perhaps, is cultivated, while that of the inferior workman lies waste. The statesman may have a wide comprehension of human affairs, while the tools he employs are ignorant of the system in which they are themselves combined. The general officer may be a great proficient in the knowledge of war, while the soldier is confined to a few motions of the hand and the foot. The former may have gained, what the latter has lost; and being occupied in the conduct of disciplined armies, may practise on a larger scale, all the arts of preservation, of deception, and of stratagem, which the savage exerts in leading a small party, or merely in defending himself.

The practitioner of every art and profession may afford matter of general speculation to the man of science; and thinking itself, in this age of separations, may become a peculiar craft. In the bustle of civil pursuits and occupations, men appear in a variety of lights, and suggest matter of inquiry and fancy, by which conversation is enlivened, and greatly enlarged. The productions of ingenuity are brought to the market; and men are willing to pay for whatever has a tendency to inform or amuse. By this means the idle, as well as the busy, contribute to forward the progress of arts, and bestow on polished nations that air of superior ingenuity, under which they appear to have gained the ends that were pursued by the savage in his forest, knowledge, order, and wealth.

# Chapter 12*

# From *Reflections on the Formation and the Distribution of Riches*

**Anne Robert Jacques Turgot**

## §. FIRST

*Impossibility of commerce upon the supposition of an equal division of lands, wherein every man should possess only what was necessary for his own support.*

If the land were so distributed among all the inhabitants of a country that each of them had precisely the quantity of it necessary for his support and nothing more, it is evident that, all being equal, no one would be willing to work for others. No one, besides, would possess anything with which to pay for the labor of another; for each, having only as much land as he needed to produce his subsistence, would consume all that he had gathered, and would have nothing that he could exchange for the labor of the others.

---

* Taken from *Reflections on The Formation and The Distribution of Riches*, Augustus M. Kelley, New York, 1963, pp. 3–6, and p. 42

## §. II

*The above hypothesis has never existed, and could not have continued. The diversity of soil and the multiplicity of wants lead to the exchange of the products of the land for other products.*

This hypothesis can never have existed, because the lands have been cultivated before they have been divided; that very cultivation having been the sole motive for division and for the law which assures to each his property. Now the first who have cultivated have probably cultivated as much ground as their forces permitted, and consequently more than was necessary for their support.

Even if this state could have existed, it could not possibly have been durable; each man, as he got from his field nothing but his subsistence, and had nothing wherewith to pay the labor of the others, could only supply his other wants in the way of shelter, clothing, etc., by his own labor; and this would be almost impossible; *every piece of land by no means producing everything.*

He whose land was only fit for grain and would produce neither cotton nor hemp would be without cloth wherewith to clothe himself. Another would have a piece of land fit for cotton which would not produce grain. A third would be without wood wherewith to warm himself, while a fourth would be without grain wherewith to feed himself. Experience would soon teach each what was the kind of product for which his land would be best adapted, and he would limit himself to the cultivation of that particular crop, in order to procure for himself the things he was devoid of by means of exchange with his neighbours; and these, having in their turn made the same reflections, would have cultivated the crop best suited to their field and abandoned the cultivation of all the others.

## §. III

*The products of the land require preparations long and difficult, in order to render them fit to satisfy the wants of man.*

The crops which the land produces to satisfy the different wants of man cannot serve that purpose, for the most part, in the state in which nature gives them; they must undergo various changes and be prepared by art. Wheat must be converted into flour and then into bread; hides must be tanned or dressed; wool and cotton must be spun; silk must be drawn from the cocoons; hemp and flax must be soaked, peeled, and spun; next, different textures must be made from them; and then they must be cut and sewn into garments, foot-gear, etc. If the man who causes his land to produce all these different things and uses them to supply his wants were himself obliged to put them through all these intermediate stages, it is certain that he would succeed very badly. The greater part of these preparations demand an amount of care, of attention, of long experience, such as are only to be acquired by working continuously and on a great quantity of materials. Take for example the preparation of hides; what laborer could attend to all the details necessary in this operation, which lasts several months and sometimes several years? If he could, would he be able to, for a single hide? What loss of time, of space, of material, which might have served either at the same time or successively to tan a great quantity of hides! But even should he succeed in tanning a single hide, he only needs one pair of shoes; what shall he do with the rest? Shall he kill an ox to have this pair of shoes? Shall he cut down a tree to make himself a pair of sabots? One might say the same thing concerning all the other wants of each man, who, if he were reduced to his own field and his own labor, would consume much time and trouble to be very badly equipped in every respect, and would cultivate his land very badly.

## §. IV

*The necessity of these preparations brings about the exchange of produce for labor.*

The same motive which has established the exchange of crop for crop between the cultivators of different kinds of soil must, then, have necessarily brought about the exchange of crop for labor between the cultivators and another part of the society, which shall have preferred the occupation of preparing and working up the produce of the land to that of growing it. Everyone profited by this arrangement, for each by devoting himself to a single kind of work succeeded much better in it. The husbandman obtained from his field the greatest amount of produce possible, and procured for himself much more easily all the other things he needed by the exchange of his surplus than he would have done by his own labor. The shoe-maker, by making shoes for the husbandman, obtained for himself a part of the latter's harvest. Each workman labored to satisfy the wants of the workmen of all the other kinds, who, on their side, all labored for him.

## §. XLVIII

*The practice of using money has greatly facilitated the separation of different labor among the different Members of Society.*

The more money came to stand for everything else, the more possible did it become for each person, by devoting himself entirely to the kind of cultivation or industry he had chosen, to relieve himself of all care for the satisfaction of his other wants, and to think only how he could obtain as much money as possible by the sale of his fruits or his labor, very sure that by means of this money he can get all the rest. It is thus that the employment of money has prodigiously hastened the progress of Society.

# Chapter 13*

# From *The Wealth of Nations*

**Adam Smith**

## Book I Chapter I Of the Division of Labor

The greatest improvement in the productive powers of labor, and the greater part of the skill, dexterity, and judgment with which it is any where directed, or applied, seem to have been the effects of the division of labor.

The effects of the division of labor, in the general business of society, will be more easily understood, by considering in what manner it operates in some particular manufactures. It is commonly supposed to be carried furthest in some very trifling ones; not perhaps that it really is carried further in them than in others of more importance: but in those trifling manufactures which are destined to supply the small wants of but a small number of people, the whole number of workmen must necessarily be small; and those employed in every different branch of the work can often be collected into the same workhouse, and placed at once under the view of the spectator. In those great manufactures, on the contrary, which are destined to supply the great wants of the great body of the people, every different branch of the work employs so great a number of workmen, that it is impossible to collect them all into the

* Taken from *An Inquiry Into the Nature and Causes of the Wealth of Nations*, edited by R. H. Campbell, A. S. Skinner and W. B. Todd, Clarendon Press, Oxford, 1976, Vol. 1, pp. 13-44, 277, 377-8, 446-8; and Vol. 2, pp. 781-4 (text only, without notes).

same workhouse. We can seldom see more, at one time, than those employed in one single branch. Though in such manufactures, therefore, the work may really be divided into a much greater number of parts, than in those of a more trifling nature, the division is not near so obvious, and has accordingly been much less observed.

To take an example, therefore, from a very trifling manufacture; but one in which the division of labor has been very often taken notice of, the trade of the pin-maker; a workman not educated to this business (which the division of labor has rendered a distinct trade), nor acquainted with the use of the machinery employed in it (to the invention of which the same division of labor has probably given occasion), could scarce, perhaps, with his utmost industry, make one pin in a day, and certainly could not make twenty. But in the way in which this business is now carried on, not only the whole work is a peculiar trade, but it is divided into a number of branches, of which the greater part are likewise peculiar trades. One man draws out the wire, another straights it, a third cuts it, a fourth points it, a fifth grinds it at the top for receiving the head; to make the head requires two or three distinct operations; to put it on, is a peculiar business, to whiten the pins is another; it is even a trade by itself to put them into the paper; and the important business of making a pin is, in this manner, divided into about eighteen distinct operations, which, in some manufactories, are all performed by distinct hands, though in others the same man will sometimes perform two or three of them. I have seen a small manufactory of this kind where ten men only were employed, and where some of them consequently performed two or three distinct operations. But though they were very poor, and therefore but indifferently accommodated with the necessary machinery, they could, when they exerted themselves, make among them about twelve pounds of pins in a day. There are in a pound upwards of four thousand pins of a middling size. Those ten persons, therefore, could make among them upwards of forty-eight thousand pins in a day. Each person, therefore, making a tenth part of forty-eight thousand pins, might be considered as making four thousand eight hundred pins in a day. But if they had all wrought separately and independently, and without any of them having been educated to this peculiar business, they certainly could not each of them have made twenty, perhaps not one pin in a day; that is, certainly, not the two hundred and fortieth, perhaps not the four thousand eight hundredth part of what they are at present capable of performing, in consequence of a proper division and combination of their different operations.

In every other art and manufacture, the effects of the division of labor are similar to what they are in this very trifling one; though, in many of them, the labor can neither be so much subdivided, nor reduced to so great a simplicity of operation. The division of labor, however, so far as it can be introduced, occasions, in every art, a proportionable increase of the productive powers of labor. The separation of different trades and employments from one another, seems to have taken place, in consequence of this advantage. This separation too is generally carried furthest in those countries which enjoy the highest degree of industry and improvement; what is the work of one man, in a rude state of society, being generally that of several in an improved one. In every improved society, the farmer is generally nothing but a farmer; the manufacturer, nothing but a manufacturer. The labor too which is necessary to produce anyone complete manufacture, is almost always divided among a great number of hands. How many different trades are employed in each branch of the linen and woollen manufactures, from the growers of the flax and the wool, to the bleachers and smoothers of the linen, or to the dyers and dressers of the cloth! The nature of agriculture, indeed, does not admit of so many subdivisions of labor, nor of so complete a separation of one business from another, as manufactures. It is impossible to separate so entirely, the business of the grazier from that of the corn-farmer, as the trade of the carpenter is commonly separated from that of the smith. The spinner is almost always a distinct person from the weaver; but the ploughman, the harrower, the sower of the seed, and the reaper of the corn, are often the same. The occasions for those different sorts of labor returning with the different seasons of the year, it is impossible that one man should be constantly employed in anyone of them. This impossibility of making so complete and entire a separation of all the different branches of labor employed in agriculture, is perhaps the reason why the improvement of the productive powers of labor in this art, does not always keep pace with their improvement in manufactures. The most opulent nations; indeed, generally excel all their neighbours in agriculture as well as in manufactures; but they are commonly more distinguished by their superiority in the latter than in the former. Their lands are in general better cultivated, and having more labor and expence bestowed upon them, produce more, in proportion to the extent and natural fertility of the ground. But this superiority of produce is seldom much more than in proportion to the superiority of labor and expence. In agriculture, the labor of the rich country is not always much more productive than that of the poor; or, at least, it is never so much more productive, as it commonly is in manufactures. The corn of the rich country, therefore, will not always, in the same degree of goodness, come cheaper to market than that of the poor. The corn of Poland, in the same degree of goodness, is as cheap as that of France, notwithstanding the superior opulence and improvement of the latter country. The corn of France is, in the corn provinces, fully as good, and in most years nearly about the same price with the corn of England, though, in opulence and improvement, France is perhaps inferior to England. The corn-lands of England, however, are better cultivated than those of France, and the corn-lands of France are said to be much better cultivated than those of Poland. But though the poor country, notwithstanding the inferiority of its cultivation, can, in some measure, rival the rich in the cheapness and goodness of its corn, it can pretend to no such competition in its manufactures; at least if those manufactures suit the soil, climate, and situation of the rich country. The silks of France are better and cheaper than those of England, because the silk manufacture, at least under the present high duties upon the importation of raw silk, does not so well suit the climate of England as that of France. But the hard-ware and the coarse woollens of England are beyond all comparison superior to those of France, and much cheaper too in the same degree of goodness. In Poland there are said to be scarce any manufactures of any kind, a few of those coarser household manufactures excepted, without which no country can well subsist.

This great increase of the quantity of work which, in consequence of the division of labor, the same number of people are capable of performing, is owing to three different circumstances; first, to the increase of dexterity in every particular workman; secondly, to the saving of the time which is commonly lost in passing from one species of work to another; and lastly, to the invention of a great number of machines which facilitate and abridge labor, and enable one man to do the work of many.

First, the improvement of the dexterity of the workman necessarily increases the quantity of the work he can perform, and the division of labor, by reducing every man's business to some one simple operation, and by making this operation the sole employment of his life, necessarily increases very much the dexterity of the workman. A common smith, who, though accustomed to handle the hammer, has never been used to make nails, if upon some particular occasion he is obliged to attempt it, will scarce, I am assured, be able to make above two or three hundred nails in a day, and those too very bad ones. A smith who has been accustomed to make nails, but whose sole or principal business has not been that of a nailer, can seldom with his utmost diligence make more than eight hundred or a thousand nails in a day. I have seen several boys under twenty years of age who had never exercised any other trade but that of making nails, and who, when they exerted themselves, could make, each of them, upwards of two thousand three hundred nails in a day. The making of a nail, however, is by no means one of the simplest operations. The same person blows the bellows, stirs or mends the fire as there is occasion, heats the iron, and forges every part of the nail: In forging the head too he is obliged to change his tools. The different operations into which the making of a pin, or of a metal button, is subdivided, are all of them much more simple, and the dexterity of the person, of whose life it has been the sole business to perform them, is usually much greater. The rapidity with which some of the operations of those manufactures are performed, exceeds what the human hand could, by those who had never seen them, be supposed capable of acquiring.

Secondly, the advantage which is gained by saving the time commonly lost in passing from one sort of work to another, is much greater than we should at first view be apt to imagine it. It is impossible to pass very quickly from one kind of work to another, that is carried on in a different place, and with quite different tools. A country weaver, who cultivates a small farm, must lose a good deal of time in passing from his loom to the field, and from the field to his loom. When the two trades can be carried on in the same workhouse, the loss of time is no doubt much less. It is even in this case, however, very considerable. A man commonly saunters a little in turning his hand from one sort of employment to another. When he first begins the new work he is seldom very keen and hearty; his mind, as they say, does not go to it, and for some time he rather trifles than applies to good purpose. The habit of sauntering and of indolent careless application, which is naturally, or rather necessarily acquired by every country workman who is obliged to change his work and his tools every half hour, and to apply his hand in twenty different ways almost every day of his life; renders him almost always slothful and lazy, and incapable of any vigorous application even on the most pressing occasions. Independent, therefore, of his deficiency in point of dexterity, this cause alone must always reduce considerably the quantity of work which he is capable of performing.

Thirdly, and lastly, every body must be sensible how much labor is facilitated and abridged by the application of proper machinery. It is unnecessary to give any example. I shall only observe, therefore, that the invention of all those machines by which labor is so much facilitated and abridged, seems to have been originally owing to the division of labor. Men are much more likely to discover easier and readier methods of attaining any object, when the whole attention of their minds is directed towards that single object, than when it is dissipated among a great variety of things. But in consequence of the division of labor, the whole of every man's attention comes naturally to be directed towards some one very simple object. It is naturally to be expected, therefore, that some one or other of those who are employed in each particular branch of labor should soon find out easier and readier methods of performing their own particular work, wherever the nature of it admits of such improvement. A great part of the machines made use of in those manufactures in which labor is most subdivided, were originally the inventions of common workmen, who, being each of them employed in some very simple operation, naturally turned their thoughts towards finding out easier and readier methods of performing it. Whoever has been much accustomed to visit such manufactures, must frequently have been shewn very pretty machines, which were the inventions of such workmen, in order to facilitate and quicken their own particular part of the work. In the first fire-engines, a boy was constantly employed to open and shut alternately the communication between the boiler and the cylinder, according as the piston either ascended or descended. One of those boys, who loved to play with his companions, observed that, by tying a string from the handle of the valve which opened this communication to another part of the machine, the valve would open and shut without his assistance, and leave him at liberty to divert himself with his play-fellows. One of the greatest improvements that has been made upon this machine, since it was first invented, was in this manner the discovery of a boy who wanted to save his own labor.

All the improvements in machinery, however, have by no means been the inventions of those who had occasion to use the machines. Many improvements have been made by the ingenuity of the makers of the machines, when to make them became the business of a peculiar trade; and some by that of those who are called philosophers or men of speculation, whose trade it is not to do any thing, but to observe every thing; and who, upon that account, are often capable of combining together the powers of the most distant and dissimilar objects. In the progress of society, philosophy or speculation becomes, like every other employment, the principal or sole trade and occupation of a particular class of citizens. Like every other employment too, it is subdivided into a great number of different branches, each of which affords occupation to a peculiar tribe or class of philosophers; and this subdivision of employment in philosophy, as well as in every other business, improves dexterity, and saves time. Each individual becomes more expert in his own peculiar branch, more work is done upon the whole, and the quantity of science is considerably increased by it.

It is the great multiplication of the productions of all the different arts, in consequence of the division of labor, which occasions, in a well-governed society, that universal opulence which extends itself to the lowest ranks of the people. Every workman has a great quantity of his own work to dispose of beyond what he himself has occasion for; and every other workman being exactly in the same situation, he is enabled to exchange a great quantity of his own goods for a great quantity, or, what comes to the same thing, for the price of a great quantity of theirs. He supplies them abundantly with what they have occasion for, and they accommodate him as amply with what he has occasion for, and a general plenty diffuses itself through all the different ranks of the society.

Observe the accommodation of the most common artificer or day-laborer in a civilized and thriving country, and you will perceive that the number of people of whose industry a part, though but a small part, has been employed in procuring him this accommodation, exceeds all computation. The woollen coat, for example, which covers the day-laborer, as coarse and rough as it may appear, is the produce of the joint labor of a great multitude of workmen. The shepherd, the sorter of the wool, the wool-comber or carder, the dyer, the scribbler, the spinner, the weaver, the fuller, the dresser, with many others, must all join their different arts in order to complete even this homely production. How many merchants and carriers, besides, must have been employed in transporting the materials from some of those workmen to others who often live in a very distant part of the country! How much commerce and navigation in particular, how many ship-builders, sailors, sail-makers, rope-makers, must have been employed in order to bring together the different drugs made use of by the dyer, which often come from the remotest comers of the world! What a variety of labor too is necessary in order to produce the tools of the meanest of those workmen! To say nothing of such complicated machines as the ship of the sailor, the mill of the fuller, or even the loom of the weaver, let us consider only what a variety of labor is requisite in order to form that very simple machine, the shears with which the shepherd clips the wool. The miner, the builder of the furnace for smelting the ore, the feller of the timber, the burner of the charcoal to be made use of in the smelting-house, the brick-maker, the brick-layer, the workmen who attend the furnace, the mill-wright, the forger, the smith, must all of them join their different arts in order to produce them. Were we to examine, in the same manner, all the different parts of his dress and household furniture, the coarse linen shirt which he wears next his skin, the shoes which cover his feet, the bed which he lies on, and all the different parts which compose it, the kitchen-grate at which he prepares his victuals, the coals which he makes use of for that purpose, dug from the bowels of the earth, and brought to him perhaps by a long sea and a long land carriage, all the other utensils of his kitchen, all the furniture of his table, the knives and forks, the earthen or pewter plates upon which he serves up and divides his victuals, the different hands employed in preparing his bread and his beer, the glass window which lets in the heat and the light, and keeps out the wind and the rain, with all the knowledge and art requisite for preparing that beautiful and happy invention, without which these northern parts of the world could scarce have afforded a very comfortable habitation, together with the tools of all the different workmen employed in producing those different conveniencies; if we examine, I say, all these things, and consider what a variety of labor is employed about each of them, we shall be sensible that without the assistance and co-operation of many thousands, the very meanest person in a civilized country could not be provided, even according to, what we very falsely imagine, the easy and simple manner in which he is commonly accommodated. Compared, indeed, with the more extravagant luxury of the great, his accommodation must no doubt appear extremely simple and easy; and yet it may be true, perhaps, that the accommodation of an European prince does not always so much exceed that of an industrious and frugal peasant, as the accommodation of the latter exceeds that of many an African king, the absolute master of the lives and liberties of ten thousand naked savages.

## Book I Chapter II Of the Principle Which Gives Occasion to the Division of Labor

This division of labor, from which so many advantages are derived, is not originally the effect of any human wisdom, which foresees and intends that general opulence to which it gives occasion. It is the necessary, though very slow and gradual, consequence of a certain propensity in human nature which has in view no such extensive utility; the propensity to truck, barter, and exchange one thing for another.

Whether this propensity be one of those original principles in human nature, of which no further account can be given; or whether, as seems more probable, it be the necessary consequence of the faculties of reason and speech, it belongs not to our present subject to enquire. It is common to all men, and to be found in no other race of animals, which seem to know neither this nor any other species of contracts. Two greyhounds, in running down the same hare, have sometimes the appearance of acting in some sort of concert. Each turns her towards his companion, or endeavours to intercept her when his companion turns her towards himself. This, however, is not the effect of any contract, but of the accidental concurrence of their passions in the same object at that particular time. Nobody ever saw a dog make a fair and deliberate exchange of one bone for another with another dog. Nobody ever saw one animal by its gestures and natural cries signify to another, this is mine, that yours; I am willing to give this for that. When an animal wants to obtain something either of a man or of another animal, it has no other means of persuasion but to gain the favour of those whose service it requires. A puppy fawns upon its dam, and a spaniel endeavours by a thousand attractions to engage the attention of its master who is at dinner, when it wants to be fed by him. Man sometimes uses the same arts with his brethren, and when he has no other means of engaging them to act according to his inclinations, endeavours by every servile and fawning attention to obtain their good will. He has not time, however, to do this upon every occasion. In civilized society he stands at all times in need of the co-operation and assistance of great multitudes, while his whole life is scarce sufficient to gain the friendship of a few persons. In almost every other race of animals each individual, when it is grown up to maturity, is entirely independent, and in its natural state has occasion for the assistance of no other living creature. But man has almost constant occasion for the help of his brethren, and it is in vain for him to expect it from their benevolence only. He will be more likely to prevail if he can interest their self-love in his favour, and show them that it is for their own advantage to do for him what he requires of them. Whoever offers to another a bargain of any kind, proposes to do this. Give me that which I want, and you shall have this which you want, is the meaning of every such offer; and it is in this manner that we obtain from one another the far greater part of those good offices which we stand in need of. It is not from the benevolence of the butcher, the brewer, or the baker, that we expect our dinner, but from their regard to their own interest. We address ourselves, not to their humanity but to their self-love, and never talk to them of our own necessities but of their advantages. Nobody but a beggar chuses to depend chiefly upon the benevolence of his fellow-citizens. Even a beggar does not depend upon it entirely. The charity of well-disposed people, indeed, supplies him with the whole fund of his subsistence. But though this principle ultimately provides him with all the necessaries of life which he has occasion for, it neither does nor can provide him with them as he has occasion for them. The greater part of his occasional wants are supplied in the same manner as those of other people, by treaty, by barter, and by purchase. With the money which one man gives him he purchases food. The old cloaths which another bestows upon him he exchanges for other old cloaths which suit him better, or for lodging, or for food, or for money, with which he can buy either food, cloaths, or lodging, as he has occasion.

As it is by treaty, by barter, and by purchase, that we obtain from one another the greater part of those mutual good offices which we stand in need of, so it is this same trucking disposition which originally gives occasion to the division of labor. In a tribe of hunters or shepherds a particular person makes bows and arrows, for example, with more readiness and dexterity than any other. He frequently exchanges them for cattle or for venison with his companions; and he finds at last that he can in this manner get more cattle and venison, than if he himself went to the field to catch them. From a regard to his own interest, therefore, the making of bows and arrows grows to be his chief business, and he becomes a sort of armourer. Another excels in making the frames and covers of their little huts or moveable houses. He is accustomed to be of use in this way to his neighbours, who reward him in the same manner with cattle and with venison, till at last he finds it his interest to dedicate himself entirely to this employment, and to become a sort of house-carpenter. In the same manner a third becomes a smith or a brazier, a fourth a tanner or dresser of hides or skins, the principal part of the clothing of savages. And thus the certainty of being able to exchange all that surplus part of the produce of his own labor, which is over and above his own consumption, for such parts of the produce of other men's labor as he may have occasion for, encourages every man to apply himself to a particular occupation, and to cultivate and bring to perfection whatever talent or genius he may possess for that particular species of business.

The difference of natural talents in different men is, in reality, much less than we are aware of; and the very different genius which appears to distinguish men of different professions, when grown up to maturity, is not upon many occasions so much the cause, as the effect of the division of labor. The difference between the most dissimilar characters, between a philosopher and a common street porter, for example, seems to arise not so much from nature, as from habit, custom, and education. When they came into the world, and for the first six or eight years of their existence, they were, perhaps, very much alike, and neither their parents nor play-fellows could perceive any remarkable difference. About that age, or soon after, they come to be employed in very different occupations. The difference of talents comes then to be taken notice of, and widens by degrees, till at last the vanity of the philosopher is willing to acknowledge scarce any resemblance. But without the disposition to truck, barter, and exchange, every man must have procured to himself every necessary and conveniency of life which he wanted. All must have had the same duties to perform, and the same work to do, and there could have been no such difference of employment as could alone give occasion to any great difference of talents.

As it is this disposition which forms that difference of talents, so remarkable among men of different professions, so it is this same disposition which renders that difference useful. Many tribes of animals acknowledged to be all of the same species, derive from nature a much more remarkable distinction of genius, than what, antecedent to custom and education, appears to take place among men. By nature a philosopher is not in genius and disposition half so different from a street porter, as a mastiff is from a greyhound, or a greyhound from a spaniel, or this last from a shepherd's dog. Those different tribes of animals, however, though all of the same species, are of scarce any use to one another. The strength of the mastiff is not, in the least, supported either by the swiftness of the greyhound, or by the sagacity of the spaniel, or by the docility of the shepherd's dog. The effects of those different geniuses and talents, for want of the power or disposition to barter and exchange, cannot be brought into a common stock, and do not in the least contribute to the better accommodation and conveniency of the species. Each animal is still obliged to support and defend itself, separately and independently, and derives no sort of advantage from that variety of talents with which nature has distinguished its fellows. Among men, on the contrary, the most dissimilar geniuses are of use to one another; the different produces of their respective talents, by the general disposition to truck, barter, and exchange, being brought, as it were, into a common stock, where every man may purchase whatever part of the produce of other men's talents he has occasion for.

## Book I Chapter III That the Division of Labor Is Limited by the Extent of the Market

As it is the power of exchanging that gives occasion to the division of labor, so the extent of this division must always be limited by the extent of that power, or, in other words, by the extent of the market. When the market is very small, no person can have any encouragement to dedicate himself entirely to one employment, for want of the power to exchange all that surplus part of the produce of his own labor, which is over and above his own consumption, for such parts of the produce of other men's labor as he has occasion for.

There are some sorts of industry, even of the lowest kind, which can be carried on no where but in a great town. A porter, for example, can find employment and subsistence in no other place. A village is by much too narrow a sphere for him; even an ordinary market town is scarce large enough to afford him constant occupation. In the lone houses and very small villages which are scattered about in so desert a country as the Highlands of Scotland, every farmer must be butcher, baker and brewer for his own family. In such situations we can scarce expect to find even a smith, a carpenter, or a mason, within less than twenty miles of another of the same trade. The scattered families that live at eight or ten miles distance from the nearest of them, must learn to perform themselves a great number of little pieces of work, for which, in more populous countries, they would call in the assistance of those workmen. Country workmen are almost every where obliged to apply themselves to all the different branches of industry that have so much affinity to one another as to be employed about the same sort of materials. A country carpenter deals in every sort of work that is made of wood: a country smith in every sort of work that is made of iron. The former is not only a carpenter, but a joiner, a cabinet-maker, and even a carver in wood, as well as a wheel-wright, a plough-wright, a cart and waggon maker. The employments of the latter are still more various. It is impossible there should be such a trade as even that of a nailer in the remote and inland parts of the Highlands of Scotland. Such a workman at the rate of a thousand nails a day, and three hundred working days in the year, will make three hundred thousand nails in the year. But in such a situation it would be impossible to dispose of one thousand, that is, of one day's work in the year.

As by means of water-carriage a more extensive market is opened to every sort of industry than what land-carriage alone can afford it, so it is upon the sea-coast, and along the banks of navigable rivers, that industry of every kind naturally begins to subdivide and improve itself, and it is frequently not till a long time after that those improvements extend themselves to the inland parts of the country. A broad-wheeled waggon, attended by two men, and drawn by eight horses, in about six weeks time carries and brings back between London and Edinburgh near four ton weight of goods. In about the same time a ship navigated by six or eight men, and sailing between the ports of London and Leith, frequently carries and brings back two hundred ton weight of goods. Six or eight men, therefore, by the help of water-carriage, can carry and bring back in the same time the same quantity of goods between London and Edinburgh, as fifty broad-wheeled waggons, attended by a hundred men, and drawn by four hundred horses. Upon two hundred tons of goods, therefore, carried by the cheapest land-carriage from London to Edinburgh, there must be charged the maintenance of a hundred men for three weeks, and both the maintenance, and, what is nearly equal to the maintenance, the wear and tear of four hundred horses as well as of fifty great waggons. Whereas, upon the same quantity of goods carried by water, there is to be charged only the maintenance of six or eight men, and the wear and tear of a ship of two hundred tons burden, together with the value of the superior risk, or the difference of the insurance between land and water-carriage. Were there no other communication between those two places, therefore, but by land-carriage, as no goods could be transported from the one to the other, except such whose price was very considerable in proportion to their weight, they could carry on but a small part of that commerce which at present subsists between them, and consequently could give but a small part of that encouragement which they at present mutually afford to each other's industry. There could be little or no commerce of any kind between the distant parts of the world. What goods could bear the expence of land-carriage between London and Calcutta? Or if there were any so precious as to be able to support this expence, with what safety could they be transported through the territories of so many barbarous nations? Those two cities, however, at present carry on a very considerable commerce with each other, and by mutually affording a market, give a good deal of encouragement to each other's industry.

Since such, therefore, are the advantages of water-carriage, it is natural that the first improvements of art and industry should be made where this conveniency opens the whole world for a market to the produce of every sort of labor, and that they should always be much later in extending themselves into the inland parts of the country. The inland parts of the country can for a long time have no other market for the greater part of their goods, but the country which lies round about them, and separates them from the sea-coast, and the great navigable rivers. The extent of their market, therefore, must for a long time be in proportion to the riches and populousness of that country, and consequently their improvement must always be posterior to the improvement of that country. In our North American colonies the plantations have constantly followed either the sea-coast or the banks of the navigable rivers, and have scarce any where extended themselves to any considerable distance from both.

The nations that, according to the best authenticated history, appear to have been first civilized, were those that dwelt round the coast of the Mediterranean sea. That sea, by far the greatest inlet that is known in the world, having no tides, nor consequently any waves except such as are caused by the wind only, was, by the smoothness of its surface, as well as by the multitude of its islands, and the proximity of its neighbouring shores, extremely favourable to the infant navigation of the world; when, from their ignorance of the compass, men were afraid to quit the view of the coast, and from the imperfection of the art of ship-building, to abandon themselves to the boisterous waves of the ocean. To pass beyond the pillars of Hercules, that is, to sail out of the Streights of Gibraltar, was, in the ancient world, long considered as a most wonderful and dangerous exploit of navigation. It was late before even the Phenicians and Carthaginians, the most skilful navigators and ship-builders of those old times, attempted it, and they were for a long time the only nations that did attempt it.

Of all the countries on the coast of the Mediterranean sea, Egypt seems to have been the first in which either agriculture or manufactures were cultivated and improved to any considerable degree. Upper Egypt extends itself nowhere above a few miles from the Nile, and in Lower Egypt that great river breaks itself into many different canals, which, with the assistance of a little art, seem to have afforded a communication by water-carriage, not only between all the great towns, but between all the considerable villages, and even to many farm-houses in the country; nearly in the same manner as the Rhine and the Maese do in Holland at present. The extent and easiness of this inland navigation was probably one of the principal causes of the early improvement of Egypt.

The improvements in agriculture and manufactures seem likewise to have been of very great antiquity in the provinces of Bengal in the East Indies, and in some of the eastern provinces of China; though the great extent of this antiquity is not authenticated by any histories of whose authority we, in this part of the world, are well assured. In Bengal the Ganges and several other great rivers form a great number of navigable canals in the same manner as the Nile does in Egypt. In the Eastern provinces of China too, several great rivers form, by their different branches, a multitude of canals, and by communicating with one another afford an inland navigation much more extensive than that either of the Nile or the Ganges, or perhaps than both of them put together. It is remarkable that neither the antient Egyptians, nor the Indians, nor the Chinese, encouraged foreign commerce, but seem all to have derived their great opulence from this inland navigation.

All the inland parts of Africa, and all that part of Asia which lies any considerable way north of the Euxine and Caspian seas, the antient Scythia, the modern Tartary and Siberia, seem in all ages of the world to have been in the same barbarous and uncivilized state in which we find them at present. The sea of Tartary is the frozen ocean which admits of no navigation, and though some of the greatest rivers in the world run through that country, they are at too great a distance from one another to carry commerce and communication through the greater part of it. There are in Africa none of those great inlets, such as the Baltic and Adriatic seas in Europe, the Mediterranean and Euxine seas in both Europe and Asia, and the gulphs of Arabia, Persia, India, Bengal, and Siam, in Asia, to carry maritime commerce into the interior parts of that great continent: and the great rivers of Africa are at too great a distance from one another to give occasion to any considerable inland navigation. The commerce besides which any nation can carry on by means of a river which does not break itself into any great number of branches or canals, and which runs into another territory before it reaches the sea, can never be very considerable; because it is always in the power of the nations who possess that other territory to obstruct the communication between the upper country and the sea. The navigation of the Danube is of very little use to the different states of Bavaria, Austria and Hungary, in comparison of what it would be if any of them possessed the whole of its course till it falls into the Black Sea.

## Book I Chapter IV Of the Origin and Use of Money

When the division of labor has been once thoroughly established, it is but a very small part of a man's wants which the produce of his own labor can supply. He supplies the far greater part of them by exchanging that surplus part of the produce of his own labor, which is over and above his own consumption, for such parts of the produce of other men's labor as he has occasion for. Every man thus lives by exchanging, or becomes in some measure a merchant, and the society itself grows to be what is properly a commercial society.

But when the division of labor first began to take place, this power of exchanging must frequently have been very much clogged and embarrassed in its operations. One man, we shall suppose, has more of a certain commodity than he himself has occasion for, while another has less. The former consequently would be glad to dispose of, and the latter to purchase, a part of this superfluity. But if this latter should chance to have nothing that the former stands in need of, no exchange can be made between them. The butcher has more meat in his shop than he himself can consume, and the brewer and the baker would each of them be willing to purchase a part of it. But they have nothing to offer in exchange, except the different productions of their respective trades, and the butcher is already provided with all the bread and beer which he has immediate occasion for. No exchange can, in this case, be made between them. He cannot be their merchant, nor they his customers; and they are all of them thus mutually less serviceable to one another. In order to avoid the inconveniency of such situations, every prudent man in every period of society, after the first establishment of the division of labor, must naturally have endeavoured to manage his affairs in such a manner, as to have at all times by him, besides the peculiar produce of his own industry, a certain quantity of some one commodity or other, such as he imagined few people would be likely to refuse in exchange for the produce of their industry.

Many different commodities, it is probable, were successively both thought of and employed for this purpose. In the rude ages of society, cattle are said to have been the common instrument of commerce; and, though they must have been a most inconvenient one, yet in old times we find things were frequently valued according to the number of cattle which had been given in exchange for them. The armour of Diomede, says Homer, cost only nine oxen; but that of Glaucus cost an hundred oxen. Salt is said to be the common instrument of commerce and exchanges in Abyssinia; a species of shells in some parts of the coast of India; dried cod at Newfoundland; tobacco in Virginia; sugar in some of our West India colonies; hides or dressed leather in some other countries; and there is at this day a village in Scotland where it is not uncommon, I am told, for a workman to carry nails instead of money to the baker's shop or the alehouse.

In all countries, however, men seem at last to have been determined by irresistible reasons to give the preference, for this employment, to metals above every other commodity. Metals can not only be kept with as little loss as any other commodity, scarce any thing being less perishable that they are, but they can likewise, without any loss, be divided into any number of parts, as by fusion those parts can easily be re-united again; a quality which no other equally durable commodities possess, and which more than any other quality renders them fit to be the instruments of commerce and circulation. The man who wanted to buy salt, for example, and had nothing but cattle to give in exchange for it, must have been obliged to buy salt to the value of a whole ox, or a whole sheep at a time. He could seldom buy less than this, because what he was to give for it could seldom be divided without loss; and if he had a mind to buy more, he must, for the same reasons, have been obliged to buy double or triple the quantity, the value, to wit, of two or three oxen, or of two or three sheep. If, on the contrary, instead of sheep or oxen, he had metals to give in exchange for it, he could easily proportion the quantity of the metal to the precise quantity of the commodity which he had immediate occasion for.

Different metals have been made use of by different nations for this purpose. Iron was the common instrument of commerce among the ancient Spartans; copper among the ancient Romans; and gold and silver among all rich and commercial nations.

Those metals seem originally to have been made use of for this purpose in rude bars, without any stamp or coinage. Thus we are told by Pliny, upon the authority of Timaeus, an ancient historian, that, till the time of Servius Tullius, the Romans had no coined money, but made use of unstamped bars of copper to purchase whatever they had occasion for. These rude bars, therefore, performed at this time the function of money.

The use of metals in this rude state was attended with two very considerable inconveniencies; first, with the trouble of weighing; and, secondly, with that of assaying them. In the precious metals, where a small difference in the quantity makes a great difference in the value, even the business of weighing, with proper exactness, requires at least very accurate weights and scales. The weighing of gold in particular is an operation of some nicety. In the coarser metals, indeed, where a small error would be of little consequence, less accuracy would, no doubt, be necessary. Yet we should find it excessively troublesome, if every time a poor man had occasion either to buy or sell a farthing's worth of goods, he was obliged to weigh the farthing. The operation of assaying is still more difficult, still more tedious, and, unless a part of the metal is fairly melted in the crucible, with proper dissolvents, any conclusion that can be drawn from it, is extremely uncertain. Before the institution of coined money, however, unless they went through this tedious and difficult operation, people must always have been liable to the grossest frauds and impositions, and instead of a pound weight of pure silver, or pure copper, might receive in exchange for their goods, an adulterated composition of the coarsest and cheapest materials, which had, however, in their outward appearance, been made to resemble those metals. To prevent such abuses, to facilitate exchanges, and thereby to encourage all sorts of industry and commerce, it has been found necessary, in all countries that have made any considerable advances towards improvement, to affix a public stamp upon certain quantities of such particular metals, as were in those countries commonly made use of to purchase goods. Hence the origin of coined money, and of those public offices called mints; institutions exactly of the same nature with those of the aulnagers and stampmasters of woollen and linen cloth. All of them are equally meant to ascertain, by means of a public stamp, the quantity and uniform goodness of those different commodities when brought to market.

The first public stamps of this kind that were affixed to the current metals, seem in many cases to have been intended to ascertain, what it was both most difficult and most important to ascertain, the goodness or fineness of the metal, and to have resembled the sterling mark which is at present affixed to plate and bars of silver, or the Spanish mark which is sometimes affixed to ingots of gold, and which being struck only upon one side of the piece, and not covering the whole surface, ascertains the fineness, but not the weight of the metal. Abraham weighs to Ephron the four hundred shekels of silver which he had agreed to pay for the field of Machpelah. They are said however to be the current money of the merchant, and yet are received by weight and not by tale, in the same manner as ingots of gold and bars of silver are at present. The revenues of the antient Saxon kings of England are said to have been paid, not in money but in kind, that is, in victuals and provisions of all sorts. William the Conqueror introduced the custom of paying them in money. This money, however, was, for a long time; received at the exchequer, by weight and not by tale.

The inconveniency and difficulty of weighing those metals with exactness gave occasion the institution of coins, of which the stamp, covering entirely both sides of the piece and sometimes the edges too, was supposed to ascertain not only the fineness, but the weight of the metal. Such coins, therefore, were received by tale as at present, without the trouble of weighing.

The denominations of those coins seem originally to have expressed the weight or quantity of metal contained in them. In the time of Servius Tullius, who first coined money at Rome, the Roman As or Pondo contained a Roman pound of good copper. It was divided in the same manner as our Troyes pound, into twelve ounces, each of which contained a real ounce of good copper. The English pound sterling, in the time of Edward I., contained a pound, Tower weight, of silver of a known fineness. The Tower pound seems to have been something more than the Roman pound, and something less than the Troyes pound. This last was not introduced into the mint of England till the 18th of Henry VIII. The French livre contained in the time of Charlemagne a pound, Troyes weight, of silver of a known fineness. The fair of Troyes in Champaign was at that time frequented by all the nations of Europe, and the weights and measures of so famous a market were generally known and esteemed. The Scots money pound contained, from the time of Alexander the First to that of Robert Bruce, a pound of silver of the same weight and fineness with the English pound sterling. English, French, and Scots pennies too, contained all of them originally a real pennyweight of silver, the twentieth part of an ounce, and the two-hundred-and-fortieth part of a pound. The shilling too seems originally to have been the denomination of a weight. *When wheat is at twelve shillings the quarter,* says an antient statute of Henry III. *then wastel bread of a farthing shall weigh eleven shillings and four pence.* The proportion, however, between the shilling and either the penny on the one hand, or the pound on the other, seems not to have been so constant and uniform as that between the penny and the pound. During the first race of the kings of France, the French sou or shilling appears upon different occasions to have contained five, twelve, twenty, and forty pennies. Among the antient Saxons a shilling appears at one time to have contained only five pennies, and it is not improbable that it may have been as variable among them as among their neighbours, the antient Franks. From the time of Charlemagne among the French, and from that of William the Conqueror among the English, the proportion between the pound, the shilling, and the penny, seems to have been uniformly the same as at present, though the value of each has been very different. For in every country of the world, I believe, the avarice and injustice of princes and sovereign states, abusing the confidence of their subjects, have by degrees diminished the real quantity of metal, which had been originally contained in their coins. The Roman As, in the latter ages of the Republic, was reduced to the twenty-fourth part of its original value, and, instead of weighing a pound, came to weigh only half an ounce. The English pound and penny contain at present about a third only; the Scots pound and penny about a thirty-sixth; and the French pound and penny about a sixty-sixth part of their original value. By means of those operations the princes and sovereign states which performed them were enabled, in appearance, to pay their debts and to fulfil their engagements with a smaller quantity of silver than would otherwise have been requisite. It was indeed in appearance only; for their creditors were really defrauded of a part of what was due to them. All other debtors in the state were allowed the same privilege, and might pay with the same nominal sum of the new and debased coin whatever they had borrowed in the old. Such operations, therefore, have always proved favourable to the debtor, and ruinous to the creditor, and have sometimes produced a greater and more universal revolution in the fortunes of private persons, than could have been occasioned by a very great public calamity.

It is in this manner that money has become in all civilized nations the universal instrument of commerce, by the intervention of which goods of all kinds are bought and sold, or exchanged for one another.

## Book II Of the Nature, Accumulation, and Employment of Stock. Introduction

IN that rude state of society in which there is no division of labor, in which exchanges are seldom made, and in which every man provides every thing for himself, it is not necessary that any stock should be accumulated or stored up beforehand in order to carry on the business of the society. Every man endeavours to supply by his own industry his own occasional wants as they occur. When he is hungry, he goes to the forest to hunt; when his coat is worn out, he cloaths himself with the skin of the first large animal he kills: and when his hut begins to go to ruin, he repairs it, as well as he can, with the trees and the turf that are nearest it.

But when the division of labor has once been thoroughly introduced, the produce of a man's own labor can supply but a very small part of his occasional wants. The far greater part of them are supplied by the produce of other men's labor, which he purchases with the produce, or, what is the same thing, with the price of the produce of his own. But this purchase cannot be made till such time as the produce of his own labor has not only been completed, but sold. A stock of goods of different kinds, therefore, must be stored up somewhere sufficient to maintain him, and to supply him with the materials and tools of his work till such time, at least, as both these events can be brought about. A weaver cannot apply himself entirely to his peculiar business, unless there is beforehand stored up somewhere, either in his own possession or in that of some other person, a stock sufficient to maintain him, and to supply him with the materials and tools of his work, till he has not only completed, but sold his web. This accumulation must, evidently, be previous to his applying his industry for so long a time to such a peculiar business.

As the accumulation of stock must, in the nature of things, be previous to the division of labor, so labor can be more and more subdivided in proportion only as stock is previously more and more accumulated. The quantity of materials which the same number of people can work up, increases in a great proportion as labor comes to be more and more subdivided; and as the operations of each workman are gradually reduced to a greater degree of simplicity, a variety of new machines come to be invented for facilitating and abridging those operations. As the division of labor advances, therefore, in order to give constant employment to an equal number of workmen, an equal stock of provisions, and a greater stock of materials and tools than what would have been necessary in a ruder state of things, must be accumulated beforehand. But the number of workmen in every branch of business generally increases with the division of labor in that branch, or rather it is the increase of their number which enables them to class and subdivide themselves in this manner.

As the accumulation of stock is previously necessary for carrying on this great improvement in the productive powers of labor, so that accumulation naturally leads to this improvement. The person who employs his stock in maintaining labor, necessarily wishes to employ it in such a manner as to produce as great a quantity of work as possible. He endeavours, therefore, both to make among his workmen the most proper distribution of employment, and to furnish them with the best machines which he can either invent or afford to purchase. His abilities in both these respects are generally in proportion to the extent of his stock, or to the number of people whom it can employ. The quantity of industry, therefore, not only increases in every country with the increase of the stock which employs it, but, in consequence of that increase, the same quantity of industry produces a much greater quantity of work.

## Book III Chapter I Of the Natural Progress of Opulence

The great commerce of every civilized society, is that carried on between the inhabitants of the town and those of the country. It consists in the exchange of rude for manufactured produce, either immediately, or by the intervention of money, or of some sort of paper which represents money. The country supplies the town with the means of subsistence, and the materials of manufacture. The town repays this supply by sending back a part of the manufactured produce to the inhabitants of the country. The town, in which there neither is nor can be any reproduction of substances, may very properly be said to gain its whole wealth and subsistence from the country. We must not, however, upon this account, imagine that the gain of the town is the loss of the country. The gains of both are mutual and reciprocal, and the division of labor is in this, as in all other cases, advantageous to all the different persons employed in the various occupations into which it is subdivided. The inhabitants of the country purchase of the town a greater quantity of manufactured goods, with the produce of a much smaller quantity of their own labor, than they must have employed had they attempted to prepare them themselves. The town affords a market for the surplus produce of the country, or what is over and above the maintenance of the cultivators, and it is there that the inhabitants of the country exchange it for something else which is in demand among them. The greater the number and revenue of the inhabitants of the town, the more extensive is the market which it affords to those of the country; and the more extensive that market, it is always the more advantageous to a great number. The corn which grows within a mile of the town, sells there for the same price with that which comes from twenty miles distance. But the price of the latter must generally, not only pay the expence of raising and bringing it to market, but afford too the ordinary profits of agriculture to the farmer. The proprietors and cultivators of the country, therefore, which lies in the neighbourhood of the town, over and above the ordinary profits of agriculture, gain, in the price of what they sell, the whole value of the carriage of the like produce that is brought from more distant parts, and they save, besides, the whole value of this carriage in the price of what they buy. Compare the cultivation of the lands in the neighbourhood of any considerable town, with that of those which lie at some distance from it, and you will easily satisfy yourself how much the country is benefited by the commerce of the town. Among all the absurd speculations that have been propagated concerning the balance of trade, it has never been pretended that either the country loses by its commerce with the town, or the town by that with the country which maintains it.

As subsistence is, in the nature of things, prior to conveniency and luxury, so the industry which procures the former, must necessarily be prior to that which ministers to the latter. The cultivation and improvement of the country, therefore, which affords subsistence, must, necessarily, be prior to the increase of the town, which furnishes only the means of conveniency and luxury. It is the surplus produce of the country only, or what is over and above the maintenance of the cultivators, that constitutes the subsistence of the town, which can therefore increase only with the increase of this surplus produce. The town, indeed, may not always derive its whole subsistence from the country in its neighbourhood, or even from the territory to which it belongs, but from very distant countries; and this, though it forms no exception from the general rule, has occasioned considerable variations in the progress of opulence in different ages and nations.

That order of things which necessity imposes in general, though not in every particular country, is, in every particular country, promoted by the natural inclinations of man. If human institutions had never thwarted those natural inclinations, the towns could nowhere have increased beyond what the improvement and cultivation of the territory in which they were situated could support; till such time, at least, as the whole of that territory was compleatly cultivated and improved. Upon equal, or nearly equal profits, most men will chuse to employ their capitals rather in the improvement and cultivation of land, than either in manufactures or in foreign trade. The man who employs his capital in land, has it more under his view and command, and his fortune is much less liable to accidents than that of the trader, who is obliged frequently to commit it, not only to the winds and the waves, but to the more uncertain elements of human folly and injustice, by giving great credits in distant countries to men, with whose character and situation he can seldom be thoroughly acquainted. The capital of the landlord, on the contrary, which is fixed in the improvement of his land, seems to be as well secured as the nature of human affairs can admit of. The beauty of the country besides, the pleasures of a country life, the tranquillity of mind which it promises, and wherever the injustice of human laws does not disturb it, the independency which it really affords, have charms that more or less attract every body; and as to cultivate the ground was the original destination of man, so in every stage of his existence he seems to retain a predilection for this primitive employment.

Without the assistance of some artificers, indeed, the cultivation of land cannot be carried on, but with great inconveniency and continual interruption. Smiths, carpenters, wheel-wrights, and plough-wrights, masons, and bricklayers, tanners, shoemakers, and taylors, are people, whose service the farmer has frequent occasion for. Such artificers too stand, occasionally, in need of the assistance of one another; and as their residence is not, like that of the farmer, necessarily tied down to a precise spot, they naturally settle in the neighbourhood of one another, and thus form a small town or village. The butcher, the brewer, and the baker, soon join them, together with many other artificers and retailers, necessary or useful for supplying their occasional wants, and who contribute still further to augment the town. The inhabitants of the town and those of the country are mutually the servants of one another. The town is a continual fair or market, to which the inhabitants of the country resort, in order to exchange their rude for manufactured produce. It is this commerce which supplies the inhabitants of the town both with the materials of their work, and the means of their subsistence. The quantity of the finished work which they sell to the inhabitants of the country, necessarily regulates the quantity of the materials and provisions which they buy. Neither their employment nor subsistence, therefore, can augment, but in proportion to the augmentation of the demand from the country for finished work; and this demand can augment only in proportion to the extension of improvement and cultivation. Had human institutions, therefore, never disturbed the natural course of things, the progressive wealth and increase of the towns would, in every political society, be consequential, and in proportion to the improvement and cultivation of the territory or country.

## Book IV Chapter I Of the Principle of the Commercial or Mercantile System

The importation of gold and silver is not the principal, much less the sole benefit which a nation derives from its foreign trade. Between whatever places foreign trade is carried on, they all of them derive two distinct benefits from it. It carries out that surplus part of the produce of their land and labor for which there is no demand among them, and brings back in return for it something else for which there is a demand. It gives a value to their superfluities, by exchanging them for something else, which may satisfy a part of their wants, and increase their enjoyments. By means of it, the narrowness of the home market does not hinder the division of labor in any particular branch of art or manufacture from being carried to the highest perfection. By opening a more extensive market for whatever part of the produce of their labor may exceed the home consumption, it encourages them to improve its productive powers, and to augment its annual produce to the utmost, and thereby to increase the real revenue and wealth of the society. These great and important services foreign trade is continually occupied in performing, to all the different countries between which it is carried on. They all derive great benefit from it, though that in which the merchant resides generally derives the greatest, as he is generally more employed in supplying the wants, and carrying out the superfluities of his own, than of any other particular country. To import the gold and silver which may be wanted, into the countries which have no mines, is, no doubt, a part of the business of foreign commerce. It is, however, a most insignificant part of it. A country which carried on foreign trade merely upon this account, could scarce have occasion to freight a ship in a century.

It is not by the importation of gold and silver, that the discovery of America has enriched Europe. By the abundance of the American mines, those metals have become cheaper. A service of plate can now be purchased for about a third part of the corn, or a third part of the labor, which it would have cost in the fifteenth century. With the same annual expence of labor and commodities, Europe can annually purchase about three times the quantity of plate which it could have purchased at that time. But when a commodity comes to be sold for a third part of what had been its usual price, not only those who purchased it before can purchase three times their former quantity, but it is brought down to the level of a much greater number of purchasers; perhaps to more than ten, perhaps to more than twenty times the former number. So that there may be in Europe at present not only more than three times, but more than twenty or thirty times the quantity of plate which would have been in it, even in its present state of improvement, had the discovery of the American mines never been made. So far Europe has, no doubt, gained a real conveniency, though surely a very trifling one. The cheapness of gold and silver renders those metals rather less fit for the purposes of money than they were before. In order to make the same purchases, we must load ourselves with a greater quantity of them, and carry about a shilling in our pocket where a groat would have done before. It is difficult to say which is most trifling, this inconveniency, or the opposite conveniency. Neither the one nor the other could have made any very essential change in the state of Europe. The discovery of America, however, certainly made a most essential one. By opening a new and inexhaustible market to all the commodities of Europe, it gave occasion to new divisions of labor and improvements of art, which, in the narrow circle of the antient commerce, could never have taken place for want of a market to take off the greater part of their produce. The productive powers of labor were improved, and its produce increased in all the different countries of Europe, and together with it the real revenue and wealth of the inhabitants. The commodities of Europe were almost all new to America, and many of those of America were new to Europe. A new set of exchanges, therefore, began to take place which had never been thought of before, and which should naturally have proved as advantageous to the new, as it certainly did to the old continent. The savage injustice of the Europeans rendered an event, which ought to have been beneficial to all, ruinous and destructive to several of those unfortunate countries.

## Book V Chapter V, Part III, Article II: Of the Expence of the Institutions for the Education of Youth

In the progress of the division of labor, the employment of the far greater part of those who live by labor, that is, of the great body of the people, comes to be confined to a few very simple operations; frequently to one or two. But the understandings of the greater part of men are necessarily formed by their ordinary employments. The man whose whole life is spent in performing a few simple operations, of which the effects too are, perhaps, always the same, or very nearly the same, has no occasion to exert his understanding, or to exercise his invention in finding out expedients for removing difficulties which never occur. He naturally loses, therefore, the habit of such exertion, and generally becomes as stupid and ignorant as it is possible for a human creature to become. The torpor of his mind renders him, not only incapable of relishing or bearing a part in any rational conversation, but of conceiving any generous, noble, or tender sentiment, and consequently of forming any just judgment concerning many even of the ordinary duties of private life. Of the great and extensive interests of his country, he is altogether incapable of judging; and unless very particular pains have been taken to render him otherwise, he is equally incapable of defending his country in war. The uniformity of his stationary life naturally corrupts the courage of his mind, and makes him regard with abhorrence the irregular, uncertain, and adventurous life of a soldier. It corrupts even the activity of his body, and renders him incapable of exerting his strength with vigour and perseverance, in any other employment than that to which he has been bred. His dexterity at his own particular trade seems, in this manner, to be acquired at the expence of his intellectual, social, and martial virtues. But in every improved and civilized society this is the state into which the laboring poor, that is, the great body of the people, must necessarily fall, unless government takes some pains to prevent it.

It is otherwise in the barbarous societies, as they are commonly called, of hunters, of shepherds, and even of husbandmen in that rude state of husbandry which precedes the improvement of manufactures, and the extension of foreign commerce. In such societies the varied occupations of every man oblige every man to exert his capacity, and to invent expedients for removing difficulties which are continually occurring. Invention is kept alive, and the mind is not suffered to fall into that drowsy stupidity, which, in a civilized society, seems to benumb the understanding of almost all the inferior ranks of people. In those barbarous societies, as they are called, every man, it has already been observed, is a warrior. Every man too is in some measure a statesman, and can form a tolerable judgment concerning the interest of the society, and the conduct of those who govern it. How far their chiefs are good judges in peace, or good leaders in war, is obvious to the observation of almost every single man among them. In such a society indeed, no man can well acquire that improved and refined understanding, which a few men sometimes possess in a more civilized state. Though in a rude society there is a good deal of variety in the occupations of every individual, there is not a great deal in those of the whole society. Every man does, or is capable of doing, almost every thing which any other man does, or is capable of doing. Every man has a considerable degree of knowledge, ingenuity, and invention; but scarce any man has a great degree. The degree, however, which is commonly possessed, is generally sufficient for conducting the whole simple business of the society. In a civilized state, on the contrary, though there is little variety in the occupations of the greater part of individuals, there is an almost infinite variety in those of the whole society. These varied occupations present an almost infinite variety of objects to the contemplation of those few, who, being attached to no particular occupation themselves, have leisure and inclination to examine the occupations of other people. The contemplation of so great a variety of objects necessarily exercises their minds in endless comparisons and combinations, and renders their understandings, in an extraordinary degree, both acute and comprehensive. Unless those few, however, happen to be placed in some very particular situations, their great abilities, though honourable to themselves, may contribute very little to the good government or happiness of their society. Notwithstanding the great abilities of those few, all the nobler parts of the human character may be, in a great measure, obliterated and extinguished in the great body of the people.

# Part III. Classical Political Economy

## Chapter 14*

# From *The Principles of Political Economy and Taxation*

**David Ricardo**

The same rule which regulates the relative value of commodities in one country does not regulate the relative value of the commodities exchanged between two or more countries.

Under a system of perfectly free commerce, each country naturally devotes its capital and labor to such employments as are most beneficial to each. This pursuit of individual advantage is admirably connected with the universal good of the whole. By stimulating industry, by rewarding ingenuity, and by using most efficaciously the peculiar powers bestowed by nature, it distributes labor most effectively and most economically: while, by increasing the general mass of productions, it diffuses general benefit, and binds together, by one common tie of interest and intercourse, the universal society of nations throughout the civilised world. It is this principle which determines that wine shall be made in France and Portugal, that corn sell be grown in America and Poland, and that hardware and other goods shall be manufactured in England.

In one and the same country, profits are, generally speaking, always on the same level; or differ only as the employment of capital may be more or less secure and agreeable. It is not so between different countries. If the profits of capital employed in Yorkshire should exceed

* Taken from *The Principles of Political Economy and Taxation,* David Ricardo, J. M. Dent & Sons Ltd., 1965, pp. 81–2.

those of capital employed in London, capital would speedily move from London to Yorkshire, and an equality of profits would be effected; but if in consequence of the diminished rate of production in the lands of England from the increase of capital and population wages should rise and profits fall, it would not follow that capital and population would necessarily move from England to Holland, or Spain, or Russia, where profits might be higher.

If Portugal had no commercial connection with other countries, instead of employing a great part of her capital and industry in the production of wines, with which she purchases for her own use the cloth and hardware of other countries, she would be obliged to devote a part of that capital to the manufacture of those commodities, which she would thus obtain probably inferior in quality as well as quantity.

The quantity of wine which she shall give in exchange for the cloth of England is not determined by the respective quantities of labor devoted to the production of each, as it would be if both commodities were manufactured in England, or both in Portugal.

England may be so circumstanced that to produce the cloth may require the labor of 100 men for one year; and if she attempted to make the wine, it might require the labor of 120 men for the same time. England would therefore find it her interest to import wine, and to purchase it by the exportation of cloth.

To produce the wine in Portugal might require only the labor of 80 men for one year, and to produce the cloth in the same country might require the labor of 90 men for the same time. It would therefore be advantageous for her to export wine in exchange for cloth. This exchange might even take place notwithstanding that the commodity imported by Portugal could be produced there with less labor than in England. Though she could make the cloth with the labor of 90 men, she would import it from a country where it required the labor of 100 men to produce it, because it would be advantageous to her rather to employ her capital in the production of wine, for which she would obtain more cloth from England, than she could produce by diverting a portion of her capital from the cultivation of vines to the manufacture of cloth.

Thus England would give the produce of the labor of 100 men for the produce of the labor of 80. Such an exchange could not take place between the individuals of the same country. The labor of 100 Englishmen cannot be given for that of 80 Englishmen, but the produce of the labor of 100 Englishmen may be given for the produce of the labor of 80 Portuguese, 60 Russians, or 120 East Indians. The difference in this respect, between a single country and many, is easily accounted for, by considering the difficulty with which capital moves from one country to another, to seek a more profitable employment, and the activity with which it invariably passes from one province to another in the same country.[1]

It would undoubtedly be advantageous to the capitalists of England, and to the consumers in both countries, that under such circumstances the wine and the cloth should both be made in Portugal, and therefore that the capital and labor of England employed in making cloth should be removed to Portugal for that purpose. In that case, the relative value of these commodities would be regulated by the same principle as if one were the produce of Yorkshire and the other of London: and in every other case, if capital freely flowed towards those countries where it could be most profitably employed, there could be no difference in the rate of profit, and no other difference in the real or labor price of commodities than the additional quantity of labor required to convey them to the various markets where they were to be sold.

Experience, however, shows that the fancied or real insecurity of capital, when not under the immediate control of its owner, together with the natural disinclination which every man has to quit the country of his birth and connections, and intrust himself, with all his habits fixed, to a strange government and new laws, check the emigration of capital. These feelings, which I should be sorry to see weakened, induce most men of

---

[1] It will appear, then, that a country possessing very considerable advantages in machinery and skill, and which may therefore be enabled to manufacture commodities with much less labor than her neighbours may, in return for such commodities, import a portion of the corn required for its consumption, even if its land were more fertile and corn could be grown with less labor than in the country from which it was imported. Two men can both make shoes and hats, and one is superior to the other in both employments; but in making hats he can only exceed his competitor by one-fifth or 20 per cent., and in making shoes he can excel him by one-third or 33 per cent; — will it not be for the interest of both that the superior man should employ himself exclusively in making shoes, and the inferior man in making hats?

property to be satisfied with a low rate of profits in their own country, rather than seek a more advantageous employment for their wealth in foreign nations.

# Chapter 15*

# From *The Economy of Machinery and Manufactures*

**Charles Babbage**

## On the Division of Labor

Perhaps the most important principle on which the economy of a manufacture depends, is the *division of labor* amongst the persons who perform the work. The first application of this principle must have been made in a very early stage of society; for it must soon have been apparent, that a larger number of comforts and conveniences could be acquired by each individual, if one man restricted his occupation to the art of making bows, another to that of building houses, a third boats, and so on. This division of labor into trades was not, however, the result of an opinion that the general riches of the community would be increased by such an arrangement; but it must have arisen from the circumstance of each individual so employed discovering that he himself could thus make a greater profit of his labor than by pursuing more varied occupations. Society must have made considerable advances before this principle could have been carried into the workshop; for it is only in countries which have attained a high degree of civilization, and in articles in which there is a great competition amongst the producers, that the most perfect system of the division of labor is to be observed. The various principles

* Taken from *The Economy of Machinery and Manufactures*, ed. Martin Campbell-Kelly, William Pickering, London, 1989, Vol. 8, pp. 121–5, 130-40 and p. 143.

on which the advantages of this system depend, have been much the subject of discussion amongst writers on political economy; but the relative importance of their influence does not appear, in all cases, to have been estimated with sufficient precision. It is my intention, in the first instance, to state shortly those principles, and then to point out what appears to me to have been omitted by those who have previously treated the subject.

1. *Of the time required for learning.* It will readily be admitted, that the portion of time occupied in the acquisition of any art will depend on the difficulty of its execution; and that the greater the number of distinct processes, the longer will be the time which the apprentice must employ in acquiring it. Five or seven years have been adopted, in a great many trades, as the time considered requisite for a lad to acquire a sufficient knowledge of his art, and to enable him to repay by his labor, during the latter portion of his time, the expense incurred by his master at its commencement. If, however, instead of learning *all* the different processes for making a needle, for instance, his attention be confined to one operation, the portion of time consumed unprofitably at the commencement of his apprenticeship will be small, and all the rest of it will be beneficial to his master: and, consequently, if there be any competition amongst the masters, the apprentice will be able to make better terms, and diminish the period of his servitude. Again, the facility of acquiring skill in a single process, and the early period of life at which it can be made a source of profit, will induce a greater number of parents to bring up their children to it; and from this circumstance also, the number of workmen being increased, the wages will soon fall.

2. *Of waste of materials in learning.* A certain quantity of material will, in all cases, be consumed unprofitably, or spoiled by every person who learns an art; and as he applies himself to each new process, he will waste some of the raw material, or of the partly manufactured commodity. But if each man commit this waste in acquiring successively every process, the quantity of waste will be much greater than if each person confine his attention to one process; in this view of the subject, therefore, the division of labor will diminish the price of production.

3. Another advantage resulting from the division of labor is, *the saving of that portion of time which is always lost in changing from one*

*occupation to another.* When the human hand, or the human head, has been for some time occupied in any kind of work, it cannot instantly change its employment with full effect. The muscles of the limbs employed have acquired a flexibility during their exertion, and those not in action a stiffness during rest, which renders every change slow and unequal in the commencement. Long habit also produces in the muscles exercised a capacity for enduring fatigue to a much greater degree than they could support under other circumstances. A similar result seems to take place in any change of mental exertion; the attention bestowed on the new subject not being so perfect at first as it becomes after some exercise.

4. *Change of tools.* The employment of different tools in the successive processes is another cause of the loss of time in changing from one operation to another. If these tools are simple, and the change is not frequent, the loss of time is not considerable; but in many processes of the arts the tools are of great delicacy, requiring accurate adjustment every time they are used; and in many cases the time employed in adjusting bears a large proportion to that employed in using the tool. The sliding-rest, the dividing and the drilling-engine, are of this kind; and hence, in manufactories of sufficient extent, it is found to be good economy to keep one machine constantly employed in one kind of work: one lathe, for example, having a screw motion to its sliding-rest along the whole length of its bed, is kept constantly making cylinders; another, having a motion for equalizing the velocity of the work at the point at which it passes the tool, is kept for facing surfaces; whilst a third is constantly employed in cutting wheels.

5. *Skill acquired by frequent repetition of the same processes.* The constant repetition of the same process necessarily produces in the workman a degree of excellence and rapidity in his particular department, which is never possessed by a person who is obliged to execute many different processes. This rapidity is still further increased from the circumstance that most of the operations in factories, where the division of labor is carried to a considerable extent, are paid for as piece-work. It is difficult to estimate in numbers the effect of this cause upon production. In nail-making, Adam Smith has stated, that it is almost three to one; for, he observes, that a smith accustomed to make nails, but

whose whole business has not been that of a nailer, can make only from eight hundred to a thousand per day; whilst a lad who had never exercised any other trade, can make upwards of two thousand three hundred a day.

In different trades, the economy of production arising from the last-mentioned cause will necessarily be different. The case of nail-making is, perhaps, rather an extreme one. It must, however, be observed, that, in one sense, this is not a permanent source of advantage; for, though it acts at the commencement of an establishment, yet every month adds to the skill of the workmen; and at the end of three or four years they will not be very far behind those who have never practised any other branch of their art. Upon an occasion when a large issue of bank-notes was required, a clerk at the Bank of England signed his name, consisting of seven letters, including the initial of his Christian name, five thousand three hundred times during eleven working hours, besides arranging the notes he had signed in parcels of fifty each.

6. *The division of labor suggests the contrivance of tools and machinery to execute its processes.* When each processes, by which any article is produced, is the sole occupation of one individual, his whole attention being devoted to a very limited and simple operation, improvements in the form of his tools, or in the mode of using them, are much more likely to occur to his mind, than if it were distracted by a greater variety of circumstances. Such an improvement in the tool is generally the first step towards a machine. If a piece of metal is to be cut in a lathe, for example, there is one particular angle at which the cutting-tool must be held to insure the cleanest cut; and it is quite natural that the idea of fixing the tool at that angle should present itself to an intelligent workman. The necessity of moving the tool slowly, and in a direction parallel to itself, would suggest the use of a screw, and thus arises the sliding-rest. It was probably the idea of mounting a chisel in a frame, to prevent its cutting too deeply, which gave rise to the common carpenter's plane. In cases where a blow from a hammer is employed, experience teaches the proper force required. The transition from the hammer held in the hand to one mounted upon an axis, and lifted regularly to a certain height by some mechanical contrivance, requires perhaps a greater degree of invention than those just instanced; yet it is not difficult to

perceive, that, if the hammer always falls from the same height, its effect must be always the same.

When each process has been reduced to the use of some simple tool, the union of all these tools, actuated by one moving power, constitutes a machine. In contriving tools and simplifying processes, the operative workmen are, perhaps, most successful; but it requires far other habits to combine into one machine these scattered arts. A previous education as a workman in the peculiar trade, is undoubtedly a valuable preliminary; but in order to make such combinations with any reasonable expectation of success, an extensive knowledge of machinery, and the power of making mechanical drawings, are essentially requisite. These accomplishments are now much more common than they were formerly; and their absence was, perhaps, one of the causes of the multitude of failures in the early history of many of our manufactures.

Such are the principles usually assigned as the causes of the advantage resulting from the division of labor. As in the view I have taken of the question, the most important and influential cause has been altogether unnoticed, I shall restate those principles in the words of Adam Smith:

> The great increase in the quantity of work, which, in consequence of the division of labor, the same number of people are capable of performing, is owing to three different circumstances: first. to the increase of dexterity in every particular workman; secondly, to the saving of time, which is commonly lost in passing from one species of work to another; and, lastly, to the invention of a great number of machines which facilitate and abridge labor, and enable one man to do the work of many. [a]

Now although all these are important causes, and each has its influence on the result; yet it appears to me, that any explanation of the cheapness of manufactured articles, as consequent upon the division of labor, would be incomplete if the following principle were omitted to be stated.

*That the master manufacturer, by dividing the work to be executed into different processes, each requiring different degrees of skill or of*

---

[a] Adam Smith, *The wealth of nations* (1776), Vol. 1, Book 1, Chap. 1.

*force, can purchase exactly that precise quantity of both which is necessary for each process; whereas, if the whole work were executed by one workman, that person must possess sufficient skill to perform the most difficult, and sufficient strength to execute the most laborious, of the operations into which the art is divided.* *

As the clear apprehension of this principle, upon which a great part of the economy arising from the division of labor depends, is of considerable importance, it may be desirable to point out its precise and numerical application in some specific manufacture. The art of making needles is, perhaps, that which I should have selected for this illustration. as comprehending a very large number of processes remarkably different in their nature; but the less difficult art of pin-making, has some claim to attention, from its having been used by Adam Smith; and I am confirmed in the choice of it, by the circumstance of our possessing a very accurate and minute description of that art, as practised in France above half a century ago.

Having thus generally described the various processes of pin-making, and having stated the usual cost of each, it will be convenient to present a tabular view of the time occupied by each process, and its cost, as well as the sums which can be earned by the persons who confine themselves solely to each process. As the rate of wages is itself fluctuating, and as the prices paid and quantities executed have been given only between certain limits, it is not to be expected that this table can represent the cost of each part of the work with the minutest accuracy, nor even that it shall accord perfectly with the prices above given: but it has been drawn up with some care, and will be quite sufficient to serve as the basis of those reasonings which it is meant to illustrate. A table nearly similar will be subjoined, which has been deduced from a statement of M. Perronet, respecting the art of pin-making in France, above seventy years ago.

---

* I have already stated that this principle presented itself to me after a personal examination of a number of manufactories and workshops devoted to different purposes; but I have since found that it had been distinctly pointed out, in the work of Gioja, *Nuovo Prospetto delle Scienze Economiche,* 6 tom. 4to. Milano. 1815, tom. i. capo iv.

**English manufacture**

Pins, *Elevens,* 5546 weigh one pound; *one dozen* = 6932 pins weigh twenty ounces, and require six ounces of paper.

| Name of the process | Work men | Time for making 1 lb of pins | Cost of making 1 lb of pins | Workman earns per day | | Price of making each part of a single pin in millionths of a penny |
|---|---|---|---|---|---|---|
| | | Hours | Pence | s. | d. | |
| 1. Drawing wire | Man | .3636 | 1.2500 | 3 | 3 | 225 |
| 2. Straightening wire | Woman | .3000 | .2840 | 1 | 0 | 51 |
| | Girl | .3000 | .1420 | 0 | 6 | 26 |
| 3. Pointing | Man | .3000 | 1.7750 | 5 | 3 | 319 |
| 4. Twisting and cutting heads | Boy | .0400 | .0147 | 0 | 4.5 | 3 |
| | Man | 0.0400 | .2103 | 5 | 4.5 | 38 |
| 5. Heading | Woman | 4.0000 | 5.0000 | 1 | 3 | 901 |
| 6. Tinning, or whitening | Man | .1071 | .6666 | 6 | 0 | 121 |
| | Woman | .1071 | .3333 | 3 | 0 | 60 |
| 7. Papering | Woman | 2.1314 | 3.1973 | 1 | 6 | 576 |
| | | 7.6892 | 12.8732 | | | 2320 |

Number of persons employed: Men, 4; Women, 4; Children, 2. Total, 10.

**French manufacture**

Cost of 12,000 pins, No.6, each being eight-tenths of an English inch in length – as they were manufactured in France about 1760; with the cost of each operation: deduced from the observations and statement of M. Perronet.

| | *Time for making twelve thousand pins* | *Cost of making twelve thousand pins* | *Workman usually earns per day* | *Expense of tools and materials* |
|---|---|---|---|---|
| | *Hours* | *Pence* | *Pence* | *Pence* |
| 1. Wire | — | — | — | 24.75 |
| 2. Straightening and cutting | 1.2 | .5 | 4.5 | — |
| 3. Coarse pointing | 1.2 | .625 | 10.0 | — |
| Turning wheel* | 1.2 | .875 | 7.0 | — |
| Fine pointing | .8 | .5 | 9.375 | — |
| Turning wheel | 1.2 | .5 | 4.75 | — |
| Cutting off pointed ends | .6 | .375 | 7.5 | — |
| 4. Turning spiral | .5 | .125 | 3.0 | — |
| Cutting off heads | .8 | .375 | 5.625 | — |
| Fuel to anneal ditto | — | — | — | .125 |
| 5. Heading | 12.0 | .333 | 4.25 | — |
| 6. Tartar for cleaning | — | — | — | .5 |
| Tartar for whitening | — | — | — | .5 |
| 7. Papering | 4.8 | .5 | 2.0 | — |
| Paper | — | — | — | 1.0 |
| Wear of tools | — | — | — | 2.0 |
| | 24.3 | 4.708 | | |

*The great expense of turning the wheel appears to have arisen from the person so occupied being unemployed during half his time, whilst the pointer went to another manufactory.

It appears from the analysis we have given of the art of pin-making, that it occupies rather more than seven hours and a half of time, for ten different individuals working in succession on the same material, to convert it into a pound of pins; and that the total expense of their labor, each being paid in the joint ratio of his skill and of the time he is employed, amounts very nearly to 1*s.* 1*d.* But from an examination of the first of these tables, it appears that the wages earned by the persons employed vary from 4.5*d.* per day up to 6*s.*, and consequently the skill which is required for their respective employments may be measured by those sums. Now it is evident, that if one person were required to make the whole pound of pins, he must have skill enough to earn about *5s. 3d.* per day, whilst he is pointing the wires or cutting off the heads from the spiral coils – and *6s,* when he is whitening the pins; which three operations together would occupy little more than the seventeenth part of his time. It is also apparent, that during more than one half of his time he must be earning only 1*s.* 3*d.* per day, in putting on the heads; although his skill, if properly employed, would, in the same time, produce nearly five times as much. If, therefore, we were to employ, for all the processes, the man who whitens the pins, and who earns *6s.* per day, even supposing that he could make the pound of pins in an equally short time, yet we must pay him for his time 46.14 pence, or about 3*s.* 10*d.* *The pins would therefore cost, in making, three times and three quarters as much as they now do by the application of the division of labor.*

The higher the skill required of the workman in any one process of a manufacture, and the smaller the time during which it is employed, so much the greater will be the advantage of separating that process from the rest, and devoting one person's attention entirely to it. Had we selected the art of needle-making as our illustration, the economy arising from the division of labor would have been still more striking; for the process of tempering the needles requires great skill, attention, and experience, and although from three to four thousand are tempered at once, the workman is paid a very high rate of wages. In another process of the same manufacture, dry-pointing, which also is executed with great rapidity, the wages earned by the workman reach from *7s.* to 12*s.*, 15*s.*, and even, in some instances, to *20s.* per day; whilst other processes are carried on by children paid at the rate of *6d.* per day.

Some further reflections suggested by the preceding analysis, will be reserved until we have placed before the reader a brief description of a machine for making pins, invented by an American. It is highly ingenious in point of contrivance, and, in respect to its economical principles, will furnish a strong and interesting contrast with the manufacture of pins by the human hand. In this machine a coil of brass wire is placed on an axis; one end of this wire is drawn by a pair of rollers through a small hole in a plate of steel, and is held there by a forceps. As soon as the machine is put in action —

1. The forceps draws the wire on to a distance equal in length to one pin: a cutting edge of steel then descends close to the hole through which the wire entered, and severs the piece drawn out.

2. The forceps holding the piece thus separated moves on, till it brings the wire to the centre of the *chuck* of a small lathe, which opens to receive it. Whilst the forceps is returning to fetch another piece of wire, the lathe revolves rapidly, and grinds the projecting end of the wire upon a steel mill, which advances towards it.

3. After this first or coarse pointing, the lathe stops, and another forceps takes hold of the half-pointed pin, (which is instantly released by the opening of the *chuck),* and conveys it to a similar *chuck* of an adjacent lathe, which receives it, and finishes the pointing on a finer steel mill.

4. This mill again stops, and another forceps removes the pointed pin into a pair of strong steel clams, having a small groove in them by which they hold the pin very firmly. A part of this groove, which terminates at that edge of the steel clams which is intended to form the head of the pin, is made conical. A small round steel punch is now driven forcibly against the end of the wire thus clamped, and the head of the pin is partially formed by compressing the wire into the conical cavity.

5. Another pair of forceps now removes the pin to another pair of clams, and the head of the pin is completed by a blow from a second punch, the end of which is slightly concave. Each pair of forceps returns as soon as it has delivered its burden; and thus there are always five pieces of wire at the same moment in different stages of advance towards a finished pin.

The pins so formed are received in a tray, and whitened and papered in the usual manner. About sixty pins can thus be made by this machine in one minute; but each process occupies exactly the same time.

In order to judge of the value of such a machine, compared with hand labor, it would be necessary to ascertain: 1. The defects to which pins so made are liable. 2. Their advantages, if any, over those made in the usual way. 3. The prime cost of the machine for making them. 4. The expense of keeping it in repair. 5. The expense of moving the machine and of attending to it.

1. Pins made by the machine are more likely to bend, because the head being 'punched up', the wire must be in a soft state to admit of that operation. 2. Pins made by the machine are better than common ones, because they are not subject to losing their heads. 3. With respect to the prime cost of a machine, it would be very much reduced if a large number should be required. 4. With regard to its wear and tear, experience only can decide: but it may be remarked, that the steel clams or dies in which the heads are punched up, will wear quickly unless the wire has been softened by annealing; and that if softened, the bodies of the pins will bend too readily. Such an inconvenience might be remedied, either by making the machine spin the heads and fix them on, or by annealing only that end of the wire which is to become the head of the pin; but this would cause a delay between the operations, since the brass is too brittle, while heated, to bear a blow without crumbling. 5. On comparing the time occupied by the machine with that stated in the analysis, we find that, except in the heading, the human hand is more rapid. Three thousand six hundred pins are pointed by the machine in one hour, whilst a man can point fifteen thousand six hundred in the same time. But in the process of heading, the rapidity of the machine is two and a half times that of the human hand. It must, however, be observed, that the grinding in the machine does not require the application of a force equal to that of one man; for all the processes are executed at once by the machine, and a single laborer can easily work it.

**On the Division of Mental Labor**

We have already mentioned what may, perhaps, appear paradoxical to some of our readers — that the division of labor can be applied with equal success to mental as to mechanical operations, and that it ensures in both the same economy of time. A short account of its practical application, in the most extensive series of calculations ever executed, will offer an interesting illustration of this fact, whilst at the same time it will afford an occasion for showing that the arrangements which ought to regulate the interior economy of a manufactory, are founded on principles of deeper root than may have been supposed, and are capable of being usefully employed in preparing the road to some of the sublimest investigations of the human mind.

In the midst of that excitement which accompanied the Revolution of France and the succeeding wars, the ambition of the nation, unexhausted by its fatal passion for military renown, was at the same time directed to some of the nobler and more permanent triumphs which mark the era of a people's greatness — and which receive the applause of posterity long after their conquests have been wrested from them, or even when their existence as a nation may be told only by the page of history. Amongst their enterprises of science, the French Government was desirous of producing a series of mathematical tables, to facilitate the application of the decimal system which they had so recently adopted. They directed, therefore, their mathematicians to construct such tables, on the most extensive scale. Their most distinguished philosophers, responding fully to the call of their country, invented new methods for this laborious task; and a work, completely answering the large demands of the Government, was produced in a remarkably short period of time. M. Prony, to whom the superintendence of this great undertaking was confided, in speaking of its commencement, observes:[a] *Je m'y livrai avec route l'ardeur dont j'étois capable, et je m'occupai d'abord du plan général de l'exécution.*

---

[a] *Translation:* I devoted myself to it with all the enthusiasm I could muster, and I first concerned myself with the general plan of execution. The many conditions which I had to fulfil called for the use of a large number of calculators; and it soon occurred to me that I could use in the making of these tables of *the division of labor,* such as is turned to such good account by the Commercial Arts in the perfection of work and the saving of time.

*Toutes les conditions que j'avois à remplir nécessitoient l'emploi d'un grand nombre de calculateurs,. et il me vint bientôt à la pensée d'appliquer à la confection de ces Tables* la division du travail, *dont les Arts de Commerce tirent un parti si avantageux pour réunir à la perfection de main-d'œuvre l'économie de la dépense et du temps.* The circumstance which gave rise to this singular application of the principle of *the division of labor* is so interesting, that no apology is necessary for introducing it from a small pamphlet printed at Paris a few years since, when a proposition was made by the English to the French Government, that the two countries should print these tables at their joint expense.

The origin of the idea is related in the following extract:[b]

C'est à un chapitre d'un ouvrage Anglais (*An Enquiry into the Nature and Causes of the Wealth of Nations*, by Adam Smith), justement célèbre, (I.) qu'est probablement due l'existence de l'ouvrage dont le gouvernement Britannique veut faire jouir le monde savant:

> Voici l'anecdote: M. de Prony s'était engagé, avec les comités de gouvernement, à composer pour la division centesimale du cercle, des tables logarithmiques et trigonometriques, qui, non seulement ne laissassent rien à

---

[b] *Translation:* The work by which the British Government wishes to benefit the world of learning probably owes its existence to a chapter in a justly famous English work:

Here is the anecdote: M. de Prony undertook, on behalf of the Government committees, to produce *logarithmic and trigonometrical tables for the decimal division of the circle, which, not only would leave nothing to be desired concerning accuracy, but would also form the greatest and most imposing monument of calculation ever made, or even thought of* The logarithms for the numbers 1 to 200,000 were a necessary and imperative supplement to this labor. It was easy for M. de Prony to determine that even with the help of three or four skilled collaborators, the greatest of possible life expectancies would not suffice to fulfil his commitment. He was concerned with this annoying thought when, finding himself at a bookshop, he saw the fine 1776 London edition of Smith in English; he opened the book at random and chanced on the first chapter, which deals with *the division of labor,* and where the manufacture of pins is given as an example. He had hardly perused the first pages before, by some inspiration, he had the idea of *manufacturing* his logarithms like pins. At that time he was studying at the Ecole Polytechnique an area of analysis which was connected with this type of work, *the method of differences,* and its application to *interpolation.* He went off to spend a few days in the country, and returned to Paris with the *manufacturing* plan, which was subsequently executed. He formed two workshops, which worked separately on the same calculations, and made use of reciprocal verification of the results.

desirer quant à l'exactitude, mais qui formassent le monument de calcul le plus vaste et le plus imposant qui eût jamais été execute, ou même concu. Les logarithmes des nombres de 1 à 200,000 formaient à ce travail un supplement nécessaire et exigé. Il fut aisé à M. de Prony de s'assurer que même en s'associant trois ou quatre habiles co-operateurs, la plus grande durée presumable de sa vie, ne lui suffirai pas pour remplir ses engagements. Il était occupé de cette fâcheuse pensée lorsque, se trouvant devant la boutique d'un marchand de livres, il appercut la belle edition Anglaise de Smith, donnée a Londres en 1776; il ouvrit le livre au hazard, et tomba sur le premier chapitre, qui traite de la division du travail, et où la fabrication des épingles est citée pour exemple. A peine avait-il parcouru les premières pages, que, par une espèce d'inspiration, il concut l'expédient de mettre ses logarithmes en manufacture comme les épingles. Il faisait, en ce moment, à l'école polytechnique, des lecons sur une partie d'analyse liée à ce genre de travail, la methode des differences, et ses applications à l'interpolation. Il alla passer quelques jours à la campagne, et revint à Paris avec le plan de fabrication, qui a été suivi dans l'exécution. Il rassembla deux ateliers, qui faisaient séparément les mêmes calculs, et se servaient de vérification reciproque.*

The ancient methods of computing tables were altogether inapplicable to such a proceeding. M. Prony, therefore, wishing to avail himself of all the talent of his country in devising new methods, formed the first section of those who were to take part in this enterprise out of five or six of the most eminent mathematicians in France.

*First section.* The duty of this first section was to investigate, amongst the various analytical expressions which could be found for the same function, that which was most readily adapted to simple numerical calculation by many individuals employed at the same time. This section had little or nothing to do with the actual numerical work. When its labors were concluded, the formulae on the use of which it had decided, were delivered to the second section.

---

* *Note sur la publication, proposée par le gouvemement / Anglais des grandes tables logarithmiques et trigonometriques de M. de Prony.* De l'imprimerie de F. Didot. December 1, 1820, p. 7.

*Second section.* This section consisted of seven or eight persons of considerable acquaintance with mathematics: and their duty was to convert into numbers the formulae put into their hands by the first section – an operation of great labor; and then to deliver out these formulae to the members of the third section, and receive from them the finished calculations. The members of this second section had certain means of verifying the calculations without the necessity of repeating, or even of examining, the whole of the work done by the third section.

*Third section.* The members of this section, whose number varied from sixty to eighty, received certain numbers from the second section, and, using nothing more than simple addition and subtraction, they returned to that section the tables in a finished state. It is remarkable that nine-tenths of this class had no knowledge of arithmetic beyond the two first rules which they were thus called upon to exercise, and that these persons were usually found more correct in their calculations, than those who possessed a more extensive knowledge of the subject.

When it is stated that the tables thus computed occupy seventeen large folio volumes, some idea may perhaps be formed of the labor. From that part executed by the third class, which may almost be termed mechanical, requiring the least knowledge and by far the greatest exertions, the first class were entirely exempt. Such labor can always be purchased at an easy rate. The duties of the second class, although requiring considerable skill in arithmetical operations, were yet in some measure relieved by the higher interest naturally felt in those more difficult operations. The exertions of the first class are not likely to require, upon another occasion, so much skill and labor as they did upon the first attempt to introduce such a method; but when the completion of a calculating engine shall have produced a substitute for the whole of the third section of computers, the attention of analysts will naturally be directed to simplifying its application, by a new discussion of the methods of converting analytical formulae into numbers.

The proceeding of M. Prony, in this celebrated system of calculation, much resembles that of a skilful person about to construct a cotton or silk mill, or any similar establishment. Having, by his own genius, or through the aid of his friends, found that some improved machinery may be successfully applied to his pursuit, he makes drawings of his plans of the machinery, and may himself be considered as constituting the first section. He next requires the assistance of operative engineers capable of executing the machinery he has designed, some of whom should understand the nature of the processes to be carried on; and these constitute his second section. When a sufficient number of machines have been made, a multitude of other persons, possessed of a lower degree of skill, must be employed in using them; these form the third section: but their work, and the just performance of the machines, must be still superintended by the second class.

As the possibility of performing arithmetical calculations by machinery may appear to non-mathematical readers to be rather too large a postulate, and as it is connected with the subject of the *division of labor,* I shall here endeavour, in a few lines, to give some slight perception of the manner in which this can be done - and thus to remove a small portion of the veil which covers that apparent mystery.

That nearly all tables of numbers which follow any law, however complicated, may be formed, to a greater or less extent, solely by the proper arrangement of the successive addition and subtraction of numbers befitting each table, is a general principle which can be demonstrated to those only who are well acquainted with mathematics; but the mind, even of the reader who is but very slightly acquainted with that science, will readily conceive that it is not impossible, by attending to the following example.

The subjoined table is the beginning of one in very extensive use, which has been printed and reprinted very frequently in many countries, and is called a *table of square numbers.*

| Terms of table | A table | B First difference | C Second difference |
|---|---|---|---|
| 1 | 1 | | |
| | | 3 | |
| 2 | 4 | | 2 |
| | | 5 | |
| 3 | 9 | | 2 |
| | | 7 | |
| 4 | 16 | | 2 |
| | | 9 | |
| 5 | 25 | | 2 |
| | | 11 | |
| 6 | 36 | | 2 |
| | | 13 | |
| 7 | 49 | | |

Any number in the table, column A, may be obtained, by multiplying the number which expresses the distance of that term from the commencement of the table by itself; thus, 25 is the fifth term from the beginning of the table, and 5 multiplied by itself, or by 5, is equal to 25. Let us now subtract each term of this table from the next succeeding term, and place the results in another column (B), which may be called first difference column. If we again subtract each term of this first difference from the succeeding term, we find the result is always the number 2, (column C); and that the same number will always recur in that column, which may be called the second difference, will appear to any person who takes the trouble to carry on the table a few terms further. Now when once this is admitted, it is quite clear that, provided the first term (1) of the table, the first term (3) of the first differences, and the first term (2) of the second or constant difference, are originally given, we can continue the table of square numbers to any extent, merely by addition: for the series of first differences may be formed by repeatedly adding the constant difference (2) to (3) the first number in column B, and we then have the series of numbers, 3, 5, 7, etc.[1]: and again, by successively adding each of these to the first number (1) of the table, we produce the square numbers.

[1] Mistaken as "3, 5, 6 etc." in C. Babbage 1989. --- Guang-Zhen Sun

The *division of labor* cannot be successfully practised unless there exists a great demand for its produce; and it requires a large capital to be employed in those arts in which it is used. In watchmaking it has been carried, perhaps, to the greatest extent. It was stated in evidence before a committee of the House of Commons, that there are a hundred and two distinct branches of this art, to each of which a boy may be put apprentice: and that he only learns his master's department, and is unable, after his apprenticeship has expired, without subsequent instruction, to work at any other branch. The watch-finisher, whose business is to put together the scattered parts, is the only one, out of the hundred and two persons, who can work in any other department than his own.

In one of the most difficult arts, that of mining, great improvements have resulted from the judicious distribution of the duties; and under the arrangements which have gradually been introduced, the whole system of the mine and its government is now placed under the control of the following officers.

1. A manager, who has the general knowledge of all that is to be done, and who may be assisted by one or more skilful persons.

2. Underground captains direct the proper mining operations, and govern the working miners.

3. The purser and book-keeper manage the accounts.

4. The engineer erects the engines, and superintends the men who work them.

5. A chief pitman has charge of the pumps and the apparatus of the shafts.

6. A surface-captain, with assistants, receives the ores raised, and directs the dressing department, the object of which is to render them marketable.

7. The head carpenter superintends many constructions.

8. The foreman of the smiths regulates the ironwork and tools.

9. A materials man selects, purchases, receives and delivers all articles required.

10. The roper has charge of ropes and cordage of all sorts.

# Chapter 16*

# From *The Philosophy of Manufactures*

**Andrew Ure**

When Adam Smith wrote his immortal elements of economics, automatic machinery being hardly known, he was properly led to regard the division of labor as the grand principle of manufacturing improvement; and he showed, in the example of pin-making, how each handicraftsman, being thereby enabled to perfect himself by practice in one point, became a quicker and cheaper workman. In each branch of manufacture he saw that some parts were, on that principle, of easy execution, like the cutting of pin wires into uniform lengths, and some were comparatively difficult, like the formation and fixation of their heads; and therefore he concluded that to each a workman of appropriate value and cost was naturally assigned. This appropriation forms the very essence of the division of labor, and has been constantly made since the origin of society. The ploughman, with powerful hand and skilful eye, has been always hired at high wages to form the furrow, and the ploughboy at low wages, to lead the team. But what was in Dr. Smith's time a topic of useful illustration, cannot now be used without risk of misleading the public mind as to the right principle of manufacturing industry. In fact, the division, or rather adaptation of labor to the different talents of men, is little thought of in factory employment. On the contrary, wherever a process requires peculiar dexterity and steadiness of

---

* Taken from *The Philosophy of Manufactures*, Andrew Ure, Frank Cass & Co. Ltd., 1967, pp. 19–23 and p. 30.

hand, it is withdrawn as soon as possible from the cunning workman, who is prone to irregularities of many kinds, and it is placed in charge of a peculiar mechanism, so self-regulating, that a child may superintend it. Thus, — to take an example from the spinning of cotton — the first operation in delicacy and importance, is that of laying the fibres truly parallel in the spongy slivers, and the next is that of drawing these out into slender spongy cords, called rovings, with the least possible twist; both being perfectly uniform throughout their total length. To execute either of these processes tolerably by a hand-wheel, would require a degree of skill not to be met with in one artisan out of a hundred. But fine yarn could not be made in factory-spinning except by taking these steps, nor was it ever made by machinery till Arkwright's sagacity contrived them. Moderately good yarn may be spun indeed on the *hand-wheel* without any drawings at all, and with even indifferent rovings, because the thread, under the two-fold action of twisting and extension, has a tendency to equalize itself.

The principle of the factory system then is, to substitute mechanical science for hand skill, and the partition of a process into its essential constituents, for the division or graduation of labor among artisans. On the handicraft plan, labor more or less skilled, was usually the most expensive element of production — *Materiam superabat opus*; but on the automatic plan, skilled labor gets progressively superseded, and will, eventually, be replaced by mere overlookers of machines,

By the infirmity of human nature it happens, that the more skilful the workman, the more self-willed and intractable he is apt to become, and, of course, the less fit a component of a mechanical system, in which, by occasional irregularities, he may do great damage to the whole. The grand object therefore of the modern manufacturer is, through the union of capital and science, to reduce the task of his work-people to the exercise of vigilance and dexterity, — faculties, when concentred to one process, speedily brought to perfection in the young. In the infancy of mechanical engineering, a machine-factory displayed the division of labor in manifold gradations — the file, the drill, the lathe, having each its different work-men in the order of skill: but the dexterous hands of the filer and driller are now superseded by the planning, the key-groove cutting, and the drilling-machines; and those of the iron and brass turners, by the self-acting slide-lathe. Mr. Anthony Strutt, who conducts the mechanical department of the great cotton factories of Belper and Milford, has so thoroughly departed from the old routine of the schools, that he will employ no man who has learned his craft by regular apprenticeship; but in contempt, as it were, of the division of labor principle, he sets a ploughboy to turn a shaft of perhaps several tons weight, and never has reason to repent his preference, because he infuses into the turning apparatus a precision of action, equal, if not superior, to the skill of the most experienced journeyman.

An eminent mechanician in Manchester told me, that he does not choose to make any steam-engines at present, because with his existing means, he would need to resort to the old principle of the division of labor, so fruitful of jealousies and strikes among workmen; but he intends to prosecute that branch of business whenever he has prepared suitable arrangements on the equalization of labor, or automatic plan. On the graduation system, a man must serve an apprenticeship of many years before his hand and eye become skilled enough for certain mechanical feats; but on the system of decomposing a process into its constituents, and embodying each part in an automatic machine, a person of common care and capacity may be entrusted with any of the said elementary parts after a short probation, and may be transferred from one to another, on any emergency, at the discretion of the master. Such translations are utterly at variance with the old practice of the division of labor, which fixed one man to shaping the head of a pin, and another to sharpening its point, with most irksome and spirit-wasting uniformity, for a whole life.

It was indeed a subject of regret to observe how frequently the workman's eminence, in any craft, had to be purchased by the sacrifice of his health and comfort. To one unvaried operation, which required unremitting dexterity and diligence, his hand and eye were constantly on the strain, or if they were suffered to swerve from their task for a time, considerable loss ensued, either to the employer, or the operative, according as the work was done by the day or by the piece. But on the equalization plan of self-acting machines, the operative needs to call his faculties only into agreeable exercise; he is seldom harassed with anxiety or fatigue, and may find many leisure moments for either amusement or meditation, without detriment to his master's interests or his own. As his business consists in tending the work of a well regulated mechanism, he can learn it in a short period; and when he transfers his services from one machine to another, he varies his task, and enlarges his views, by thinking on those general combinations which result from his and his companions' labors. Thus, that cramping of the faculties, that narrowing of the mind, that stunting of the frame, which were ascribed, and not unjustly, by moral writers, to the division of labor, cannot, in common circumstances, occur under the equable distribution of industry. How superior in vigour and intelligence are the factory mechanics in Lancashire, where the latter system of labor prevails, to the handicraft artisans of London, who, to a great extent, continue slaves to the former! The one set is familiar with almost every physico-mechanical combination, while the other seldom knows anything beyond the pin-head sphere of his daily task.

It is, in fact, the constant aim and tendency of every improvement in machinery to supersede human labor altogether, or to diminish its cost, by substituting the industry of women and children for that of men; or that of ordinary laborers, for trained artisans. In most of the water-twist, or throstle cotton mills, the spinning is entirely managed by females of sixteen years and upwards. The effect of substituting the self-acting mule for the common mule, is to discharge the greater part of the men spinners, and to retain adolescents and children. The proprietor of a factory near Stockport states, in evidence to the commissioners, that by such substitution, he would save 50l. a week in wages, in consequence of dispensing with nearly forty male spinners, at about 25*s*. of wages each. This tendency to employ merely children with watchful eyes and nimble fingers, instead of journeymen of long experience, shows how the scholastic dogma of the division of labor into degrees of skill has been exploded by our enlightened manufacturers.

Improvements in machinery have a three-fold bearing: —

1st. They make it possible to fabricate some articles which, but for them, could not be fabricated at all.

2d. They enable an operative to turn out a greater quantity of work than he could before, — time, labor, and quality of work remaining constant.

3d. They effect a substitution of labor comparatively unskilled, for that which is more skilled.

# Chapter 17*

# From *A Commentary on An Inquiry into the Nature and Causes of the Wealth of Nations*

**Edward Gibbon Wakefield**

## Notes to Chapter One "Of the Division of Labor"

No one will deny, however, that there is a wide difference between an operation, work, or business, which is performed by labor, and the labor which performs it. The muscular exertion by which a house is built, is not the same thing as the operation of building a house; the operation of making a pin is something entirely distinct from the muscular exertion by means of which the pin is made. These different things are, over and over again, confounded by Adam Smith. To establish this position, it will be sufficient to mark a number of instances in which he expresses by some other term than "division of labor," what he generally employs that term to express.

"The important *business* of making a pin is, in this manner, divided into about eighteen *distinct operations.*"

"The separation of different *trades* and *employments* from one another."

" How many different *trades* are employed [pursued] in each branch of the linen and woollen manufactures."

"So complete a separation of one *business from* another."

---

* Taken from *A Commentary on An Inquiry into the Nature and Causes of the Wealth of Nations,* London: Charles Knight and Co., 1835, pp. 22–30 and 77-82.

"It is impossible to separate so entirely the *business* of the grazier from that of the corn-farmer, as the *trade* of the carpenter is commonly separated from that of the smith."

"Philosophy or speculation becomes, like every other *employment,* the principal or sole *trade* or *occupation* of a particular class of citizens. Like every other *employment,* too, it is subdivided into a great number of different branches."

"The subdivision of *employment* in philosophy, as well as in every other *business,* improves dexterity and saves time."

In all these instances, and not a few more, division is said to take place, not, as the writer says elsewhere, in the labor which performs operations, but in the operations which are performed by labor. The impropriety of using terms so dissimilar, to express the same meaning, is obvious enough; but this is not a dispute about terms merely, as will be seen by the following curious remarks; curious, that is, as appearing in a treatise on the *division* of labor.

"Observe the accommodation of the most common artificer or day-labourer in a civilized and thriving country, and you will perceive that the *number of people* of whose industry a part, though but a small part, has been employed in procuring him this accommodation, exceeds *all computation.* The woollen coat, for examples which covers the day-labourer, as coarse and rough as it may appear, is the produce of the *joint labor* of a great multitude of workmen.". "Without the assistance and *co-operation of many thousands;* the very meanest person in a civilized country could not be provided, even according to, what we very falsely imagine, the easy and simple manner in which he is commonly accommodated."

Here, then, labor is said to be united, as in fact it is whenever employments are divided. Nature has divided labor into single pairs of hands. The greatest division of labor takes place amongst those exceedingly barbarous savages who never help each other, who work separately from each other; and division of employments, with all its great results, depends altogether on combination of labor, or co-operation. Such important consequences spring from this principle, that it deserves the most ample illustration.

"Suppose," says Dr. Whately, "a number of travellers proceeding through some nearly desert country, such as many parts of America, and journeying together in a kind of cafila or caravan for the sake of mutual security: when they came to a halting-place for the night, they would not fail to make some kind of extemporaneous arrangement, that some should unlade and fodder the cattle, while others should fetch fire-wood from the nearest thicket, and others water from the spring: some, in the meantime, would be occupied in' pitching tents, or erecting sheds of boughs; others in preparing food for the whole party; while some, again, with their arms in readiness, would be posted as centinels, in suitable spots, to watch that the rest might not be surprised by bands of robbers. It would be evident to them that, but for such an arrangement, each man would have to go to the spring for water, and to the wood for fuel; would have to prepare his own meal with almost as much trouble as it costs to dress food for the whole, and would have to perform all these tasks encumbered by his arms, and on the watch for a hostile attack."

All this would be evident to them; they would perceive, in short, the great utility of separating the different occupations required for their ease and safety. But in order that the travellers should thus apportion those different occupations amongst their whole body, it would be necessary that they should first combine their labor by agreeing to travel together, and to help each other on the way. If each of them had travelled alone, each man's labor would have been separated or divided, not only from that of all the others, but again amongst the several occupations of going to the wood for fire, and to the spring for water, &c.: if the labor of the travellers had been so divided, there could not have been any, the slightest division of their employments. In like manner, the division of employments which takes place in a pin-factory, results from, and is wholly dependent on, the union, generally under one roof, of all the labor by which the pins are made. Though no entire pin be made by anyone person, each pin is the produce of many persons' united labor; many persons whose labor is united, in order that the whole operation which it is to perform, may be separated into distinct parts, and easily apportioned amongst the workmen. It appears, therefore, not only that "division of labor" is a most improper term as commonly used; not only that this is the proper term for expressing a state of things under which what is commonly expressed by it — namely, division of employments — cannot possibly take place; but that all writers on political economy, from Adam Smith downwards, while treating of the "causes of improvement in the productive powers of labor," have overlooked a principle of first-rate importance.

This principle is, that all improvements in the productive powers of labor, including division of employments, depend upon co-operation.

Co-operation appears to be of two distinct kinds: first, such co-operation as takes place when several persons help each other in the same employment; secondly, such co-operation as takes place when several persons help each other in different employments. These may be termed simple co-operation; and complex co-operation. It will be seen presently, that, until men help each other in simple operations, they cannot well help each other in operations which consist of several parts.

The advantage of simple co-operation is illustrated by the case of two greyhounds running together, which, it is said, will kill more hares than four greyhounds running separately. In a vast number of simple operations performed by human exertion, it is quite obvious that two men working together will do more than four, or four times four men, each of whom should work alone. In the lifting of heavy weights, for example, in the felling of trees, in the sawing of timber, in the gathering of much hay or corn during a short period of fine weather, in draining a large extent of land during the short season when such a work may be properly conducted, in the pulling of ropes on board ship, in the rowing of large boats, in some mining operations, in the erection of a scaffolding for building, and in the breaking of stones for the repair of a road, so that the whole of the road shall always be kept in good order; in all these simple operations, and thousands more, it is absolutely necessary that many persons should work together, at the same time, in the same place, and in the same way. The savages of New Holland never help each other, even in the most simple operations; and their condition is hardly superior, in some respects it is inferior, to that of the wild animals which they now and then catch. Let any one imagine that the laborers of England should suddenly desist from helping each other in simple employments, and he will see at once the prodigious advantages of simple co-operation. In a countless number of employments, the produce of labor is, up to a certain point, in proportion to such mutual assistance amongst the workmen. This is the first step in social improvement. A single person, working entirely by himself, either in hunting, or in cultivating the earth, will not, it seems plain, obtain more food than what lie requires for his own subsistence: several persons combining their labor, in the most simple operations either of the chace or of agriculture, will obtain more food than they require; they will obtain a surplus produce, which surplus produce may either be used as capital for the employment of more laborers, whereby the produce, in proportion to the hands at work, will be' still further increased; or it may be given in exchange for some other kind of produce, provided always that some other body of workmen have combined their labor, and have so obtained, of some other kind of produce, more than they require for themselves. This possession of capital, and this power of exchanging, both of them being strictly dependent on the greater productiveness of labor arising from simple co-operation, constitute the second step in social improvement. One body of men having combined their labor to raise more food than they require, another body of men are induced to combine their labor for the purpose of producing more clothes than they require, and, with those surplus clothes, buying the surplus food of the other body of laborers; while, if both bodies together have produced more food and clothes than they both require, both bodies obtain, by means of exchange, a proper capital for setting more laborers to work in their respective occupations. What is true of two bodies of men, applies to any number of bodies, however great the difference in their occupations; and thus we perceive, that the division of employments, the power of exchanging, and the possession of a capital as well, depend on the combination of labor in simple operations.

The use of capital, and not the power, but the act of exchanging, and further the division of employments, are still dependent on something else than simple co-operation; they are all dependent also upon arrangements, agreements, concert, or combination, of a general kind, in which the whole society takes a part, and which, for want of a better expression, may be termed complex co-operation.

When a body of men raise more food than they want, and employ that surplus food as capital, paying it in wages to other laborers, those other laborers act in concert or combination with those capitalists: it is only by means of concert or co-operation, that the body who raise more food than they want, can exchange with the body who raise more clothes than they want; and if the two bodies were separated, either by distance or disinclination — unless the two bodies should virtually form themselves into one, for the common object of raising enough food and clothes for the whole — they could not divide into two distinct parts the whole operation of producing a sufficient quantity of food and clothes. The division of pursuits, then, into the management of capital, and such occupations as are carried on by muscular exertion, all division of employments, and all exchanges, result from co-operation amongst men; not only simple co-operation, which first raises capital, and surplus produce for exchange, but also complex co-operation, which enable the rich man to employ his capital, and the poor one to consume it, and which includes all the means over and above surplus produce, for practising exchange, and division of employments amongst different bodies of men.

Before we proceed to the practical conclusions which may be drawn from this principle, it seems right to notice an important distinction between simple and complex co-operation. Of the former, one is always conscious at the time of practising it: it is obvious to the most ignorant and vulgar eye. Of the latter, but a very few of the vast numbers who practise it are in any degree conscious. The cause of this distinction is easily seen. When several men are employed in lifting the same weight, or pulling the same rope, at the same time, and in the same place, there can be no sort of doubt that they co-operate with each other; the fact is impressed on the mind by the mere sense of sight: but when several men, or bodies of men, are employed at different times and places, and in different pursuits, their co-operation with each other, though it may be quite as certain, is not so readily perceived as in the other case: in order to perceive it, a complex operation of the mind is required.

## Notes to Chapter Three "That the Division of Labor is Limited by the Extent of the Market"

The energy at labor as well as the division of employments, — the wealth of individuals and of nations, — being limited by the power of exchanging, a question of the greatest interest occurs: what are the circumstances on which the power of exchanging chiefly depends?

The power of exchanging seems to depend upon a great number of circumstances. Adam Smith has noticed only two of them, viz., the facilities afforded by water-carriage, and by the use of money. No other writer, as far as I know, has noticed all of them. A sufficient notice of all of them, supposing that they have all been discovered, would almost convert this commentary into, what I am far from intending it to be, a treatise on the principles of political economy. A profound thinker and powerful reasoner attaches so much importance to those circumstances, that he has proposed to call the science of political economy the *Science of Exchanges**. Let us hope that he may yet employ his great talents in giving an account of all those circumstances. Meanwhile, one of them appears to exert so peculiar and vast an influence on the production of wealth, that I am tempted to seize this opportunity for saying a few words concerning it.

Human labor is engaged in two grand classes of employments: those which relate to the means of subsistence, and those which promote enjoyments over and above the means of subsistence. If all the objects enjoyed by mankind were divided into two classes, — those which are indispensable to existence, and those which are not, — the list of comforts and luxuries would be found much more numerous than the list of necessaries; and the same result would be obtained by a comparison of the two classes of employment. Moreover, a great, if not the greater part of the exchanges which take place in the world, consist of the exchange of objects which are indispensable to existence, for those which are not. Now, a very brief inquiry will show that the production of all comforts and luxuries, the pursuit of all the different employments concerned in that production, and all the exchanges of necessary objects for objects

---

* Dr. Whately. See his *Introductory Lectures on Political Economy*.

which are not necessary, wholly depend on the productiveness of labor employments which relate to the means of subsistence.

Before anyone can engage in the production of comforts or luxuries, he must be assured of the means of subsistence. If no one of those who are engaged in raising food, could produce more than enough for his own family, nothing beyond the means of subsistence could be anywhere produced. It is the surplus produce of agriculture, beyond what maintains the producers, that provides the means of subsistence for persons not engaged in agriculture. What proportion, therefore, of the people in any society shall engage in employment which relate to comforts and luxuries, depends upon the productiveness of agricultural industry. One-third of the people of England, it has been already observed, raise food for the whole; so that two-thirds are set free to engage in other occupations; while, in France, only one-third can engage in employments which relate to comforts and luxuries, because two-thirds are occupied in raising food for the whole number. In Portugal, it has been reckoned, four-fifths of the people are engaged in agriculture: if so, only one-fifth remains to engage in other pursuits. The superiority of the English over the French and Portuguese with respect to the power of exchanging, obviously arises from the greater productiveness of their agriculture.

The productiveness of agriculture appears to depend upon two different circumstances; upon the natural fertility of soil and climate, and upon the degree of skill with which labor is applied to agriculture. With a very unfruitful soil and climate, the utmost skill will not raise a large surplus produce; nor will the most fruitful soil and climate yield a large surplus produce to very unskilful labor. Good examples of these extreme cases are furnished by the smallness of the produce, in proportion to the number of laborers, raised by very skilful labor on the poorest soils of England, and the smallness of the produce, always in proportion to the number of laborers, raised by very unskilful, because much divided labor, on the rich virgin soils of Canada. But these extreme cases are noticed only for the purpose of showing that, in every case, the nature of the soil and climate from which a society derive their means of subsistence, and the degree of skill with which they apply their labor to agriculture, must, taken together, determine the extent of their power to engage in the production of comforts and luxuries, and, therefore, in great measure, the extent of their power of exchanging. It is by means of superior skill in the application of labor to agriculture, that England enjoys a greater power of exchanging than Portugal 'or France. On the other hand, the influence of soil and climate affords perhaps, a better explanation than that which has been given by Adam Smith, of the early improvement of Egypt, Bengal, and some provinces of China, and of the barbarous and uncivilized state, in all ages of the world, of the parched interior of Africa, and the frozen regions of the north of Asia.

Soil and climate are beyond the control of man; but not so the degree of skill with which labor is applied to agriculture. In France and Ireland, certain tenures of land tend, as we have seen already, to prevent that simple combination of labor, and that complex combination of labor for division of employments, to which England owes her great superiority in agriculture. The produce of agriculture, in proportion to the hands at work, is greatly augmented by a complete separation of that employment from all other employments, and a division of that employment into many distinct parts. Considering the influence on the power of exchanging, of the proportion between the produce of agriculture and the number of hands at work, it would seem to follow that the converse of the proposition at the head of this chapter is not less true than the proposition itself; that while division of employments is limited by the extent of the market, the extent of the market is, in great measure, at least, limited by the division of employments.

Adam Smith, himself, would not have objected to this conclusion; for in his chapter on what he calls the division of labor, he says, "It is the great multiplication of the productions of all the different arts, *in consequence of* the division of labor, which occasions, in a well-governed society, that universal opulence which extends itself to the lowest ranks of the people. Every workman has a great quantity of his own work to dispose of beyond what he himself has occasion for; and every other workman being exactly in the same situation, he is *enabled to exchange* a great quantity of his own goods for a great quantity, or, what comes to the same thing, for the price of a great quantity of theirs. He *supplies them abundantly* with what they have occasion for, and they *accommodate him as amply* with what he has occasion for, and a general plenty diffuses itself through all the ranks of the society."

There is nothing contradictory in the conclusion thus supported by Adam Smith. As, in walking, the use of either leg depends on the use of the other, so, in political economy, the division of employments and the power of exchanging are mutually dependent means of increasing human enjoyments. At the same time, however, it must be confessed, that the power of exchanging has not been thoroughly analyzed by any writer on the subject. Of what elements that complex power is composed, and by what circumstances it is apt to be increased or diminished; these are questions which would occupy much space in a complete treatise on the principles of political economy.

# Chapter 18*

# From *Principles of Political Economy*

**John Stuart Mill**

## Of Co-operation, or The Combination of Labor

§ 1. In the enumeration of the circumstances which promote the productiveness of labor, we have left one untouched, which, because of its importance, and of the many topics of discussion which it involves, requires to be treated apart. This is co-operation, or the combined action of numbers. Of this great aid to production, a single department, known by the name of Division of labor, has engaged a large share of the attention of political economists' most deservedly indeed, but to the exclusion of other cases and exemplifications of the same comprehensive law. Mr. Wakefield was, I believe, the first to point out, that a part of the subject had, with injurious effect, been mistaken for the whole; that a more fundamental principle lies beneath that of the division of labor, and comprehends it.

Co-operation, he observes,† is "of two distinct kinds: first, such co-operation as takes place when several persons help each other in the same employment; secondly, such co-operation as takes place when several persons help each other in different employments. These may be termed Simple Co-operation and Complex Co-operation.

---

* Taken from *Principles of Political Economy*, ed. W. J. Ashley, Longmans and Co. Ltd., 1940, pp. 116–22, pp. 132-4 and pp. 142–4.

† Note to Wakefield's edition of Adam Smith, vol. i. p. 26.

"The advantage of simple co-operation is illustrated by the case of two greyhounds running together, which, it is said, will kill more hares than four greyhounds running separately. In a vast number of simple operations performed by human exertion, it is quite obvious that two men working together will do more than four, or four times four men, each of whom should work alone. In the lifting of heavy weights, for example, in the felling of trees, in the sawing of timber, in the gathering of much hay or corn during a short period of fine weather, in draining a large extent of land during the short season when such a work may be properly conducted, in the pulling of ropes on board ship, in the rowing of large boats, in some mining operations, in the erection of a scaffolding for building, and in the breaking of stones for the repair of a road, so that the whole of the road shall always be kept in good order: in all these simple operations, and thousands more, it is absolutely necessary that many persons should work together, at the same time, in the same place, and in the same way. The savages of New Holland never help each other, even in the most simple operations; and their condition is hardly superior, in some respects it is inferior, to that of the wild animals which they now and then catch. Let any one imagine that the laborers of England should suddenly desist from helping each other in simple employments, and he will see at oncc the prodigious advantages of simple co-operation. In a countless number of employments, the produce of labor is, up to a certain point, in proportion to such mutual assistance amongst the workmen. This is the first step in social improvement." The second is, when "one body of men having combined their labor to raise more food than they require, another body of men are induced to combine their labor for the purpose of producing more clothes than they require, and with those surplus clothes buying the surplus food of the other body of laborers; while, if both bodies together have produced more food and clothes than they both require, both bodies obtain, by means of exchange, a proper capital for setting more laborers to work in their respective occupations." To simple co-operation is thus superadded what Mr. Wakefield terms Complex Co-operation. The one is the combination of several laborers to help each other in the same set of operations; the other is the combination of several laborers to help one another by a division of operations.

There is "an important distinction between simple and complex co-operation. Of the former, one is always conscious at the time of practising it: it is obvious to the most ignorant and vulgar eye. Of the latter, but a very few of the vast numbers who practise it are in any degree conscious. The cause of this distinction is easily seen. When several men are employed in lifting the same weight, or pulling the same rope, at the same time, and in the same place, there can be no sort of doubt that they co-operate with each other ; the fact is impressed on the mind by the mere sense of sight; but when several men, or bodies of men, are employed at different times and places, and in different pursuits, their co-operation with each other, though it may be quite as certain, is not so readily perceived as in the other case: in order to perceive it, a complex operation of the mind is required."

In the present state of society the breeding and feeding of sheep is the occupation of one set of people, dressing the wool to prepare it for the spinner is that of another, spinning it into thread of a third, weaving the thread into broadcloth of a fourth, dyeing the cloth of a fifth, making it into a coat of a sixth, without counting the multitude of carriers, merchants, factors, and retailers, put in requisition at the successive stages of this progress. All these persons, without knowledge of one another or previous understanding, co-operate in the production of the ultimate result, a coat. But these are far from being all who co-operate in it; for each of these persons requires food, and many other articles of consumption, and unless he could have relied that other people would produce these for him, he could not have devoted his whole time to one step in the succession of operations which produces one single commodity, a coat. Every person who took part in producing food or erecting houses for this series of producers, has, however unconsciously on his part, combined his labors with theirs. It is by a real, though unexpressed, concert, "that the body who raise more food than they want, can exchange with the body who raise more clothes than they want; and if the two bodies were separated, either by distance or disinclination — unless the two bodies should virtually form themselves into one, for the common object of raising enough food and clothes for the whole — they could not divide into two distinct parts the whole operation of producing a sufficient quantity of food and clothes."

§ 2. The influence exercised on production by the separation of employments, is more fundamental than, from the mode in which the subject is usually treated, a reader might be induced to suppose. It is not merely that when the production of different things becomes the sole or principal occupation of different persons, a much greater quantity of each kind of article is produced. The truth is much beyond this. Without some separation of employments, very few things would be produced at all.

Suppose a set of persons, or a number of families, all employed precisely in the same manner; each family settled on a piece of its own land, on which it grows by its labor the food required for its own sustenance, and as there are no persons to buy any surplus produce where all are producers, each family has to produce within itself whatever other articles it consumes. In such circumstances, if the soil was tolerably fertile, and population did not tread too closely on the heels of subsistence, there would be, no doubt, some kind of domestic manufactures; clothing for the family might perhaps be spun and woven within it, by the labor probably of the women (a first step in the separation of employments); and a dwelling of some sort would be erected and kept in repair by their united labor. But beyond simple food (precarious, too, from the variations of the seasons), coarse clothing, and very imperfect lodging, it would be scarcely possible that the family should produce anything more. They would, in general, require their utmost exertions to accomplish so much. Their power even of extracting food from the soil would be kept within narrow limits by the quality of their tools, which would necessarily be of the most wretched description. To do almost anything in the way of producing for themselves articles of convenience or luxury, would require too much time, and, in many cases, their presence in a different place. Very few kinds of industry, therefore, would exist; and that which did exist, namely the production of necessaries, would be extremely inefficient, not solely from imperfect implements, but because, when the ground and the domestic industry fed by it had been made to supply the necessaries of a single family in tolerable abundance, there would be little motive, while the numbers of the family remained the same, to make either the land or the labor produce more.

But suppose an event to occur, which would amount to a revolution in the circumstances of this little settlement. Suppose that a company of artificers, provided with tools, and with food sufficient to maintain them for a year, arrive in the country and establish themselves in the midst of the population. These new settlers occupy themselves in producing articles of use or ornament adapted to the taste of a simple people; and before their food is exhausted they have produced these in considerable quantity, and are ready to exchange them for more food. The economical position of the landed population is now most materially altered. They have an opportunity given them of acquiring comforts and luxuries. Things which, while they depended solely on their own labor, they never could have obtained, because they could not have produced, are now accessible to them if they can succeed in producing an additional quantity of food and necessaries. They are thus incited to increase the productiveness of their industry. Among the conveniences for the first time made accessible to them, better tools are probably one: and apart from this, they have a motive to labor more assiduously, and to adopt contrivances for making their labor more effectual. By these means they will generally succeed in compelling their land to produce, not only food for themselves, but a surplus for the new comers, wherewith to buy from them the products of their industry. The new settlers constitute what is called a *market* for surplus agricultural produce: and their arrival has enriched the settlement not only by the manufactured article which they produce, but by the food which would not have been produced unless they had been there to consume it.

There is no inconsistency between this doctrine, and the proposition we before maintained, that a market for commodities does not constitute employment for labor.* The labor of the agriculturists was already provided with employment; they are not indebted to the demand of the new comers for being able to maintain themselves. What that demand does for them is, to call their labor into increased vigour and efficiency; to stimulate them, by new motives, to new exertions. Neither do the new comers owe their maintenance and employment to the demand of the agriculturists: with a year's subsistence in store, they could have settled

---

* Supra, pp 79-00.

side by side with the former inhabitants, and produced a similar scanty stock of food and necessaries. Nevertheless we see of what supreme importance to the productiveness of the labor of producers, is the existence of other producers within reach, employed in a different kind of industry. The power of exchanging the products of one kind of labor for those of another, is a condition, but for which, there would almost always be a smaller quantity of labor altogether. When a new market is opened for any product of industry, and a greater quantity of the article is consequently produced, the increased production is not always obtained at the expense of some other product; it is often a new creation, the result of labor which would otherwise have remained unexerted; or of assistance rendered to labor by improvements or by modes of co-operation to which recourse would not have been had if an inducement had not been offered for raising a larger produce.

§ 3. From these considerations it appears that a country will seldom have a productive agriculture, unless it has a large town population, or the only available substitute, a large export trade in agricultural produce to supply a population elsewhere. I use the phrase town population for shortness, to imply a population non-agricultural; which will generally be collected in towns or large villages, for the sake of combination of labor. The application of this truth by Mr. Wakefield to the theory of colonization has excited much attention, and is doubtless destined to excite much more. It is one of those great practical discoveries, which, once made, appears so obvious that the merit of making them seems less than it is. Mr. Wakefield was the first to point out that the mode of planting new settlements, then commonly practised — setting down a number of families side by side, each on its piece of land, all employing themselves in exactly the same manner, — though in favourable circumstances it may assure to those families a rude abundance of mere necessaries, can never be other than unfavourable to great production or rapid growth: and his system consists of arrangement for securing that every colony shall have from the first a town population bearing due proportion to its agricultural, and that the cultivators of the soil shall not be so widely scattered as to be deprived by distance of the benefit of that town population as a market for their produce. The principle on which the scheme is founded, does not depend on any theory respecting the superior productiveness of land held in large portions, and cultivated by hired labor. Supposing it true that land yields the greatest produce when divided into small properties and cultivated by peasant proprietors. a town population will be just as necessary to induce those proprietors to raise that larger produce: and if they were too far from the nearest seat of non-agricultural industry to use it as a market for disposing of their surplus, and thereby supplying their other wants, neither that surplus nor any equivalent for it would, generally speaking, be produced.

It is, above all, the deficiency of town population which limits the productiveness of the industry of a country like India. The agriculture of India is conducted entirely on the system of small holdings. There is, however, a considerable amount of combination of labor. The village institutions and customs, which are the real framework of Indian society, make provision for joint action in the cases in which it is seen to be necessary; or where they fail to do so, the government (when tolerably well administered) steps in, and by an outlay from the revenue, executes by combined labor the tanks, embankments, and works of irrigation, which are indispensable. The implements and processes of agriculture are however so wretched, that the produce of the soil, in spite of great natural fertility and a climate highly favourable to vegetation, is miserably small: and the land might be made to yield food in abundance for many more than the present number of inhabitants, without departing from the system of small holdings. But to this the stimulus is wanting, which a large town population, connected with the rural districts by easy and unexpensive means of communication, would afford. That town population, again, does not grow up, because the few wants and unaspiring spirit of the cultivators (joined until lately with great insecurity of property, from military and fiscal rapacity) prevent them from attempting to become consumers of town produce. In these circumstances the best chance of an early development of the productive resources of India, consists in the rapid growth of its export of agricultural produce (cotton, indigo, sugar, coffee, etc.) to the markets of Europe. The producers of these articles are consumers of food supplied by their fellow-agriculturists in India; and the market thus opened for surplus food will, if accompanied by good government, raise up by degrees more extended wants and desires, directed either towards European commodities, or towards things which will require for their production in India a larger manufacturing population.

## Of Production on a Large, and Production on a Small Scale

§ 1. From the importance of combination of labor, it is an obvious conclusion, that there are many cases in which production is made much more effective by being conducted on a large scale. Whenever it is essential to the greatest efficiency of labor that many laborers should combine, even though only in the way of Simple Co-operation, the scale of the enterprise must be such as to bring many labourers together, and the capital must be large enough to maintain them. Still more needful is this when the nature of the employment allows, and the extent of the possible market encourages, a considerable division of labor. The larger the enterprise, the farther the division of labor may be carried. This is one of the principal causes of large manufactories. Even when no additional subdivision of the work would follow an enlargement of the operations, there will be good economy in enlarging them to the point at which every person to whom it is convenient to assign a special occupation, will have full employment in that occupation. This point is well illustrated by Mr. Babbage.*

"If machines be kept working through the twenty-four hours (which is evidently the only economical mode of employing them,) "it is necessary that some person shall attend to admit the workmen at the time they relieve each other; and whether the porter or other person so employed admit one person or twenty, his rest will be equally disturbed. It will also be necessary occasionally to adjust or repair the machine; and this can be done much better by a workman accustomed to machine-making, than by the person who uses it. Now, since the good performance and the duration of machines depend, to a very great extent, upon correcting every shake or imperfection in their parts as soon as they

* Page 214 et seq.

appear, the prompt attention of a workman resident on the spot will considerably reduce the expenditure arising from the wear and tear of the machinery. But in the case of a single lace-frame, or a single loom, this would be too expensive a plan. Here then arises another circumstance which tends to enlarge the extent of a factory. It ought to consist of such a number of machines as shall occupy the whole time of one workman in keeping them in order: if extended beyond that number, the same principle of economy would point out the necessity of doubling or tripling the number of machines, in order to employ the whole time of two or three skilful workmen."

"When one portion of the workman's labor consists in the exertion of mere physical force, as in weaving, and in many similar arts, it will soon occur to the manufacturer, that if that part were executed by a steam-engine, the same man might, in the case of weaving, attend to two or more looms at once: and, since we already suppose that one or more operative engineers have been employed, the number of looms may be so arranged that their time shall be fully occupied in keeping the steam-engine and the looms in order."

"Pursuing the same principles, the manufactory becomes gradually so enlarged, that the expense of lighting during the night amounts to a considerable sum: and as there are already attached to the establishment persons who are up all night, and can therefore constantly attend to it, and also engineers to make and keep in repair any machinery, the addition of an apparatus for making gas to light the factory leads to a new extension, at the same time that it contributes, by diminishing the expense of lighting, and the risk of accidents from fire, to reduce the cost of manufacturing.

"Long before a factory has reached this extent, it will have been found necessary to establish an accountant's department, with clerks to pay the workmen, and to see that they arrive at their stated times; and this department must be in communication with the agents who purchase the raw produce, and with those who sell the manufactured article." It will cost these clerks and accountants little more time and trouble to pay a large number of workmen than a small number; to check the accounts of large transactions, than of small. If the business doubled itself, it would probably be necessary to increase, but certainly not to double, the number either of accountants, or of buying and selling agents. Every increase of business would enable the whole to be carried on with a proportionately smaller amount of labor."

As a general rule, the expenses of a business do not increase by any means proportionally to the quantity of business. Let us take as an example, a set of operations which we are accustomed to see carried on by one great establishment, that of the Post Office. Suppose that the business, let us say only of the London letter-post, instead of being centralized in a single concern, were divided among five or six competing companies. Each of these would be obliged to maintain almost as large an establishment as is now sufficient for the whole. Since each must arrange for receiving and delivering letters in all parts of the town, each must send letter-carriers into every street, and almost every alley, and this too as many times in the day as is now done by the Post Office, if the service is to be as well performed. Each must have an office for receiving letters in every neighbourhood, with all subsidiary arrangements for collecting the letters from the different offices and re-distributing them. To this must be added the much greater number of superior officers who would be required to check and control the subordinates, implying not only a greater cost in salaries for such responsible officers, but the necessity, perhaps, of being satisfied in many instances with an inferior standard of qualification, and so failing in the object.

Whether or not the advantages obtained by operating on a large scale preponderate in any particular case over the more watchful attention, and greater regard to minor gains and losses, usually found in small establishments, can be ascertained, in a state of free competition, by an unfailing test. Wherever there are large and small establishments in the same business, that one of the two which in existing circumstances carries on the production at greatest advantage will be able to undersell the other. The power of permanently underselling can only, generally speaking, be derived from increased effectiveness of labor; and this, when obtained by a more extended division of employment, or by a classification tending to a better economy of skill, always implies a greater produce from the same labor, and not merely the same produce from less labor: it increases not the surplus only, but the gross produce of industry. If an increased quantity of the particular article is not required, and part of the laborers in consequence lose their employment, the capital which maintained and employed them is also set at liberty; and the general produce of the country is increased by some other application of their labor.

§ 3. The possibility of substituting the large system of production for the small, depends, of course, in the first place, on the extent of the market. The large system can only be advantageous when a large amount of business is to be done: it implies, therefore, either a populous and flourishing community, or a great opening for exportation. Again, this as well as every other change in the system of production is greatly favoured by a progressive condition of capital. It is chiefly when the capital of a country is receiving a great annual increase, that there is a large amount of capital seeking for investment: and a new enterprise is much sooner and more easily entered upon by new capital, than by withdrawing capital from existing employments. The change is also much facilitated by the existence of large capitals in few hands. It is true that the same amount of capital can be raised by bringing together many small sums. But this (besides that it is not equally well suited to all branches of industry) supposes a much greater degree of commercial confidence and enterprise diffused through the community, and belongs altogether to a more advanced stage of industrial progress.

In the countries in which there are the largest markets, the widest diffusion of commercial confidence and enterprise, the greatest annual increase of capital, and the greatest number of large capitals owned by individuals, there is a tendency to substitute more and more, in one branch of industry after another, large establishments for small ones. In England, the chief type of all these characteristics, there is a perpetual growth not only of large manufacturing establishments, but also, wherever a sufficient number of purchasers are assembled, of shops and warehouses for conducting retail business on a large scale. These are almost always able to undersell the smaller tradesmen, partly, it is understood, by means of division of labor, and the economy occasioned by limiting the employment of skilled agency to cases where skill is required; and partly, no doubt, by the saving of labor arising from the great scale of the transactions; as it costs no more time, and not much more exertion of mind, to make a large purchase, for example, than a small one, and very much less than to make a number of small ones.

With a view merely to production, and to the greatest efficiency of labor, this change is wholly beneficial. In some cases it is attended with drawbacks, rather social than economical, the nature of which has been already hinted at. But whatever disadvantages may be supposed to attend on the change from a small to a large system of production, they are not applicable to the change from a large to a still larger. When, in any employment, the regime of independent small producers has either never been possible, or has been superseded, and the system of many work-people under one management has become fully established, from that time any further enlargement in the scale of production is generally an unqualified benefit. It is obvious, for example, how great an economy of labor would be obtained if London were supplied by a single gas or water company instead of the existing plurality. While there are even as many as two, this implies double establishments of all sorts, when one only, with a small increase, could probably perform the whole operation equally well; double sets of machinery and works, when the whole of the gas or water required could generally be produced by one set only; even double sets of pipes, if the companies did not prevent this needless expense by agreeing upon a division of the territory. Were there only one establishment, it could make lower charges, consistently with obtaining the rate of profit now realized. But would it do so! Even if it did not, the community in the aggregate would still be a gainer: since the share-holders are a part of the community, and they would obtain higher profits while the consumers paid only the same. It is, however, an error to suppose that the prices are ever permanently kept down by the com-petition of these companies. Where competitors are so few, they always end by agreeing not to compete. They may run a race of cheapness to ruin a new candidate, but as soon as he has established his footing they come to terms with him. When, therefore, a business of real public importance can only be carried on advantageously upon so large a scale as to render the liberty of competition almost illusory, it is an unthrifty dispensation of the public resources that several costly sets of arrangements should be kept up for the purpose of rendering to the community this one service. It is much better to treat it at once as a public function; and if it be not such as the government itself could beneficially undertake, it should be made over entire to the company or association which will perform it on the best terms for the public. In the case of railways, for example, no one can desire to see the enormous waste of capital and land (not to speak of increase nuisance) involved in the construction of a second railway to connect the same places already united by an existing one; while the two would not do the work better than it could be done by one, and after a short time would probably be amalgamated. Only one ought to be permitted, but the control over that line never ought to be parted with by the State, unless on a temporary concession, as in France; and the vested right which Parliament has allowed to be acquired by the existing companies, like all other proprietary rights which are opposed to public utility, is morally valid only as a claim to compensation.

# Chapter 19*

# From *Capital*

**Karl Marx**

## Division of Labor in Manufacture, and Division of Labor in Society

We first considered the origin of manufacture, then its simple elements, the specialized worker and his tools, and finally the total mechanism. We shall now lightly touch on the relation between the division of labor in manufacture, and the social division of labor which forms the foundation of all commodity production.

If we keep labor alone in view, we may designate the division of social production into its main *genera* such as agriculture, industry, etc. as division of labor in general, and the splitting-up of these broad divisions into species and sub-species as division of labor in particular. Finally, we may designate the division of labor within the workshop as division of labor in detail.[1]

---

* Taken from *Capital*, Karl Marx, translated by Ben Fowkes, Penguin Books in association with New Left Review (Edition and Notes copyright holder), 1976, Volume One, Book 1, Part 4, Ch 14, Section 4, pp. 470–80.

[1] 'Division of labor proceeds from the separation of the most widely different professions to that division where several workers divide between them the preparation of one and the same product, as in manufacture' (Storch, *Cours d'économie politique,* Paris edition, Vol. I, p. 173). 'Among peoples which have reached a certain level of civilization, we meet with three kinds of division of labor: the first, which we shall call general, brings about the division of the producers into agriculturalists, manufacturers, and shop-keepers, it corresponds to the three main branches of the nation's labor; the second, which one could call particular, is the division of each branch of labor into species. . . the third division of labor, which one should designate as a division of tasks, or of labor properly

The division of labor within society develops from one starting-point; the corresponding restriction of individuals to particular vocations or callings develops from another starting-point, which is diametrically opposed to the first. This second starting-point is also that of the division of labor within manufacture. Within a family[1] and, after further development, within a tribe, there springs up naturally a division of labor caused by differences of sex and age, and therefore based on a purely physiological foundation. More material for this division of labor is then provided by the expansion of the community, the increase of its population and, in particular, conflicts between the different tribes and the subjugation of one tribe by another. On the other hand, as I have already remarked,[*] the exchange of products springs up at the points where different families, tribes or communities come into contact; for at the dawn of civilization it is not private individuals but families, tribes, etc. that meet on an independent footing. Different communities find different means of production and different means of subsistence in their natural environment. Hence their modes of production and living, as well as their products, are different. It is this spontaneously developed difference which, when different communities come into contact, calls forth the mutual exchange of products and the consequent gradual conversion of those products into commodities. Exchange does not create the differences between spheres of production but it does bring the different spheres into a relation, thus converting them into more or less interdependent branches of the collective production of a whole society. In this case, the social division of labor arises from the exchange between spheres of production which are originally distinct from and independent of one another. In the other case, where the physiological division of

---

so called, is that which grows up in the individual crafts and trades. . . and takes root in the majority of the workshops and factories' (F. Skarbek, *Théorie des richesses socials,* 2nd ed. Paris, 1839, Vol 1, pp. 84-5).

[1] [Note by Engels to the third German edition:] Subsequent and very thorough investigations into the primitive condition of man led the author to the conclusion that it was not the family that originally developed into the tribe, but that, on the contrary, the tribe was the primitive and spontaneously developed form of human association, based on consanguinity, and that out of the first incipient loosening of the tribal bonds, the many and various forms of the family were afterwards developed.

[*] See above, p. 182.

labor is the starting-point, the particular organs of a compact whole become separated from each other and break off. This process of disintegration receives its main impetus from the exchange of commodities with foreign communities. Afterwards, these organs attain such a degree of independence that the sole bond still connecting the various kinds of work is the exchange of the products as commodities. In the one case, what was previously independent has been made dependent; in the other case, what was previously dependent has been made independent.

The foundation of every division of labor which has attained a certain degree of development, and has been brought about by the exchange of commodities, is the separation of town from country.[1] One might well say that the whole economic history of society is summed up in the movement of this antithesis. However, for the moment we shall not go into this.

Just as a certain number of simultaneously employed workers is the material pre-condition for the division of labor within manufacture, so the number and density of the population, which here corresponds to the collection of workers together in one workshop, is a pre-condition for the division of labor within society,[2] Nevertheless, this density is more or

---

[1] Sir James Steuart has provided the best treatment of this question. How little his book, which appeared ten years before the *Wealth of Nations,** is known, even at the present time, may be judged from the fact that the admirers of Malthus do not know that the first edition of the latter's work on population contains, except in the purely declamatory part, very little but extracts from Steuart, as well as from the clerics Wallace[†] and Townsend.[‡]

*Steuart's Inquiry into the Principles of Political Economy was first published in 1767, the Wealth of Nations in 1776.

[†]Robert Wallace (1697-1771) was a Scottish Presbyterian minister, and author *of* treatises on population which are reputed *to* have influenced Malthus, namely *A Dissertation* on the *Numbers of Mankind in Ancient and Modern Times* (1753), and *Various Prospects of Mankind, Nature, and Providence* (1761).

[‡]Rev. Joseph Townsend (1739-1816) was a Methodist clergyman who, in *A Dissertation* on *the Poor Laws* (1786), advanced a theory *of* population later taken over by Malthus.

[2] 'There is a certain density of population which is convenient, both for social intercourse, and for that combination of powers by which the produce of labor is increased' (James Mill, *Elements of Political Economy*, London, 1821, p. 50). 'As the number of laborers increases, the productive power of society augments in the compound ratio of that increase, multiplied by the effects of the division of labor' (Thomas Hodgskin, *Popular Political Economy*, London, 1827, pp. 125-6).

less relative. A relatively thinly populated country, with well-developed means of communication, has a denser population than a more numerously populated country with badly developed means of communication. In this sense, the northern states of the U.S.A. for instance, are more thickly populated than India.[1]

Since the production and the circulation of commodities are the general prerequisites of the capitalist mode of production, division of labor in manufacture requires that a division of labor within society should have already attained a certain degree of development. Inversely, the division of labor in manufacture reacts back upon that in society, developing and multiplying it further. With the differentiation of the instruments of labor, the trades which produce these instruments themselves become more and more differentiated.[2] If the system of manufacture seizes upon a trade which was previously carried on in connection with others, either as a chief or a subordinate trade, and by one producer, these trades immediately break their connection and assert their independence of each other. If it seizes upon a particular stage in the production of a commodity, the other stages of its production become converted into as many independent trades. It has already been stated that where the finished article consists merely of a number of parts fitted together, the specialized operations may re-establish themselves as genuine and separate handicrafts. In order to accomplish the division of labor in manufacture more completely, a single branch of production is split up into numerous and to some extent entirely new manufactures, according to the varieties of its raw material or the various forms that the same piece of raw material may assume. Thus in France alone, in the first half of the eighteenth century, over 100 different kinds of silk stuffs were woven, and in Avignon, for instance, it was legally required that 'every apprentice should devote himself to only one sort of fabrication, and

---

[1] As a result of the great demand for cotton after 1861, its production was extended at the expense of rice cultivation in some otherwise thickly populated districts of eastern India. In consequence there arose local famines, because, owing to deficiencies in the means of communication, and hence the absence of physical links, failures of the rice crop in one district could not be compensated for by importing supplies from other districts.

[2] Thus the manufacture of shuttles formed a special branch of industry in Holland as early as the seventeenth century.

should not learn the preparation of several kinds of stuff at once'. The territorial division of labor, which confines special branches of production to special districts of a country, acquires fresh stimulus from the system of manufacture, which exploits all natural peculiarities.[1] The colonial system and the extension of the world market, both of which form part of the general conditions for the existence of the manufacturing period, furnish us with rich materials for displaying the division of labor in society. This is not the place, however, for us to show how division of labor seizes upon, not only the economic, but every other sphere of society, and everywhere lays the foundation for that specialization, that development in a man of one single faculty at the expense of all others, which already caused Adam Ferguson, the master of Adam Smith, to exclaim: 'We make a nation of Helots, and have no free citizens.'[2]

But in spite of the numerous analogies and links connecting them, the division of labor in the interior of a society, and that in the interior of a workshop, differ not only in degree, but also in kind. The analogy appears most indisputable where there is an invisible bond uniting the various branches of trade. For instance the cattle-breeder produces hides, the tanner makes the hides into leather and the shoemaker makes the leather into boots. Here the product of each man is merely a step towards the final form, which is the combined product of their specialized labors. There are, besides, all the various trades which supply the cattle-breeder, the tanner and the shoemaker with their means of production. Now it is quite possible to imagine, with Adam Smith, that the difference between the above social division of labor, and the division in manufacture, is merely subjective, exists merely for the observer, who in the case of manufacture can see at a glance all the numerous operations being performed on one spot, while in the instance given above, the spreading-out of the work over great areas and the great number of people

---

1 'Whether the Woollen Manufacture of England is not divided into several parts or branches, appropriated to particular places, where they are only or principally manufactured; fine cloths in Somersetshire, coarse in Yorkshire, long ells at Exeter, saies [serges] at Sudbury, crapes at Norwich, linseys at Kendal, blankets at Witney, and so forth?' (Berkeley, *The Querist,* 1750, query No.520).

2 A. Ferguson, *History of Civil Society,* Edinburgh, 1767, Part IV, Section ii, p. 285.

employed in each branch of labor obscure the connection.[1] But what is it that forms the bond between the independent labors of the cattle-breeder, the tanner and the shoemaker? It is the fact that their respective products are commodities. What, on the other hand, characterizes the division of labor in manufacture? The fact that the specialized worker produces no commodities.[2] It is only the common product of all the specialized workers that becomes a commodity.[3] The division of labor within society is mediated through the purchase and sale of the products of different branches of industry, while the connection between the various partial operations in a workshop is mediated through the sale of the labor-power

---

[1] In manufacture proper, Smith says, the division of labor appears to be greater, because 'those employed in every different branch of the work can often be collected into the same workhouse, and placed at once under the view of the spectator. In those great manufactures (!), on the contrary, which are destined to supply the great wants of the great body of the people, every different branch of the work employs so great a number of workmen that it is impossible to collect them all into the same workhouse. . . the division is not near so obvious' (A. Smith. *Wealth of Nations,* Bk I, Ch. 1). The famous passage in the same chapter, which begins with the words, 'Observe the accommodation of the most common artificer or day-labourer in a civilized and thriving country', etc., and then proceeds to depict what an enormous number and variety of industries contribute to the satisfaction of the needs of an ordinary worker, is copied almost word for word from the 'Remarks' added by B. de Mandeville to his *Fable of the Bees, or Private Vices, Publick Benefits* (first edition, without the remarks, 1706; with the remarks, 1714).

[2] 'There is no longer anything which we can call the natural reward of individual labor. Each laborer produces only some part of a whole, and each part, having no value or utility in itself, there is nothing on which the laborer can seize, and say: It is my product, this I will keep to myself' (*Labour Defended against the* Claims *of Capital,* London, 1825, p.25). The author of this admirable work is Thomas Hodgskin.

[3] This distinction between the division of labor in society and in manufacture has been illustrated to the Yankees in practice. One of the new taxes devised at Washington during the Civil War was the duty of 6 per cent 'on all industrial products '. Question: What is an industrial product? Answer of the legislature: A thing is produced 'when it is made', and it is made when it is ready for sale. Now for one example out of many. The New York and Philadelphia manufacturers had previously been in the habit of 'making' umbrellas with all their accessories. But since an umbrella is a composite mixture of very heterogeneous parts, these parts by degrees became the products of various separate industries, carried on independently in different places. They entered as separate commodities into the manufacture of umbrellas, so that all the umbrella manufacturers had to do was fit them together. The Yankees have given the name 'assembled articles' to articles of this kind, and they deserve this name, for they allow taxes to be assembled together as well. Thus an umbrella 'assembles', first 6 per cent on the price of each of its elements, and a further 6 per cent on its own total price.

of several workers to one capitalist, who applies it as combined labor-power. The division of labor within manufacture presupposes a concentration of the means of production in the hands of one capitalist; the division of labor within society presupposes a dispersal of those means among many independent producers of commodities. While, within the workshop, the iron law of proportionality subjects definite numbers of workers to definite functions, in the society outside the workshop, the play of chance and caprice results in a motley pattern of distribution of the producers and their means of production among the various branches of social labor. It is true that the different spheres of production constantly tend towards equilibrium, for the following reason. On the one hand, every producer of a commodity is obliged to produce a use-value, i.e. he must satisfy a particular social need (though the extent of these needs differs quantitatively, and there exists an inner bond which attaches the different levels of need to a system which has grown up spontaneously); on the other hand, the law of the value of commodities ultimately determines how much of its disposable labor-time society can expend on each kind of commodity. But this constant tendency on the part of the various spheres of production towards equilibrium comes into play only as a reaction against the constant upsetting of this equilibrium. The planned and regulated *a priori* system on which the division of labor is implemented within the workshop becomes, in the division of labor within society, an *a posteriori* necessity imposed by nature, controlling the unregulated caprice of the producers, and perceptible in the fluctuations of the barometer of market prices. Division of labor within the workshop implies the undisputed authority of the capitalist over men, who are merely the members of a total mechanism which belongs to him. The division of labor within society brings into contact independent producers of commodities, who acknowledge no authority other than that of competition, of the coercion exerted by the pressure of their reciprocal interests, just as in the animal kingdom the 'war of all against all' more or less preserves the conditions of existence of every species. The same bourgeois consciousness which celebrates the division of labor in the workshop, the lifelong annexation of the worker to a partial operation, and his complete subjection to capital, as an organization of labor that increases its productive power, denounces with equal vigour every conscious attempt to control and regulate the process of production socially, as an inroad upon such sacred things as the rights of property, freedom and the self-determining 'genius' of the individual capitalist. It is very characteristic that the enthusiastic apologists of the factory system have nothing more damning to urge against a general organization of labor in society than that it would turn the whole of society into a factory.

If, in the society where the capitalist mode of production prevails, anarchy in the social division of labor and despotism in the manufacturing division of labor mutually condition each other, we find, on the contrary, in those earlier forms of society in which the separation of trades has been spontaneously developed, then crystallized, and finally made permanent by law, on the one hand, a specimen of the organization of the labor of society in accordance with an approved and authoritative plan, and, on the other, the entire exclusion of division of labor in the workshop or, at the least, its development on a minute scale, sporadically and accidentally.[1]

Those small and extremely ancient Indian communities, for example, some of which continue to exist to this day, are based on the possession of the land in common, on the blending of agriculture and handicrafts and on an unalterable division of labor, which serves as a fixed plan and basis for action whenever a new community is started. The communities occupy areas of from 100 up to several thousand acres, and each forms a compact whole producing all it requires. Most of the products are destined for direct use by the community itself, and are not commodities. Hence production here is independent of that division of labor brought about in Indian society as a whole by the exchange of commodities. It is the surplus alone that becomes a commodity, and a part of that surplus cannot become a commodity until it has reached the hands of the state, because from time immemorial a certain quantity of the community's production has found its way to the state as rent in kind. The form of the

---

[1] 'It can. . . be laid down as a general rule that the less authority presides over the division of labor inside society, the more the division of labor develops inside the workshop, and the more it is subjected there to the authority of a single person. Thus authority in the workshop and authority in society, in relation to the division of labor, are in *inverse ratio* to each other' (Karl Marx. *Misère de la philosophie,* pp.130-31) [English edition, p.118].

community varies in different parts of India. In the simplest communities, the land is tilled in common. and the produce is divided among the members. At the same time, spinning and weaving are carried on in each family as subsidiary industries. Alongside the mass of people thus occupied in the same way, we find the 'chief inhabitant', who is judge, police authority and tax-gatherer in one; the book-keeper, who keeps the accounts of the tillage and registers everything relating to this; another official, who prosecutes criminals, protects strangers travelling through and escorts them to the next village; the boundary man, who guards the boundaries against neighbouring communities; the water-overseer, who distributes the water from the common tanks for irrigation; the Brahmin, who conducts the religious services; the schoolmaster, who on the sand teaches the children reading and writing; the calendar-Brahmin, or astrologer, who makes known the lucky or unlucky days for seed-time and harvest, and for every other kind of agricultural work; a smith and a carpenter, who make and repair all the agricultural implements; the potter, who makes all the pottery of the village; the barber, the washerman, who washes clothes, the silversmith, here and there the poet, who in some communities replaces the silversmith, in others the schoolmaster. This dozen or so of individuals is maintained at the expense of the whole community. If the population increases, a new community is founded, on the pattern of the old one, on unoccupied land. The whole mechanism reveals a systematic division of labor; but a division like that in manufacture is impossible, since the smith, the carpenter etc find themselves faced with an unchanging market, and at the most there occur, according to the sizes of the villages, two or three smiths or carpenters, instead of one.[1] The law that regulates the division of labor in the community acts with the irresistible authority of a law of nature, while each individual craftsman, the smith, the carpenter and so on, conducts in his workshop all the operations of his handicraft in the traditional way, but independently, and without recognizing any authority. The simplicity of the productive organism in these self-

---

[1] Lieut.-Col. Mark Wilks, *Historical Sketches of the South of India.* London, 1810-17, Vol. 1, pp. 118-20. A good account of the various forms of the Indian community is to be found in George Campbell's *Modern India,* London, 1852.

sufficing communities which constantly reproduce themselves in the same form and, when accidentally destroyed, spring up again on the same spot and with the same name[1] –this simplicity supplies the key to the riddle of the unchangeability of Asiatic societies, which is in such striking contrast with the constant dissolution and refounding of Asiatic states, and their never-ceasing changes of dynasty. The structure of the fundamental economic elements of society remains untouched by the storms which blow up in the cloudy regions of politics.

The rules of the guilds, as I have said before, deliberately hindered the transformation of the single master into a capitalist, by placing very strict limits on the number of apprentices and journeymen he could employ. Moreover, he could employ his journeymen only in the handicraft in which he was himself a master. The guilds zealously repelled every encroachment by merchants' capital, the only free form of capital which confronted them. A merchant could buy every kind of commodity, but he could not buy labor as a commodity. He existed only on sufferance, as a dealer in the products of the handicrafts. If circumstances called for a further division of labor, the existing guilds split themselves up into subordinate sections, or founded new guilds by the side of the old ones. But they did this without concentrating different handicrafts in one workshop. Hence the guild organization, however much it may have contributed to creating the material conditions for the existence of manufacture by separating, isolating and perfecting the handicrafts, excluded the kind of division of labor characteristic of manufacture. On the whole, the worker and his means of production remained closely united, like the snail with its shell, and therefore the principal basis of manufacture was absent, namely the autonomy of the means of production, as capital, *vis-à-vis* the worker.

---

1 'Under this simple form . . . the inhabitants of the country have lived from time immemorial. The boundaries of the village have been but seldom altered, and though the villages themselves have been sometimes injured, and even desolated by war, famine, and disease, the same name, the same limits, the same interests, and even the same families, have continued for ages. The inhabitants give themselves no trouble about the breaking up and division of kingdoms; while the village remains entire, they care not to what power it is transferred, or to what sovereign it devolves; its internal economy remains unchanged' (T. Stamford Raffles, late Lieut.-Gov. of Java, *The History of lava,* London, 1817, Vol. 1, p. 285).

While the division of labor in society at large, whether mediated through the exchange of commodities or not, can exist in the most diverse economic formations of society, the division of labor in the workshop, as practised by manufacture, is an entirely specific creation of the capitalist mode of production.

# Chapter 20*

# From *Science of Wealth*

**Amasa Walker**

## The Limitations to the Division of Labor

But the great principle of division of labor, so very beneficial in its operations, is yet limited by certain conditions, which it cannot disregard.

1st, When the principle has been so far applied that each operation has been made as simple and fully a unit as human ingenuity can devise. Beyond this, there is no division, but only *repetition.* Any attempt to refine the process so far as to give the workman less than one naturally complete motion of the body, will only embarrass and delay industry.

2d, When the concentration of capital has become so great that interested personal supervision cannot be brought to bear upon each department, and upon the whole enterprise, with sufficient intensity to insure efficiency and fidelity on the part of those employed, and harmony in the general conduct of the business. Beyond this point, the advantages derived from the power of concentration are neutralized. It may even become mischievous. It is well that there should be limitations, because they prevent such aggregations of capital as would swallow up the whole industry of a state. Experience shows that the greatest establishments are not always or generally the most profitable. Those which are large

---

* Taken from *Science of Wealth: A Manual of Political Economy,* Amasa Walker, Little, Brown, and Company, 1874; Kraus Reprint Co., New York, 1969, Seventh Edition Revised, pp. 40-43.

enough to secure all the real advantages of concentrated capital and combined effort, yet are small enough to be brought under direct, personal, interested supervision, are the most beneficial to their owners and the public.

3d, Where the industry consists of an indefinite number of parts, yet the special circumstances will not allow each workman profitable employment in a single operation, — for example, agriculture in most of its branches: first, from the fact that its operations cannot be sufficiently localized; and, second, from the necessities of the seasons. No department is capable of so much subdivision as this; yet, in practice, none experiences so little. In mining, the fisheries, and many incidental matters, it is effected to a considerable extent; but, in most of the parts of pure agriculture, it has very limited range. Boys and women are indeed made useful in it, but they have not the same continuous and profitable employment as in manufactures. Nor does their work correspond precisely with what is required in our definition of the division of labor. They are occupied, generally, not in one operation so much as in a miscellaneous class of light duties, too variable to realize the dexterity and thoroughness obtained elsewhere.

There are other instances which seem to approach near to the conditions of the highest efficiency. Some persons are employed for an entire community to plant, to graft, or to team; but not only does the extent of territory limit their application to a single pursuit, but the change of the seasons drives them from one to another almost every month. Stock-raising, and gardening for large markets, afford the best American example in agriculture; yet each of these is not only a considerable department in itself, but whoever engages in either of them must do much not directly connected with it.

The culture of the grape realizes, perhaps, as fully the mechanical advantage of division of labor as any in agriculture.

But, generally speaking, the farmer is a laborer of a thousand duties.

This fact alone does not account for the different productiveness of the manufacturing and the agricultural interests. In the nature of their objects, it is found that machinery must be applied to them in far different proportions. The mechanic arts, which can be localized to the highest degree of concentration, and made general to all seasons of the year, admit also of prodigious multiplication by artificial agents. From these considerations, we deduce the principle, that the value of agricultural products, as a class, — that is, their power in exchange for products other than agricultural, — will be constantly increasing. A bushel of corn, in 1820, would purchase only four yards of cotton cloth. In 1860, it would purchase ten yards of the same or better quality. This difference will continue to grow wider and wider as the mechanic arts advance; but not indefinitely, inasmuch as the materials of manufactures are always themselves of agricultural origin, and hence the depreciation of the price is limited.

We have thus far spoken of the division of labor as applied only to direct, material production, affecting the laboring classes, and those immediately superintending them; but the principle has been extended to mental labor, as well as that which is simply muscular.

The professions known as the learned, and others which have an important though indirect agency in production (for, unless they have some agency in production, we have nothing to do with them here), naturally divide themselves into branches more or less numerous and special, as occasion offers. The recognition of professions and industrial classes is itself a tribute to the great principle of the division of labor; but it proceeds still further, to assign special functions, within those professions and classes, to individual members.

Thus the law, when a sufficient concentration of legal labor is secured, branches into the departments of titles and conveyances, of insurance, of marine losses, forfeiture and salvage, of patents, of criminal jurisprudence, etc. In medicine, the eye, the ear, the skin, consumption, fevers, cancers, have each their own practitioners.

That science and skill are promoted by such subdivision, and that the immediate efficiency of professional labor is greatly increased thereby, cannot be intelligently questioned.

As any community advances to a higher civilization, specialties are more and more resorted to. Individuals, finding themselves peculiarly adapted by their talents and tastes to a particular calling, or having unusual advantages for the pursuit of it, give themselves up to that object. They concentrate upon it their thoughts, their time, and their resources. They excel. They know more, and can do better, in their chosen line than those about them. This gives them position and power. They are sought for, are looked to, because they have something that is wanted. No matter how humble his station, or how minute his field of investigation, if a man understands something perfectly, his world — whether a hamlet or an empire or the race — will resort to him. He becomes a benefactor of society. He receives its honours and rewards. There is no person in any position in life, however exalted or lowly, who may not advantageously cultivate a specialty.

# Part IV. Marshallian Economics

# Chapter 21*

# From *Principles of Economics*

**Alfred Marshall**

## Industrial Organization

§I. Writers on social science from the time of Plato downwards have delighted to dwell on the increased efficiency which labor derives from organization. But in this, as in other cases, Adam Smith gave a new and larger significance to an old doctrine by the philosophic thoroughness with which he explained it, and the practical knowledge with which he illustrated it. After insisting on the advantages of the division of labor, and pointing out how they render it possible for increased numbers to live in comfort on a limited territory, he argued that the pressure of population on the means of subsistence tends to weed out those races who through want of organization or for any other cause are unable to turn to the best account the advantages of the place in which they live.

Before Adam Smith's book had yet found many readers, biologists were already beginning to make great advances towards understanding the real nature of the differences in organization which separate the higher from the lower animals; and before two more generations had elapsed, Malthus' historical account of man's struggle for existence started Darwin on that inquiry as to the effects of the struggle for existence in the animal and vegetable world, which issued in his

* Taken from *Principles of Economics*, Alfred Marshall, Ninth Edition, Macmillan and Co Limited, New York, 1961, pp.240–1, pp.250-66 and pp.318–22.

discovery of the selective influence constantly played by it. Since that time biology has more than repaid her debt; and economists have in their turn owed much to the many profound analogies which have been discovered between social and especially industrial organization on the one side and the physical organization of the higher animals on the other. In a few cases indeed the apparent analogies disappeared on closer inquiry: but many of those which seemed at first sight most fanciful, have gradually been supplemented by others, and have at last established their claim to illustrate a fundamental unity of action between the laws of nature in the physical and in the moral world. This central unity is set forth in the general rule, to which there are not very many exceptions, that the development of the organism, whether social or physical, involves an increasing subdivision of functions between its separate parts on the one hand, and on the other a more intimate connection between them.[1] Each part gets to be less and less self-sufficient, to depend for its wellbeing more and more on other parts, so that any disorder in any part of a highly-developed organism will affect other parts also.

This increased subdivision of functions, or "differentiation," as it is called, manifests itself with regard to industry is such forms as the division of labor, and the development of specialized skill, knowledge and machinery: while "integration," that is, a growing intimacy and firmness of the connections between the separate parts of the industrial organism, shows itself in such forms as the increase of security of commercial credit, and of the means and habits of communication by sea and road, by railway and telegraph, by post and printing-press.

## Industrial Organization, Continued. Division of Labor. The Influence of Machinery

§I. The first condition of an efficient organization of industry is that it should keep everyone employed at such work as his abilities and training fit him to do well, and should equip him with the best machinery and

[1] See a brilliant paper by Häckel on *Arbeitstheilung in Menschen- und Thierleben* and Schäffle's *Bau und Leben des socialen Körpers*.

other appliances for his work. We shall leave on one side for the present the distribution of work between those who carry out the details of production on the one hand, and those who manage its general arrangement and undertake its risk on the other; and confine ourselves to the division of labor between different classes of operatives, with special reference to the influence of machinery.

Everyone is familiar with the fact that "practice makes perfect," that it enables an operation, which at first seemed difficult, to be done after a time with comparatively little exertion, and yet much better than before; and physiology in some measure explains this fact. For it gives reasons for believing that the change is due to the gradual growth of new habits of more or less "reflex" or automatic action. Perfectly reflex actions, such as that of breathing during sleep, are performed by the responsibility of the local nerve centres without any reference to the supreme central authority of the thinking power, which is supposed to reside in the cerebrum. But all deliberate movements require the attention of the chief central authority: it receives information from the nerve centres or local authorities and perhaps in some cases direct from the sentient nerves, and sends back detailed and complex instructions to the local authorities, or in some cases direct to the muscular nerves, and so co-ordinates their action as to bring about the required results.[1]

---

[1] For instance, the first time a man attempts to skate he must give his whole attention to keeping his balance, his cerebrum has to exercise a direct control over every movement, and he has not much mental energy left for other things. But after a good deal of practice the action becomes semi-automatic, the local nerve centres undertake nearly all the work of regulating the muscles, the cerebrum is set free, and the man can carry on an independent train of thought; he can even alter his course to avoid an obstacle in his path, or to recover his balance after it has been disturbed by a slight unevenness, without in any way interrupting the course of his thoughts. It seems that the exercise of nerve force under the immediate direction of the thinking power residing in the cerebrum has gradually built up a set of connections, involving probably distinct physical change, between the nerves and nerve centres concerned; and these new connections may be regarded as a sort of capital of nerve force. There is probably something like an organized bureaucracy of the local nerve centres: the medulla, the spinal axis, and the larger ganglia generally acting the part of provincial authorities, and being able after a time to regulate the district and village authorities without troubling the supreme government. Very likely they send up messages as to what is going on: but if nothing much out of the way has happened, these are very little attended to. When however a new feat has to be accomplished, as for instance learning to skate backwards, the whole thinking force will

The physiological basis of purely mental work is not yet well understood; but what little we do know of the growth of brain structure seems to indicate that practice in any kind of thinking develops new connections between different parts of the brain. Anyhow we know for a fact that practice will enable a person to solve quickly, and without any considerable exertion, questions which he could have dealt with but very imperfectly a little while before, even by the greatest effort. The mind of the merchant, the lawyer, the physician, and the man of science, becomes gradually equipped with a store of knowledge and a faculty of intuition, which can be obtained in no other way than by the continual application of the best efforts of a powerful thinker for many years together to one more or less narrow class of questions. Of course the mind cannot work hard for many hours a day in one direction: and a hard-worked man will sometimes find recreation in work that does not belong to his business, but would be fatiguing enough to a person who had to do it all day long.

Some social reformers have indeed maintained that those who do the most important brain work might do a fair share of manual work also, without diminishing their power of acquiring knowledge or thinking out hard questions. But experience seems to show that the best relief from overstrain is in occupations taken up to suit the mood of the moment and stopped when the mood is passed, that is, in what popular instinct classes as "relaxation." Any occupation which is so far business-like that a person must sometimes force himself by an effort of the will to go on with it, draws on his nervous force and is not perfect relaxation: and therefore it is not economical from the point of view of the community

---

be called into requisition for the time; and will now be able by aid of the special skating-organization of the nerves and nerve centres, which has been built up in ordinary skating, to do what would have been altogether impossible without such aid.

To take a higher instance: when an artist is painting at his best, his cerebrum is fully occupied with his work: his whole mental force is thrown into it, and the strain is too great to be kept up for a long time together. In a few hours of happy inspiration he may give utterance to thoughts that exert a perceptible influence on the character of coming generations. But his power of expression had been earned by numberless hours of plodding work in which he had gradually built up an intimate connection between eye and hand, sufficient to enable him to make good rough sketches of things with which he is tolerably familiar, even while he is engaged in an engrossing conversation and is scarcely conscious that he has a pencil in his hand.

unless its value is sufficient to outweigh a considerable injury to his main work.[1]

§2. It is a difficult and unsettled question how far specialization should be carried in the highest branches of work. In science it seems to be a sound rule that the area of study should be broad during youth, and should gradually be narrowed as years go on. A medical man who has always given his attention exclusively to one class of diseases, may perhaps give less wise advice even in his special subject than another who, having learnt by wider experience to think of those diseases in relation to general health, gradually concentrates his study more and more on them, and accumulates a vast store of special experiences and subtle instincts. But there is no doubt that greatly increased efficiency can be attained through division of labor in those occupations in which there is much demand for mere manual skill.

Adam Smith pointed out that a lad who had made nothing but nails all his life could make them twice as quickly as a first-rate smith who only took to nail-making occasionally. Anyone who has to perform exactly the same set of operations day after day on things of exactly the same shape, gradually learns to move his fingers exactly as they are wanted, by almost automatic action and with greater rapidity than would be possible if every movement had to wait for a deliberate instruction of the will. One familiar instance is seen in the tying of threads by children in a cotton-mill. Again, in a clothing or a boot factory, a person who sews, whether by hand or machinery, just the same seam on a piece of leather or cloth of just the same size, hour after hour, day after day, is able to do it with far less effort and far more quickly than a worker with much greater quickness of eye and hand, and of a much higher order of general

[1] J. S. Mill went so far as to maintain that his occupations at the India Office did not interfere with his pursuit of philosophical inquiries. But it seems probable that this diversion of his freshest powers lowered the quality of his best thought more than he was aware; and though it may have diminished but little his remarkable usefulness in his own generation, it probably affected very much his power of doing that kind of work which influences the course of thought in future generations. It was by husbanding every atom of his small physical strength that Darwin was enabled to do so much work of just that kind: and a social reformer who had succeeded in exploiting Darwin's leisure hours in useful work on behalf of the community, would have done a very bad piece of business for it.

skill, who was accustomed to make the whole of a coat or the whole of a boot.[1]

Again, in the wood and the metal industries, if a man has to perform exactly the same operations over and over again on the same piece of material, he gets into the habit of holding it exactly in the way in which it is wanted, and of arranging the tools and other things which he has to handle in such positions that he is able to bring them to work on one another with the least possible loss of time and of force in the movements of his own body. Accustomed to find them always in the same position and to take them in the same order, his hands work in harmony with one another almost automatically: and with increased practice his expenditure of nervous force diminishes even more rapidly than his expenditure of muscular force.

But when the action has thus been reduced to routine it has nearly arrived at the stage at which it can be taken over by machinery. The chief difficulty to be overcome is that of getting the machinery to hold the material firmly in exactly the position in which the machine tool can be brought to bear on it in the right way, and without wasting too much time in taking grip of it. But this can generally be contrived when it is worth while to spend some labor and expense on it; and then the whole operation can often be controlled by a worker who, sitting before a machine, takes with the left hand a piece of wood or metal from a heap and puts it in a socket, while with the right he draws down a lever, or in some other way sets the machine tool at work, and finally with his left

---

[1] The best and most expensive clothes are made by highly skilled and highly paid tailors, each of whom works right through first one garment and then another: while the cheapest and worst clothes are made for starvation wages by unskilled women who take the cloth to their own homes and do every part of the sewing themselves. But clothes of intermediate qualities are made in workshops or factories, in which the division and subdivisions of labor are carried as far as the size of the staff will permit; and this method is rapidly gaining ground at both ends at the expense of the rival method. Lord Lauderdale *(Inquiry,* p. 282) quotes Xenophon's argument that the best work is done when each confines himself to one simple department, as when one man makes shoes for men, and another for women; or better when one man only sews shoes or garments, another cuts them out: the king's cooking is much better than anybody else's, because he has one cook who only boils, another who only roasts meat; one who only boils fish, another who only fries it: there is not one man to make all sorts of bread but a special man for special qualities.

hand throws on to another heap the material which has been cut or punched or drilled or planed exactly after a given pattern. It is in these industries especially that we find the reports of modern trades-unions to be full of complaints that unskilled laborers, and even their wives and children, are put to do work which used to require the skill and judgment of a trained mechanic, but which has been reduced to mere routine by the improvement of machinery and the ever-increasing minuteness of the subdivision of labor.

§3. We are thus led to a general rule, the action of which is more prominent in some branches of manufacture than others, but which applies to all. It is, that any manufacturing operation that can be reduced to uniformity, so that exactly the same thing has to be done over and over again in the same way, is sure to be taken over sooner or later by machinery. There may be delays and difficulties; but if the work to be done by it is on a sufficient scale, money and inventive power will be spent without stint on the task till it is achieved.[1]

Thus the two movements of the improvement of machinery and the growing subdivision of labor have gone together and are in some measure connected. But the connection is not so close as is generally supposed. It is the largeness of markets, the increased demand for great numbers of things of the same kind, and in some cases of things made with great accuracy, that leads to subdivision of labor; the chief effect of

---

[1] One great inventor is rumoured to have spent *£500,000* on experiments relating to textile machinery, and his outlay is said to have been abundantly returned to him. Some of his inventions were of such a kind as can be made only by a man of genius; and however great the need, they must have waited till the right man was found for them. He charged not unreasonably *£1000* as royalty for each of his combing machines; and a worsted manufacturer, being full of work, found it worth his while to buy an additional machine, and pay this extra charge for it, only six months before the expiry of the patent. But such cases are exceptional: as a rule, patented machines are not very dear. In some cases the economy of having them all produced at one place by special machinery has been so great that the patentee has found it to his advantage to sell them at a price lower than the old price of the inferior machines which they displaced: for that old price gave him so high a profit, that it was worth his while to lower the price still further in order to induce the use of the machines for new purposes and in new markets. In almost every trade many things are done by hand, though it is well known that they could easily be done by some adaptations of machines that are already in use in that or some other trade, and which are not made only because there would not as yet be enough employment for them to remunerate the trouble and expense of making them.

the improvement of machinery is to cheapen and make more accurate the work which would anyhow have been subdivided. For instance, "in organizing the works at Soho, Boulton and Watt found it necessary to carry division of labor to the furthest practicable point. There were no slide-lathes, planning machines or boring tools, such as now render mechanical accuracy of construction almost a matter of certainty. Everything depended on the individual mechanic's accuracy of hand and eye; yet mechanics generally were much less skilled then than they are now. The way in which Boulton and Watt contrived partially to get over the difficulty was to confine their workmen to special classes of work, and make them as expert in them as possible. By continued practice in handling the same tools and fabricating the same articles, they thus acquired great individual proficiency."[1] Thus machinery constantly supplants and renders unnecessary that purely manual skill, the attainment of which was, even up to Adam Smith's time, the chief advantage of division of labor. But this influence is more than countervailed by its tendency to increase the scale of manufactures and to make them more complex; and therefore to increase the opportunities for division of labor of all kinds, and especially in the matter of business management.

§4. The powers of machinery to do work that requires too much accuracy to be done by hand are perhaps best seen in some branches of the metal industries in which the system of Interchangeable Parts is being rapidly developed. It is only after long training and with much care and labor that the hand can make one piece of metal accurately to resemble or to fit into another: and after all the accuracy is not perfect. But this is just the work which a well made machine can do most easily and most perfectly. For instance, if sowing and reaping machines had to be made by hand, their first cost would be very high; and when any part of them was broken, it could be replaced only at a great cost by sending the machine back to the manufacturer or by bringing a highly skilled mechanic to the machine. But as it is, the manufacturer keeps in a store many facsimiles of the broken part, which were made by the same machinery, and are therefore interchangeable with it. A farmer in the

[1] Smiles, *Boulton and Watt,* pp. 170-1.

North-West of America, perhaps a hundred miles away from any good mechanic's shop, can yet use complicated machinery with confidence; since he knows that by telegraphing the number of the machine and the number of any part of it which he has broken, he will get by the next train a new piece which he can himself fit into its place. The import- ance of this principle of interchangeable parts has been but recently grasped; there are however many signs that it will do more than any other to extend the use of machine-made machinery to every branch of production, including even domestic and agricultural work.[1]

The influences which machinery exerts over the character of modern industry are well illustrated in the manufacture of watches. Some years ago the chief seat of this business was in French Switzerland; where the subdivision of labor was carried far, though a great part of the work was done by a more or less scattered population. There were about fifty distinct branches of trade each of which did one small part of the work. In almost all of them a highly specialized manual skill was required, but very little judgment; the earnings were generally low, because the trade had been established too long for those in it to have anything like a monopoly, and there was no difficulty in bringing up to it any child with ordinary intelligence. But this industry is now yielding ground to the American system of making watches by machinery, which requires very little specialized manual skill. In fact the machinery is becoming every year more and more automatic, and is getting to require less and less assistance from the human hand. But the more delicate the machine's power, the greater is the judgment and carefulness which is called for from those who see after it. Take for instance a beautiful machine which feeds itself with steel wire at one end, and delivers at the other tiny screws of exquisite form; it displaces a great many operatives who had indeed acquired a very high and specialized manual skill, but who lived sedentary lives, straining their eyesight through microscopes, and finding in their work very little scope for any faculty except a mere command over the use of their fingers. But the machine is intricate and costly, and

[1] The system owes its origin in great measure to Sir Joseph Whitworth's standard gauges; but it has been worked out with most enterprise and thoroughness in America. Standardization is most helpful in regard to things which are to be built up with others into complex machines, buildings, bridges, etc.

the person who minds it must have an intelligence, and an energetic sense of responsibility, which go a long way towards making a fine character; and which, though more common than they were, are yet sufficiently rare to be able to earn a very high rate of pay. No doubt this is an extreme case; and the greater part of the work done in a watch factory is much simpler. But much of it requires higher faculties than the old system did, and those engaged in it earn on the average higher wages; at the same time it has already brought the price of a trust-worthy watch within the range of the poorest classes of the community, and it is showing signs of being able soon to accomplish the very highest class of work.[1]

Those who finish and put together the different parts of a watch must always have highly specialized skill: but most of the machines which are in use in a watch factory are not different in general character from those which are used in any other of the lighter metal trades: in fact many of them are mere modifications of the turning lathes and of the slotting, punching, drilling, planning, shaping, milling machines and a few others, which are familiar to all engineering trades. This is a good illustration of the fact that while there is a constantly increasing subdivision of labor, many of the lines of division between trades which are nominally distinct are becoming narrower and less difficult to be passed. In old times it would have been very small comfort to watch-makers, who happened to be suffering from a diminished demand for their wares, to be told that the gun-making trade was in want of extra hands; but most of the operatives in a watch factory would find machines very similar to those with which they were familiar, if they strayed into a gun-making factory or sewing-machine factory, or a factory for making textile machinery. A watch factory with those who worked in it could be converted without any overwhelming loss into a sewing-machine factory: almost the only condition would be that in the new factory no one should be put to work

---

[1]The perfection which the machinery has already attained is shown by the fact that at the Inventions Exhibition held in London in 1885, the representative of an American watch factory took to pieces fifty watches before some English representatives of the older system of manufacture, and after throwing the different parts into different heaps, asked them to select for him one piece from each heap in succession; he then set these pieces up in one of the watch-cases and handed them back a watch in perfect order.

which required a higher order of general intelligence, than that to which he was already accustomed.

§5. The printing trade affords another instance of the way in which an improvement of machinery and an increase in the volume of production causes an elaborate subdivision of labor. Everyone is familiar with the pioneer newspaper editor of newly settled districts of America, who sets up the type of his articles as he composes them; and with the aid of a boy prints off his sheets and distributes them to his scattered neighbours. When however the mystery of printing was new, the printer had to do all this for himself, and in addition to make all his own appliances.[1] These are now provided for him by separate "subsidiary" trades, from whom even the printer in the backwoods can obtain everything that he wants to use. But in spite of the assistance which it thus gets from outside, a large printing establishment has to find room for many different classes of workers within its walls. To say nothing of those who organize and superintend the business, of those who do its office work and keep its stores, of the skilled "readers" who correct any errors that may have crept into the "proofs," of its engineers and repairers of machinery, of those who cast, and who correct and prepare its stereotype plates; of the warehousemen and the boys and girls who assist them, and several other minor classes; there are the two great groups of the compositors who set up the type, and the machinists and pressmen who print impressions from them. Each of these two groups is divided into many smaller groups, especially in the large centres of the printing trade. In London, for instance, a minder who was accustomed to one class of machine, or a compositor who was accustomed to one class of work, if thrown out of employment would not willingly abandon the advantage of his specialized skill, and falling back on his general knowledge of the trade seek work at another kind of machine or in another class of work.[2] These

[1] "The type-founder was probably the first to secede from the concern; then printers delegated to others the making of presses; afterwards the ink and the rollers found separate and distinct manufacturers; and there arose a class of persons who, though belonging to other trades, made printing appliances a speciality, such as printers' smiths, printers' joiners and printers' engineers" (Mr Southward in the Article on *Typography* in the *Encyclopaedia Britannica*).

[2] For instance, Mr Southward tells us "a minder may understand only book machines or only news machines; he may know all about'" machines that print from fiat surfaces or

barriers between minute subdivisions of a trade count for a great deal in many descriptions of the modern tendency towards specialization of industry; and to some extent rightly, because though many of them are so slight that a man thrown out of work in one subdivision could pass into one of its neighbours without any great loss of efficiency, yet he does not do so until he has tried for a while to get employment in his old lines; and therefore the barriers are as effective as stronger ones would be so far as the minor fluctuations of trade from week to week are concerned. But they are of an altogether different kind from the deep and broad partitions which divided one group of mediaeval handicraftsmen from another, and which caused the lifelong suffering of the handloom-weavers when their trade had left them.[1]

---

those that print from cylinders; "or of cylinders he may know only one kind. Entirely novel machines create a new class of artisans. There are men perfectly competent to manage a Walter press who are ignorant how to work two-colour or fine book-work machines. In the compositor's department division of labor is carried out to a still minuter degree. An old-fashioned printer would set up indifferently a placard, a title-page, or a book. At the present day we have jobbing hands, book hands, and news hands, the word 'hand' suggesting the factory-like nature of the business. There are jobbing hands who confine themselves to posters. Book hands comprise those who set up the titles and those who set up the body of the work. Of these latter again, while one man composes, another, the 'maker-up,' arranges the pages."

[1] Let us follow still further the progress of machinery in supplanting manual labor in some directions and opening out new fields for its employment in others. Let us watch the process by which large editions of a great newspaper are set up and printed off in a few hours. To begin with, a good part of the type-setting is itself often done by a machine; but in any case the types are in the first instance on a plane surface, from which it is impossible to print very rapidly. The next step therefore is to make a papier-maché cast of them, which is bent on to a cylinder, and is then used as the mould from which a new metal plate is cast that fits the cylinders of the printing machine. Fixed on these it rotates alternately against the inking cylinders and the paper. The paper is arranged in a huge roll at the bottom of the machine and unrolls itself automatically, first against the damping cylinders and then against the printing cylinders, the first of which prints it on one side, and the second on the other: thence to the cutting cylinders, which cut it into equal lengths, and thence to the folding apparatus, which folds it ready for sale.

More recently the casting of the type has been brought under the new methods. The compositor plays on a keyboard like that of the type-writer, and the matrix of a corresponding letter goes into line: then after spacing out, molten lead is poured on the line of matrices, and a solid line of type is ready. And in a further development each letter is cast separately from its matrix; the machine reckons up the space taken by the letters, stops when there are enough for a line, divides out the free space equally into the requisite number of small spaces between the words; and finally casts the line. It is

In the printing trades, as in the watch trade, we see mechanical and scientific appliances attaining results that would be impossible without them; at the same time that they persistently take over work that used to require manual skill and dexterity, but not much judgment; while they leave for man's hand all those parts which do require the use of judgment, and open up all sorts of new occupations in which there is a great demand for it. Every improvement and cheapening of the printer's appliances increases the demand for the judgment and discretion and literary knowledge of the reader, for the skill and taste of those who know how to set up a good title-page, or how to make ready a sheet on which an engraving is to be printed, so that light and shade will be distributed properly. It increases the demand for the gifted and highly-trained artists who draw or engrave on wood and stone and metal, and for those who know how to give an accurate report in ten lines of the substance of a speech that occupied ten minutes—an intellectual feat the difficulty of which we underrate, because it is so frequently performed. And again, it tends to increase the work of photographers and electrotypers, and stereotypers, of the makers of printer's machinery, and many others who get a higher training and a higher income from their work than did those layers on and takers off, and those folders of newspapers who have found their work taken over by iron fingers and iron arms.

§6. We may now pass to consider the effects which machinery has in relieving that excessive muscular strain which a few generations ago was the common lot of more than half the working men even in such a country as England. The most marvellous instances of the power of machinery are seen in large iron-works, and especially in those for making armour plates, where the force to be exerted is so great that man's muscles count for nothing, and where every movement, whether horizontal or vertical, has to be effected by hydraulic or steam force, and man stands by ready to govern the machinery and clear away ashes or perform some such secondary task.

---

claimed that one compositor can work several such machines simultaneously in distant towns by electric currents.

Machinery of this class has increased our command over nature, but it has not directly altered the character of man's work very much; for that which it does he could not have done without it. But in other trades machinery has lightened man's labors. The house carpenters, for instance, make things of the same kind as those used by our forefathers, with much less toil for themselves. They now give themselves chiefly to those parts of the task which are most pleasant and most interesting; while in every country town and almost every village there are found steam mills for sawing, planning and moulding, which relieve them of that grievous fatigue which not very long ago used to make them prematurely old.[1]

New machinery, when just invented, generally requires a great deal of care and attention. But the work of its attendant is always being sifted; that which is uniform and monotonous is gradually taken over by the machine, which thus becomes steadily more and more automatic and self-acting; till at last there is nothing for the hand to do, but to supply the material at certain intervals and to take away the work when finished. There still remains the responsibility for seeing that the machinery is in good order and working smoothly; but even this task is often made light by the introduction of an automatic movement, which brings the machine to a stop the instant anything goes wrong.

Nothing could be more narrow or monotonous than the occupation of a weaver of plain stuffs in the old time. But now one woman will manage four or more looms, each of which does many times as much work in the course of the day as the old hand-loom did; and her work is much less monotonous and calls for much more judgment than his did. So that for every hundred yards of cloth that are woven, the purely monotonous

[1] The jack-plane, used for making smooth large boards for floors and other purposes, used to cause heart disease, making carpenters as a rule old men by the time they were forty. Adam Smith tells us that "workmen, when they are liberally paid, are very apt to overwork themselves and to ruin their health and constitution in a few years. A carpenter in London, and in some other places, is not supposed to last in his utmost vigour above eight years....Almost every class of artificers is subject to some particular infirmity occasioned by excessive application to their peculiar species of work." *Wealth of Nations*, Book I, chapter VII.

work done by human beings is probably not a twentieth part of what it was.[1]

Facts of this kind are to be found in the recent history of many trades: and they are of great importance when we are considering the way in which the modern organization' of industry is tending to narrow the scope of each person's work, and thereby to render it monotonous. For those trades in which the work is most subdivided are those in which the chief muscular strain is most certain to be taken off by machinery; and thus the chief evil of monotonous work is much diminished. As Roscher says, it is monotony of life much more than monotony of work that is to be dreaded: monotony of work is an evil of the first order only when it involves monotony of life. Now when a person's employment requires much physical exertion, he is fit for nothing after his work; and unless his mental faculties are called forth in his work, they have little chance of being developed at all. But the nervous force is not very much exhausted in the ordinary work of a factory, at all events where there is not excessive noise, and where the hours of labor are not too long. The social surroundings of factory life stimulate mental activity in and out of working hours; and many of those factory workers, whose occupations are seemingly the most monotonous, have considerable intelligence and mental resource.[2]

---

[1] The efficiency of labor in weaving has been increased twelve-fold and that in spinning six-fold during the last seventy years. In the preceding seventy years the improvements in spinning had already increased the efficiency of labor two-hundred-fold (see Ellison's *Cotton Trade of Great Britain,* ch. IV and v).

[2] Perhaps the textile industries afford the best instance of work that used to be done by hand and is now done by machinery. They are especially prominent in England, where they give employment to nearly half a million males and more than half a million females, or more than one in ten of those persons who are earning independent incomes. The strain that is taken off human muscles in dealing even with those soft materials is shown by the fact that for every one of these million operatives there is used about one horse-power of steam, that is, about ten times as much as they would themselves exert if they were all strong men; and the history of these industries will serve to remind us that many of those who perform the more monotonous parts of manufacturing work are as a rule not skilled workers who have come down to it from a higher class of work, but unskilled workers who have risen to it. A great number of those who work in the Lancashire cotton-mills have come there from poverty-stricken districts of Ireland, while others are the descendants of paupers and people of weak physique, who were sent there in large numbers early in the last century from the most miserable conditions of life in the

It is true that the American agriculturist is an able man, and that his children rise rapidly in the world. But partly because land is plentiful, and he generally owns the farm that he cultivates, he has better social conditions than the English; he has always had to think for himself, and has long had to use and to repair complex machines. The English agricultural laborer has had many great disadvantages to contend with. Till recently he had little education; and he was in a great measure under a semi-feudal rule, which was not without its advantages, but which repressed enterprise and even in some degree self-respect. These narrowing causes are removed. He is now fairly well educated in youth. He learns to handle various machinery; he is less dependent on the good-will of any particular squire or group of farmers; and, since his work is more various, and educates intelligence more than the lowest grades of town work do, he is tending to rise both absolutely and relatively.

§7. We must now proceed to consider what are the conditions under which the economies in production arising from division of labor can best be secured. It is obvious that the efficiency of specialized machinery or specialized skill is but one condition of its economic use; the other is that sufficient work should be found to keep it well employed. As Babbage pointed out, in a large factory "the master manufacturer by dividing the work to be executed into different processes, each requiring different degrees of skill or force, can purchase exactly that precise quantity of both which is necessary for each process; whereas if the whole work were executed by one workman that person must possess sufficient skill to perform the most difficult and sufficient strength to execute the most laborious of the operations into which the work is divided.'" The economy of production requires not only that each person

---

poorest agricultural districts, where the laborers were fed and housed almost worse than the animals whom they tended. Again, when regret is expressed that the cotton factory hands of New England have not the high standard of culture which prevailed among them a century ago, we must remember that the descendants of those factory workers have moved up to higher and more responsible posts, and include many of the ablest and wealthiest of the citizens of America. Those who have taken their places are in the process of being raised; they are chiefly French Canadians and Irish, who though they may learn in their new homes some of the vices of civilization, are yet much better off and have on the whole better opportunities of developing the higher faculties of themselves and their children than they had in their old homes.

should be employed constantly in a narrow range of work, but also that, when it is necessary for him to undertake different tasks, each of these tasks should be such as to call forth as much as possible of his skill and ability. Just in the same way the economy of machinery requires that a powerful turning-lathe when specially arranged for one class of work should be kept employed as long as possible on that work; and if there is occasion to employ it on other work, that should be such as to be worthy of the lathe, and not such as could have been done equally well by a much smaller machine.

Here then, so far as the economy of production goes, men and machines stand on much the same footing: but while machinery is a mere implement of production, man's welfare is also its ultimate aim. We have already been occupied with the question whether the human race as a whole gains by carrying to an extreme that specialization of function which causes all the most difficult work to be done by a few people: but we have now to consider it more nearly with special reference to the work of business management. The main drift of the next three chapters is to inquire what are the causes which make different forms of business management the fittest to profit by their environment, and the most likely to prevail over others; but it is well that meanwhile we should have in our minds the question, how far they are severally fitted to benefit their environment.

Many of those economies in the use of specialized skill and machinery which are commonly regarded as within the reach of very large establishments, do not depend on the size of individual factories. Some depend on the aggregate volume of production of the kind in the neighbourhood; while others again, especially those connected with the growth of knowledge and the progress of the arts, depend chiefly on the aggregate volume of production in the whole civilized world. And here we may introduce two technical terms.

We may divide the economies arising from an increase in the scale of production of any kind of goods, into two classes — firstly, those dependent on the general development of the industry; and, secondly, those dependent on the resources of the individual houses of business engaged in it, on their organization and the efficiency of their management. We may call the former *external economies,* and the latter *internal economies.*

## Correlation of the Tendencies to Increasing and to Diminishing Returns

The general argument of the present Book shows that an increase in the aggregate volume of production of anything will generally increase the size, and therefore the internal economies possessed by such a representative firm; that it will always increase the external economies to which the firm has access; and thus will enable it to manufacture at a less proportionate cost of labor and sacrifice than before.

In other words, we say broadly that while the part which nature plays in production shows a tendency to diminishing return, the part which man plays shows a tendency to increasing return. The *law of increasing return* may be worded thus: — An increase of labor and capital leads generally to improved organization, which increases the efficiency of the work of labor and capital.

Therefore in those industries which are not engaged in raising raw produce an increase of labor and capital generally gives a return increased more than in proportion; and further this improved organization tends to diminish or even override any increased resistance which nature may offer to raising increased amounts of raw produce. If the actions of the laws of increasing and diminishing return are balanced we have the *law of constant return,* and an increased produce is obtained by labor and sacrifice increased just in proportion.

For the two tendencies towards increasing and diminishing return press constantly against one another. In the production of wheat and wool, for instance, the latter tendency has almost exclusive sway in an old country, which cannot import freely. In turning the wheat into flour, or the wool into blankets, an increase in the aggregate volume of production brings some new economies, but not many; for the trades of grinding wheat and making blankets are already on so great a scale that any new economies that they may attain are more likely to be the result of new inventions than of improved organization. In a country however in which the blanket trade is but slightly developed, these latter may be important; and then it may happen that an increase in the aggregate production of blankets diminishes the proportionate difficulty of manufacturing by just as much as it increases that of raising the raw material. In that case the actions of the laws of diminishing and of increasing return would just neutralize one another; and blankets would conform to the law of constant return. But in most of the more delicate branches of manufacturing, where the cost of raw material counts for little, and in most of the modern transport industries the law of increasing return acts almost unopposed.[1]

Increasing Return is a relation between a quantity of effort and sacrifice on the one hand, and a quantity of product on the other. The quantities cannot be taken out exactly, because changing methods of production call for machinery, and for unskilled and skilled labor of new kinds and in new proportions. But, taking a broad view, we may perhaps say vaguely that the output of a certain amount of labor and capital in an industry has increased by perhaps a quarter or a third in the last twenty years. To measure outlay and output in terms of money is a tempting, but a dangerous resource: for a comparison of money outlay with money returns is apt to slide into an estimate of the rate of profit on capital.[2]

§3. We may now sum up provisionally the relations of industrial expansion to social wellbeing. A rapid growth of population has often been accompanied by unhealthy and enervating habits of life in

---

[1] In an article on "The Variation of Productive Forces" in the *Quarterly Journal of Economics* 1902, Professor Bullock suggests that the term "Economy of Organization" should be substituted for Increasing Return. He shows clearly that the forces which make for Increasing Return are not of the same order as those that make for Diminishing Return: and there are undoubtedly cases in which it is better to emphasize this difference by describing causes rather than results, and contrasting Economy of Organization with the Inelasticity of Nature's response to intensive cultivation.

[2] There is no general rule that industries which yield increasing returns show also rising profits. No doubt a vigorous firm, which increases its scale of operations and obtains important (internal) economies which are peculiar to it, will show an increasing return and a rising rate of profit; because its increasing output will not materially affect the price of its produce. But profits tend to be low, as we shall see below (VI, VIII, §§1, 2.*)*, in such industries as plain weaving, because their vast scale has enabled organization in production and marketing to be carried so far as to be almost dominated by routine.

overcrowded towns. And sometimes it has started badly, outrunning the material resources of the people, causing them with imperfect appliances to make excessive demands on the soil; and so to call forth the stern action of the law of diminishing return as regards raw produce, without having the power of minimizing its effects. Having thus begun with poverty, an increase in numbers may go on to its too frequent consequences in that weakness of character which unfits a people for developing a highly organized industry.

These are serious perils: but yet it remains true that the collective efficiency of a people with a given average of individual strength and energy may increase more than in proportion to their numbers. If they can for a time escape from the pressure of the law of diminishing return by importing food and other raw produce on easy terms; if their wealth is not consumed in great wars, and increases at least as fast as their numbers; and if they avoid habits of life that would enfeeble them; then every increase in their numbers is likely *for the time* to be accompanied by a more than proportionate increase in their power of obtaining material goods. For it enables them to secure the many various economies of specialized skill and specialized machinery, of localized industries and production on a large scale: it enables them to have increased facilities of communication of all kinds; while the very closeness of their neighbourhood diminishes the expense of time and effort involved in every sort of traffic between them, and gives them new opportunities of getting social enjoyments and the comforts and luxuries of culture in every form. No doubt deduction must be made for the growing difficulty of finding solitude and quiet and even fresh air: but there is in most cases some balance of good.[1]

Taking account of the fact that an increasing density of population generally brings with it access to new social enjoyments we may give a

---

[1] The Englishman Mill bursts into unwonted enthusiasm when speaking (*Political Economy,* Book IV, ch. VI, §2) of the pleasures of wandering alone in beautiful scenery: and many American writers give fervid descriptions of the growing richness of human life as the backwoodsman finds neighbours settling around him, as the backwoods settlement develops into a village, the village into a town, and the town into a vast city. (See for instance Carey's *Principles of Social Science* and Henry George's *Progress and Poverty.*)

rather broader scope to this statement and say: — An increase of population accompanied by an equal increase in the material sources of enjoyment and aids to production is likely to lead to a more than proportionate increase in the aggregate income of enjoyment of all kinds; provided firstly, an adequate supply of raw produce can be obtained without great difficulty, and secondly there is no such overcrowding as causes physical and moral vigour to be impaired by the want of fresh air and light and of healthy and joyous recreation for the young.

The accumulated wealth of civilized countries is at present growing faster than the population: and though it may be true that the wealth per head would increase somewhat faster if the population did not increase quite so fast; yet as a matter of fact an increase of population is likely to continue to be accompanied by a more than proportionate increase of the material aids to production: and in England *at the present time,* with easy access to abundant foreign supplies of raw material, an increase of population is accompanied by a more than proportionate increase of the means of satisfying human wants other than the need for light, fresh air, etc. Much of this increase is however attributable not to the increase of industrial efficiency but to the increase of wealth by which it is accompanied: and therefore it does not necessarily benefit those who have no share in that wealth. And further, England's foreign supplies of raw produce may at any time be checked by changes in the trade regulations of other countries, and may be almost cut off by a great war, while the naval and military expenditure which would be necessary to make the country fairly secure against this last risk, would appreciably diminish the benefits that she derives from the action of the law of increasing return.

## Chapter 22*

# The Laws of Returns under Competitive Conditions[1]

**Piero Sraffa**

A striking feature of the present position of economic science is the almost unanimous agreement at which economists have arrived regarding the theory of competitive value, which is inspired by the fundamental symmetry existing between the forces of demand and those of supply, and is based upon the assumption that the essential causes determining the price of particular commodities may be simplified and grouped together so as to be represented by a pair of intersecting curves of collective demand and supply. This state of things is in such marked contrast with the controversies on the theory of value by which political economy was characterised during the past century, that it might almost be thought that from these clashes of thought the spark of an ultimate truth had at length been struck. Sceptics might perhaps think that the agreement in question is due, not so much to everyone being convinced, as to the indifference felt by the majority nowadays in regard to the theory of value — an indifference which is justified by the fact that this theory, more than any other part of economic theory, has lost much of its direct bearing upon practical politics, and particularly in regard to doctrines of social changes, which had formerly been conferred upon it

---

* From *The Economic Journal* No. 144(Vol. XXXVI December 1926), pp. 535–50.

[1] The opening pages of this article contain a summary of the conclusions of a paper on "Relazioni fra costo e quantita prodotta" published in Vol, II. of the *Annali di Economia.*

by Ricardo and afterwards by Marx, and in opposition to them by the bourgeois economists. It has been transformed more and more into "an apparatus of the mind, a technique of thinking" which does not furnish any "settled conclusions immediately applicable to policy."[1] It is essentially a pedagogic instrument, somewhat like the study of the classics, and, unlike the study of the exact sciences and law, its purposes are exclusively those of training the mind, for which reason it is hardly apt to excite the passions of men, even academical men — a theory, in short, in respect to which it is not worth while departing from a tradition which is finally accepted. However this may be, the fact of the agreement remains.

In the tranquil view which the modem theory of value presents us there is one dark spot which disturbs the harmony of the whole. This is represented by the supply curve, based upon the laws of increasing and diminishing returns. That its foundations are less solid than those of the other portions of the structure is generally recognised. That they are actually so weak as to be unable to support the weight imposed upon them is a doubt which slumbers beneath the consciousness of many, but which most succeed in silently suppressing. From time to time someone is unable any longer to resist the pressure of his doubts and expresses them openly; then, in order to prevent the scandal spreading, he is promptly silenced, frequently with some concessions and partial admission of his objections, which, naturally, the theory had implicitly taken into account. And so, with the lapse of time, the qualifications, the restrictions and the exceptions have piled up, and have eaten up, if not all, certainly the greater part of the theory. If their aggregate effect is not at once apparent, this is because they are scattered about in footnotes and articles and carefully segregated from one another.

It is not the purpose of this article to add anything to the pile, but simply to attempt to co-ordinate certain materials, separating what is still alive from what is dead in the concept of the supply curve and of its effects on competitive price determination.

---

[1] Keynes: *Introduction to Cambridge Economic Handbooks.*

At present the laws of returns are of special importance owing to the part they play in the study of the problem of value. But they are naturally much older than the particular theory of value in which they are employed, and it is precisely from their secular age and their original applications that they derive both their prestige and their weakness in their modern application. We are disposed to accept the laws of returns as a matter of course, because we have before our eyes the great and indisputable services rendered by them when performing their ancient function, and we often neglect to ask ourselves whether the old barrels are still able to hold the new wine.

The law of diminishing returns has long been associated mainly with the problem of rent, and from this point of view the law as formulated by the classical economists with reference to land was entirely adequate. It had always been perfectly obvious that its operation affected, not merely rent, but also the cost of the product; but this was not emphasised as a cause of variation in the relative price of the individual commodities produced, because the operation of diminishing returns increased in a like measure the cost of all. This remained true even when the English classical economists applied the law to the production of corn, for, as Marshall has shown, "the term 'corn' was used by them as short for agricultural produce in general" (*Principles,* VI. i. 2, note).

The position occupied in classical economics by the law of increasing returns was much less prominent, as it was regarded merely as an important aspect of the division of labor, and thus rather as a result of general economic progress than of an increase in the scale of production.

The result was that in the original laws of returns the general idea of a functional connection between cost and quantity produced was not given a conspicuous place; it appears, in fact, to have been present in the minds of the classical economists much less prominently than was the connection between demand and demand price.

The development which has emphasised the former aspect of the laws of returns is comparatively recent. At the same time it has removed both laws from the positions which, according to the traditional partition of political economy, they used to occupy, one under the heading of "distribution" and the other under "production," and has transferred them to the chapter of "exchange-value"; there, merging them in the single "law of non-proportional returns," it has derived from them a law of supply in a market such as can be co-ordinated with the corresponding law of demand; and on the symmetry of these two opposite forces it has based the modem theory of value.

In order to reach this result it was found necessary to introduce certain modifications into the form of the two laws. Very little was necessary as regards the law of diminishing returns, which merely required to be generalised from the particular case of land to every case in which there existed a factor of production of which only a constant quantity was available. The law of increasing returns, however, had to be subjected to a much more radical transformation: the part played in it by the division of labor — now limited to the case of independent subsidiary factories coming into existence as the production of an industry increases — was greatly restricted; while consideration of that greater internal division of labor, which is rendered possible by an increase in the dimensions of an individual firm, was entirely abandoned, as it was seen to be incompatible with competitive conditions. On the other hand, the importance of "external economies" was more and more emphasized — that is, of the advantage derived by individual producers from the growth, not of their own individual undertakings, but of the industry in its aggregate.

Even in their present form, however, the two laws have preserved the characteristic of originating from forces of profoundly diverse nature. Such heterogeneousness, while not constituting in itself an insurmountable obstacle when it is attempted to co-ordinate them and employ them conjointly in problems mainly relating, not to the causes, but to the effects of variations in cost, involves a fresh difficulty when it is sought to classify the various industries according as they belong to one or the other category. It is, in fact, in the very nature of the bases of the two laws that the wider the definition which we assume for "an industry"— that is, the more nearly it includes all the undertakings which employ a given *factor* of production, as, for example, agriculture or the iron industry — the more probable will it be that the forces which make for diminishing returns will play an important part in it; the more restrictive this definition — the more nearly it includes, therefore, only those undertakings which produce a given type of consumable *commodity,* as, for example, fruit or nails — the greater will be the probability that the forces which make for increasing returns will predominate in it. In its effects this difficulty is parallel to that which, as is well known, arises from the consideration of the element of time, whereby the shorter the period of time allowed for the adjustments, the greater is the likelihood of decreasing returns, while the longer that period is, the greater is the probability of increasing returns.

The really serious difficulties make their appearance when it is considered to what extent the supply curves based on the laws of returns satisfy the conditions necessary to enable them to be employed in the study of the equilibrium value of single commodities produced under competitive conditions. This point of view assumes that the conditions of production and the demand for a commodity can be considered, in respect to small variations, as being practically independent, both in regard to each other and in relation to the supply and demand of all other commodities. It is well known that such an assumption would not be illegitimate merely because the independence may not be absolutely perfect, as in fact, it never can be; and a slight degree of interdependence may be overlooked without disadvantage if it applies to quantities of the second order of smalls, as would be the case if the effect (for example, an increase of cost) of a variation in the industry which we propose to isolate were to react partially on the price of the products of other industries, and this latter effect were to influence the demand for the product of the first industry. But, of course, it is a very different matter, and the assumption becomes illegitimate, when a variation in the quantity produced by the industry under consideration sets up a force which acts directly, not merely upon its own costs, but also upon the costs of other industries; in such a case the conditions of the "particular equilibrium" which it was intended to isolate are upset, and it is no longer possible, without contradiction, to neglect collateral effects.

It unfortunately happens that it is precisely into this latter category that the applications of the laws of returns fall, in the great majority of cases. As regards diminishing returns, in fact, if in the production of a particular commodity a considerable part of a factor is employed, the total amount of which is fixed or can be increased only at a more than proportional cost, a small increase in the production of the commodity will necessitate a more intense utilisation of that factor, and this will affect in the same manner the cost of the commodity in question and the cost of the other commodities into the production of which that factor enters; and since commodities into the production of which a common special factor enters are frequently, to a certain extent, substitutes for one another (for example, various kinds of agricultural produce), the modification in their price will not be without appreciable effects upon demand in the industry concerned. If we next take an industry which employs only a small part of the "constant factor" (which appears more appropriate for the study of the particular equilibrium of a single industry), we find that a (small) increase in its production is generally met much more by drawing "marginal doses" of the constant factor from other industries than by intensifying its own utilisation of it; thus the increase in cost will be practically negligible, and anyhow it will still operate in a like degree upon all the industries of the group. Excluding these cases, and excluding — if we take a point of view embracing long periods — the numerous cases in which the quantity of a means of production may be regarded as being only temporarily fixed in respect to an unexpected demand, very little remains: the imposing structure of diminishing returns is available only for the study of that minute class of commodities in the production of which the whole of a factor of production is employed. Here, of course, by "a commodity" is to be understood an article in regard to which it is possible to construct, or at least to conceive, a demand schedule which is tolerably homogeneous and independent of the conditions of supply, and not, as is frequently implied, a collection of diverse articles, such as agricultural products or ironware.

It is not by mere chance that, notwithstanding the profoundly diverse nature of the two laws of returns, the same difficulties also arise, in almost identical form, in connection with increasing returns. Here again we find that in reality the economies of production on a large scale are not suitable for the requirements of the supply curve: their field of action is either wider or more restricted than would be necessary. On the one hand, reductions in cost which are due to "those *external* economies which result from the general progress of industrial environment" to which Marshall refers (*Principles,* V. xi. 1) must, of course, be ignored, as they are clearly incompatible with the conditions of the particular equilibrium of a commodity. On the other hand, reductions in cost connected with an increase in a firm's scale of production, arising from internal economies or from the possibility of distributing the overhead charges over a larger number of product units, must be put aside as being incompatible with competitive conditions. The only economies which could be taken into consideration would be such as occupy an intermediate position between these two extremes; but it is just in the middle that nothing, or almost nothing, is to be found. Those economies which are external from the point of view of the individual firm, but internal as regards the industry in its aggregate, constitute precisely the class which is most seldom to be met with. As Marshall has said in the work in which he has intended to approach most closely the actual conditions of industry, "the economies of production on a large scale can seldom be allocated exactly to anyone industry: they are in great measure attached to groups, often large groups, of correlated industries."[1] In any case, in so far as external economies of the kind in question exist, they are not likely to be called forth by *small* increases in production. Thus it appears that supply curves showing decreasing costs are not to be found more frequently than their opposite.

Reduced within such restricted limits, the supply schedule with variable costs cannot claim to be a general conception applicable to normal industries; it can prove a useful instrument only in regard to such exceptional industries as can reasonably satisfy its conditions. In normal cases the cost of production of commodities produced competitively — as we are not entitled to take into consideration the causes which may make it rise or fall — must be regarded as constant in respect of small variations in the quantity produced.[2] And so, as a simple way of

---

[1] *Industry and Trade,* p. 188.

[2] The absence of causes which tend to cause the cost either to increase or diminish appears to be the most obvious and plausible way from which constant costs can arise. But as these constitute the most dangerous enemy of the symmetry between demand and supply, those writers who accept this doctrine, in order to be able to relegate the constant costs to the category of theoretical limiting cases which in reality cannot exist, have persuaded themselves that they are something extremely complicated and improbable, since they "can only result from the accidental balancing of two opposite tendencies; the tendency to diminution of cost. . . and the tendency to increase of cost . . ." (Sidgwick,

approaching the problem of competitive value, the old and now obsolete theory which makes it dependent on the cost of production alone appears to hold its ground as the best available.

This first approximation, as far as it goes, is as important as it is useful: it emphasises the fundamental factor, namely, the predominant influence of cost of production in the determination of the normal value of commodities, while at the same time it does not lead us astray when we desire to study in greater detail the conditions under which exchange takes place in particular cases, for it does not conceal from us the fact that we cannot find the elements required for this purpose within the limits of its assumptions.

When we proceed to a further approximation, while keeping to the path of free competition, the complications do not arise gradually, as would be convenient; they present themselves simultaneously as a whole. If diminishing returns arising from a "constant factor" are taken into consideration, it becomes necessary to extend the field of investigation so as to examine the conditions of simultaneous equilibrium in numerous industries: a well-known conception, whose complexity, however, prevents it from bearing fruit, at least in the present state of our knowledge, which docs not permit of even much simpler schemata being applied to the study of real conditions. If we pass to external economies, we find ourselves confronted by the same obstacle, and there is also the impossibility of confining within statical conditions the circumstances from which they originate.

It is necessary, therefore, to abandon the path of free competition and turn in the opposite direction, namely, towards monopoly. Here we find a well-defined theory in which variations of cost connected with changes in the dimensions of the individual undertaking play an important part. Of course, when we are supplied with theories in respect to the two

---

*Principles of Political Economy,* 1st ed., p. 207; to the same effect see, *e.g.*, Marshall, *Principles,* IV. xiii, 2, and *Palgrave's Dictionary, sub voce* Law of Constant Return). The dictum of Edgeworth, that "to treat *variables* as *constants* is the characteristic vice of the unmathematical economist," might to-day be reversed: the mathematical economists have gone so far in correcting this vice that they can no longer conceive of a constant except as the result of the compensation of two equal and opposite variables.

extreme cases of monopoly and competition as part of the equipment required in order to undertake the study of the actual conditions in the different industries, we are warned that these generally do not fit exactly one or other of the categories, but will be found scattered along the intermediate zone, and that the nature of an industry will approximate more closely to the monopolist or the competitive system according to its particular circumstances, such as whether the number of autonomous undertakings in it is larger or smaller, or whether or not they are bound together by partial agreements, etc. We are thus led to believe that when production is in the hands of a large number of concerns entirely independent of one another as regards control, the conclusions proper to competition may be applied even if the market in which the goods are exchanged is not absolutely perfect, for its imperfections are in general constituted by frictions which may simply retard or slightly modify the effects of the active forces of competition, but which the latter ultimately succeed in substantially overcoming. This view appears to be fundamentally inadmissible. Many of the obstacles which break up that unity of the market which is the essential condition of competition are not of the nature of "frictions," but are themselves active forces which produce permanent and even cumulative effects. They are frequently, moreover, endowed with sufficient stability to enable them to be made the subject of analysis based on statical assumptions.

Of these effects two, which are closely interconnected, are of special importance because they are to be found with great frequency in industries in which competitive conditions appear to prevail; and they also possess a special interest because, as they relate to certain of the most characteristic features of the theoretical conception of competition, they show how seldom it is for these conditions to be realised in their integrity, and how a slight divergence from them suffices to render the manner in which equilibrium is attained extremely similar to that peculiar to monopoly. These two points in which the theory of competition differs radically from the actual state of things which is most general are: first, the idea that the competing producer cannot deliberately affect the market prices, and that he may therefore regard it as constant whatever the quantity of goods which he individually may throw on the market; second, the idea that each competing producer necessarily produces normally in circumstances of individual increasing costs.

Everyday experience shows that a very large number of undertakings — and the majority of those which produce manufactured consumers' goods — work under conditions of individual diminishing costs. Almost any producer of such goods, if he could rely upon the market in which he sells his products being prepared to take any quantity of them from him at the current price, without any trouble on his part except that of producing them, would extend his business enormously. It is not easy, in times of normal activity, to find an undertaking which systematically restricts its own production to an amount less than that which it could sell at the current price, and which is at the same time prevented by competition from exceeding that price. Business men, who regard themselves as being subject to competitive conditions, would consider absurd the assertion that the limit to their production is to be found in the internal conditions of production in their firm, which do not permit of the production of a greater quantity without an increase in cost. The chief obstacle against which they have to contend when they want gradually to increase their production does not lie in the cost of production — which, indeed, generally favours them in that direction — but in the difficulty of selling the larger quantity of goods without reducing the price, or without having to face increased marketing expenses. This necessity of reducing prices in order to sell a larger quantity of one's own product is only an aspect of the usual descending demand curve, with the difference that instead of concerning the whole of a commodity, whatever its origin, it relates only to the goods produced by a particular firm; and the marketing expenses necessary for the extension of its market are merely costly efforts (in the form of advertising, commercial travellers, facilities to customers, etc.) to increase the willingness of the market to buy from it — that is, to raise that demand curve artificially.

This method of regarding the matter appears the most natural, and that which adheres to the reality of things. No doubt it is possible, from the formal point of view, to reverse these relations and regard every purchaser as being perfectly indifferent in his choice between the different producers, provided the latter, in order to approach him, are prepared to incur marketing expenses varying greatly in different cases, and to reckon these increased marketing expenses in the cost of production of each. In this way increasing individual costs can be obtained to any desired extent and a perfect market in which there is an unlimited demand, at current prices, for the products of each. But the question of allocating the marketing expenses cannot be decided from the point of view of formal correctness, for on that basis the two methods are equivalent; nor can it be decided according to the fact that these charges are actually paid by the purchaser or the seller, as this does not affect their incidence or their effects in any way. What is important is to ascertain how the various forces at work can be grouped in the most homogeneous manner, so that the influence of each of them on the equilibrium resulting from their opposition may be more readily estimated. From this point of view the second of the methods mentioned must be rejected, since it entirely conceals the effects which the circumstances from which the marketing expenses originate exercise in disturbing the unity of the market. It alters in a misleading way, moreover, the customary and well defined significance of the expression "cost of production," with the result of rendering it dependent upon elements quite extraneous to the conditions under which the production of a given undertaking takes place. It consequently misrepresents the manner in which the actual process of determining the price and the quantity produced by each undertaking is affected.

By adhering to the first point of view, therefore, we are led to ascribe the correct measure of importance to the chief obstacle which hinders the free play of competition, even where this appears to predominate, and which at the same time renders a stable equilibrium possible even when the supply curve for the products of each individual firm is descending — that is, the absence of indifference on the part of the buyers of goods as between the different producers. The causes of the preference shown by any group of buyers for a particular firm are of the most diverse nature, and may range from long custom, personal acquaintance, confidence in the quality of the product, proximity, knowledge of particular requirements and the possibility of obtaining credit, to the reputation of a trade-mark, or sign, or a name with high traditions, or to such special features of modelling or design in the product as — without constituting it a distinct commodity intended for the satisfaction of particular needs — have for their principal purpose that of distinguishing it from the products of other firms. What these and the many other possible reasons for preference have in common is that they are expressed in a willingness (which may frequently be dictated by necessity) on the part of the group of buyers who constitute a firm's clientele to pay, if necessary, something extra in order to obtain the goods from a particular firm rather than from any other.

When each of the firms producing a commodity is in such a position the general market for the commodity is subdivided into a series of distinct markets. Any firm which endeavours to extend beyond its own market by invading those of its competitors must incur heavy marketing expenses in order to surmount the barriers by which they are surrounded; but, on the other hand, within its own market and under the protection of its own barrier each enjoys a privileged position whereby it obtains advantages which — if not in extent, at least in their nature — are equal to those enjoyed by the ordinary monopolist.

Nor is it necessary to stress the customary conception of monopoly to make this case fit into it. In it also, in fact, we find that the majority of the circumstances which affect the strength of a monopolist (such as the possession of unique natural resources, legal privileges, the control of a greater or less proportion of the total production, the existence of rival commodities, etc.) exercise their influence essentially by affecting the elasticity of the demand for the monopolised goods. Whatever the causes may be, this is the only decisive factor in estimating the degree of independence which monopolist has in fixing prices: the less elastic the demand product, the greater is his hold on his market. The extreme case, which may properly be called "absolute monopoly," is that in which the elasticity of the demand for the product of a firm is equal to unity[1]; in that case, however much the monopolist raises his prices, the sums

[1] The elasticity of demand for the products of a monopolist cannot, of course, be less than unity in respect to prices immediately above the equilibrium price — that is, in respect to that part of the demand curve which alone counts in regard to the determination of the power of a monopolist in his own market; a question which is quite distinct from that of the magnitude of the gains obtainable by the monopoly, as the latter is dependent, not so much on the ratio of change, as on the absolute measure of the demand and the demand price.

periodically expended in purchasing his goods are not even partially diverted into different channels of expenditure, and his price policy will not be affected at all by the fear of competition from other sources of supply. So soon as this elasticity increases, competition begins to make itself felt, and becomes ever more intense as the elasticity grows, until to infinite elasticity in the demand for the products of an individual undertaking a state of perfect competition corresponds. In the intermediate cases the significance of a moderate elasticity in the demand is that, although the monopolist has a certain freedom in fixing his prices, whenever he increases them he is forsaken by a portion of his purchasers, who prefer to spend their money in some other manner. It matters little to the monopolist if they spend it in purchasing goods very different from his own, or goods identical with them, but supplied by other producers who have not increased their price; in either case he must undergo — if only in a slight degree — actual competition from such goods, since it is precisely the possibility of buying them that leads the purchasers gradually to give up using his product as he increases the price. The direct effects are thus equal whether the sums set free as the result of an increase in price by an undertaking are expended on a large number of different commodities, or whether they are employed preponderatingly in the purchase of one or a few rival commodities which are more or less available for buyers, as occurs in the case of an undertaking which, while controlling only a small part of the total production of a commodity, has the advantage of possessing a particular market of its own. But the indirect effects in the two cases are substantially different.

The method indicated by Marshall in regard to manufactures designed for particular tastes is applicable for the study of this latter case. "When we are considering an individual producer," he writes, "we must couple his supply curve, not with the general demand curve for his commodity in a wide market, but with the particular demand curve of his own special market " *(Principles,* V. xii. 2). If we extend this method to those industries in which each firm has more or less a particular market, we must not restrict its employment to the occasions when we are considering the individual producer, but we must adhere to it also when we examine the manner in which equilibrium is attained in the trade as a whole; for it is clear that such particular curves can by no means be compounded so as to form a single pair of collective demand and supply curves. The method mentioned above is the very same as that followed in cases of ordinary monopoly, and in both cases, in fact, the individual producer determines his selling price by the well-known method which makes his monopoly revenue or his profits the maximum obtainable.

The peculiarity of the case of the firm which does not possess an actual monopoly but has merely a particular market is that, in the demand schedule for the goods produced by it, the possible buyers are entered in descending order according to the price which each of them is prepared to pay, not rather than go entirely without, but rather than not buy it from that particular producer instead of elsewhere. That is to say, that two elements enter into the composition of such demand prices — the price at which the goods can be purchased from those other producers who, in the order of a purchaser's preference, immediately follow the producer under consideration, and the monetary measure of the value (a quantity which may be positive or negative) which the purchaser puts on his preference for the products of the firm in question.

For convenience in discussion it may be assumed that initially, in an industry in which like conditions prevail, each producer sells at a price which barely covers his costs. The individual interest of each producer will urge him to increase his price quickly so as to obtain the maximum profit. But in proportion as this practice spreads throughout the trade the various demand schedules will be modified as a result; for, as each buyer finds that the prices of the substitutes upon which he was able to reckon are increased, he will be inclined to pay a higher price for the products of the firm whose customer he is. So that, even before the first increase in price has been completely carried into effect, the conditions will be created which may permit every one of the concerns to make a further increase — and so on in succession. Naturally this process speedily reaches its limit. The customers lost by a firm whenever it raises its prices have recourse in part to other suppliers, and these will return to it when the others also have raised their prices; but in part they entirely give up buying the goods and definitely drop out of the market. Thus, every business has two classes of marginal customers — those who, are at the margin only from its own individual standpoint and fix a limit for the excess of its prices over the prices generally ruling, and those who are at the margin from the standpoint of the general market and fix a limit for the general increase in price of the product.

It is, of course, possible that a general rise in the prices of a product may affect the conditions of demand and supply of certain firms in such a way as to make it advantageous for them to lower their prices rather than conform with the rise. But in an industry which has attained a certain degree of stability in its general structure, in regard of its methods of production, the number of undertakings composing it, and its commercial customs — in respect to which, therefore, statical assumptions are more nearly justified — this alternative is much less likely to be adopted than its opposite. In the first place, it involves great elasticity in the demand for the products of an individual business and rapidly diminishing costs for it — that is to say, a state of things the almost inevitable and speedy result of which is complete monopolisation, and which, therefore, is not likely to be found in a trade operated normally by a number of independent firms. In the second place, the forces which impel producers to raise prices are much more effective than those which impel them to reduce them; and this not merely owing to the fear which every seller has of spoiling his market, but mainly because an increase of profit secured by means of a cut in price is obtained *at the cost* of the competing firms, and consequently it impels them to take such defensive action as may jeopardise the greater profits secured; whereas an increase of profit obtained by means of a rise in prices not only does not injure competitors but brings them a positive *gain,* and it may therefore be regarded as having been more durably acquired. An undertaking, therefore, when confronted with the dual possibility of increasing its profits by raising its selling prices, or by reducing them, will generally adopt the first alternative unless the additional profits expected from the second are considerably greater.

These same reasons may serve to dispel the doubt, which might at first sight arise, whether in the case considered above the equilibrium may be indeterminate, as it is generally considered to be in the analogous case of multiple monopoly. In the first place, even in this case, as Edgeworth has noticed, "the extent of indeterminateness diminishes with the diminution of the degree of correlation between the articles" produced by the different monopolists[1]; that is to say, in our case, with the diminution of the elasticity of demand for the products of the individual firm — a limitation, it may be added, the effectiveness of which is the greater in proportion as the rapidity of decrease in the individual cost with the increase in the quantity produced becomes less. Both these conditions, as has been said above, are generally present to a large extent in the case we are considering. Moreover, the indeterminateness of the equilibrium in the case of multiple monopoly is necessarily dependent upon the assumption that at any moment each of the monopolists is *equally* inclined either to raise or to reduce his price, according as one or the other may suit him best from the point of view of immediate gain — a supposition which, at least in our case, is not, as we have said, justified.[2]

The conclusion that the equilibrium is in general determinate does not mean that generalising statements can be made regarding the price corresponding to that equilibrium; it may be different in the case of each undertaking, and is dependent to a great extent upon the special conditions affecting it.

The only case in which it would be possible to speak of a general price would be that of a trade in which the productive organisation of the different undertakings was uniform, and in which their particular markets were alike as regards the nature and attachment of the customers. In that case, as may readily be seen, the general price of the product, through the independent action of a number of firms, each of which is prompted only by its individual interests, would tend to reach the same level as that which would be fixed by a single monopolistic association in accordance with the ordinary principles of monopoly. This result, far from being conditioned by the existence of an almost complete isolation of the

---

[1] *The Pure Theory of Monopoly,* in Papers Relating to P. E., Vol. I. p. 121.

[2] The determinateness of the equilibrium would be more evident if, instead of regarding the various units of the same goods produced by different undertakings as rival commodities, we had regarded each unit as being composed of two commodities having, within each particular market, a joint demand, one of which (the commodity itself) is sold under competitive conditions, and the other (the special services, or the distinguishing features added to it by each producer) is sold under monopolistic conditions. This point of view, however. is more artificial and less in conformity with the customary method of regarding the matter.

individual markets, requires only a very slight degree of preference for a particular firm in each of the groups of customers. In itself, this case is of no importance, because it is extremely unlikely that such uniformity would actually be found; but it is representative of a tendency, which prevails even in actual cases where the conditions of the various undertakings differ among each other, whereby the cumulative action of slight obstacles to competition produces on prices effects which approximate to those of monopoly.

It should be noted that in the foregoing the disturbing influence exercised by the competition of new firms attracted to an industry the conditions of which permit of high monopolist profits has been neglected. This appeared justified, in the first place because the entrance of new-comers is frequently hindered by the heavy expenses necessary for setting up a connection in a trade in which the existing firms have an established goodwill — expenses which may often exceed the capital value of the profits obtainable; in the second place, this element can acquire importance only when the monopoly profits in a trade are considerably above the normal level of profits in the trade in general, which, however, does not prevent the prices from being determined up to that point in the manner which has been indicated.

It might seem, moreover, that the importance of the marketing difficulties as a limit to the development of the productive unit has been over-estimated as compared with the effect in the same direction exercised by the more than proportionate increase in the expenditure which a firm must sometimes incur in order to furnish itself with the additional means of production which it requires; but it will generally be found that such increases in costs are an effect, and not a determining cause, of the market conditions which render it necessary or desirable for a firm to restrict its production. Thus, the limited credit of many firms, which does not permit anyone of them to obtain more than a limited amount of capital at the current rate of interest, is often a direct consequence of its being known that a given firm is unable to increase its sales outside its own particular market without incurring heavy marketing expenses. If it were known that a firm which is in a position to produce an increased quantity of goods at a lower cost is also in a position to sell them without difficulty at a constant price, such a firm could encounter no obstacle in a free capital market. On the other hand, if a banker, or the owner of land on which a firm proposes to extend its own plant, or any other supplier of the firm's means of production, stands in a privileged position in respect to it, he can certainly exact from it a price higher than the current price for his supplies, but this possibility will still be a direct consequence of the fact that such a firm, being in its turn in a privileged position in regard to its particular market, also sells its products at prices above cost. What happens in such cases is that a portion of its monopoly profits are taken away from the firm, not that its cost of production is increased.

But these are mainly aspects of the process of diffusion of profits throughout the various stages of production and of the process of forming a normal level of profits throughout all the industries of a country. Their influence on the formation of the prices of single commodities is relatively unimportant, and their consideration is therefore beyond the scope of this article.

## Chapter 23*

# Increasing Returns and Economic Progress[1]

**Allyn Young**

My subject may appear alarmingly formidable, but I did not intend it to be so. The words economic progress, taken by themselves, would suggest the pursuit of some philosophy of history, of some way of appraising the results of past and possible future changes in forms of economic organisation and modes of economic activities. But as I have used them, joined to the other half of my title, they are meant merely to dispel apprehensions, by suggesting that I do not propose to discuss any of those alluring but highly technical questions relating to the precise way in which some sort of equilibrium of supply and demand is achieved in the market for the products of industries which can increase their output without increasing their costs proportionately, or to the possible advantages of fostering the development of such industries while putting a handicap upon industries whose output can be increased only at the expense of a more than proportionate increase of costs. I suspect, indeed, that the apparatus which economists have built up for dealing effectively with the range of questions to which I have just referred may stand in the way of a clear view of the more general or elementary aspects of the phenomena of increasing returns, such as I wish to comment upon in this paper.

---

* From *The Economic Journal* No.152(Vol. XXXVIII 1928), pp. 527–42.

[1] Presidential Address before Section F (Economic Science and Statistics) of the British Association for the Advancement of Science, Glasgow, September 10, 1928.

Consider, for example, Alfred Marshall's fruitful distinction between the internal productive economies which a particular firm is able to secure as the growth of the market permits it to enlarge the scale of its operations and the economies external to the individual firm which show themselves only in changes of the organisation of the industry as a whole. This distinction has been useful in at least two different ways. In the first place it is, or ought to be, a safeguard against the common error of assuming that wherever increasing returns operate there is necessarily an effective tendency towards monopoly. In the second place it simplifies the analysis of the manner in which the prices of commodities produced under conditions of increasing returns are determined. A representative firm within the industry, maintaining its own identity and devoting itself to a given range of activities, is made to be the vehicle or medium through which the economies achieved by the industry as a whole are transmitted to the market and have their effect upon the price of the product.

The view of the nature of the processes of industrial progress which is implied in the distinction between internal and external economies is necessarily a partial view. Certain aspects of those processes are illuminated, while, for that very reason, certain other aspects, important in relation to other problems, are obscured. This will be clear, I think, if we observe that, although the internal economies of some firms producing, let us say, materials or appliances may figure as the external economies of other firms, not all of the economies which are properly to be called external can be accounted for by adding up the internal economies of all the separate firms. When we look at the internal economies of a particular firm we envisage a condition of comparative stability. Year after year the firm, like its competitors, is manufacturing a particular product or group of products, or is confining itself to certain definite stages in the work of forwarding the products towards their final form. Its operations change in the sense that they are progressively adapted to an increasing output, but they are kept within definitely circumscribed bounds. Out beyond, in that obscurer field from which it derives its external economies, changes of another order are occurring. New products are appearing, firms are assuming new tasks, and new industries are coming into being. In short, change in this external field is qualitative as well as quantitative. No analysis of the forces making for economic equilibrium, forces which we might say are tangential at any moment of time, will serve to illumine this field, for movements away from equilibrium, departures from previous trends, are characteristic of it. Not much is to be gained by probing into it to see how increasing returns show themselves in the costs of individual firms and in the prices at which they offer their products.

Instead, we have to go back to a simpler and more inclusive view, such as some of the older economists took when they contrasted the increasing returns which they thought were characteristic of manufacturing industry taken as a whole with the diminishing returns which they thought were dominant in agriculture because of an increasingly unfavourable proportioning of labor and land. Most of them were disappointingly vague with respect to the origins and the precise nature of the "improvements" which they counted upon to retard somewhat the operation of the tendency towards diminishing returns in agriculture and to secure a progressively more effective use of labor in manufactures. Their opinions appear to have rested partly upon an empirical generalisation. Improvements had been made, they were still being made, and it might be assumed that they would continue to be made. If they had looked back they would have seen that there were centuries during which there were few significant changes in either agricultural or industrial methods. But they were living in an age when men had turned their faces in a new direction and when economic progress was not only consciously sought but seemed in some way to grow out of the nature of things. Improvements, then, were not something to be explained. They were natural phenomena, like the precession of the equinoxes.

There were certain important exceptions, however, to this incurious attitude towards what might seem to be one of the most important of all economic problems. Senior's positive doctrine is well known, and there were others who made note of the circumstance that with the growth of population and of markets new opportunities for the division of labor appear and new advantages attach to it. In this way, and in this way only, were the generally commonplace things which they said about "improvements" related to anything which could properly be called a doctrine of increasing returns. They added nothing to Adam Smith's famous theorem that the division of labor depends upon the extent of the market. That theorem, I have always thought, is one of the most illuminating and fruitful generalisations which can be found anywhere in the whole literature of economics. In fact, as I am bound to confess, I am taking it as the text of this paper, in much the way that some minor composer borrows a theme from one of the masters and adds certain developments or variations of his own. Today, of course, we mean by the division of labor something much broader in scope than that splitting up of occupations and development of specialised crafts which Adam Smith mostly had in mind. No one, so far as I know, has tried to enumerate all of the different aspects of the division of labor, and I do not propose to undertake that task. I shall deal with two related aspects only: the growth of indirect or roundabout methods of production and the division of labor among industries.

It is generally agreed that Adam Smith, when he suggested that the division of labor leads to inventions because workmen engaged in specialised routine operations come to see better ways of accomplishing the same results, missed the main point. The important thing, of course, is that with the division of labor a group of complex processes is transformed into a succession of simpler processes, some of which, at least, lend themselves to the use of machinery. In the use of machinery and the adoption of indirect processes there is a further division of labor, the economies of which are again limited by the extent of the market. It would be wasteful to make a hammer to drive a single nail; it would be better to use whatever awkward implement lies conveniently at hand. It would be wasteful to furnish a factory with an elaborate equipment of specially constructed jigs, gauges, lathes, drills, presses and conveyors to build a hundred automobiles; it would be better to rely mostly upon tools and machines of standard types, so as to make a relatively larger use of directly-applied and a relatively smaller use of indirectly-applied labor. Mr. Ford's methods would be absurdly uneconomical if his output were very small, and would be unprofitable even if his output were what many other manufacturers of automobiles would call large.

Then, of course, there are economies of what might be called a secondary order. How far it pays to go in equipping factories with special appliances for making hammers or for constructing specialised machinery for use in making different parts of automobiles depends again upon how many nails are to be driven and how many automobiles can be sold. In some instances, I suppose, these secondary economies, though real, have only a secondary importance. The derived demands for many types of specialised production appliances are inelastic over a fairly large range. If the benefits and the costs of using such appliances are spread over a relatively large volume of final products, their technical effectiveness is a larger factor in determining whether it is profitable to use them than any difference which producing them on a large or a small scale would commonly make in their costs. In other instances the demand for productive appliances is more elastic, and beyond a certain level of costs demand may fail completely. In such circumstances secondary economies may become highly important.

Doubtless, much of what I have said has been familiar and even elementary. I shall venture, nevertheless, to put further stress upon two points, which may be among those which have a familiar ring, but which appear sometimes to be in danger of being forgotten. (Otherwise, economists of standing could not have suggested that increasing returns may be altogether illusory, or have maintained that where they arc present they must lead to monopoly.) The first point is that the principal economies which manifest themselves in increasing returns are the economies of capitalistic or roundabout methods of production. These economies, again, are largely identical with the economies of the division of labor in its most important modern forms. In fact, these economies lie under our eyes, but we may miss them if we try to make of *large-scale* production (in the sense of production by large firms or large industries), as contrasted with *large* production, any more than an incident in the general process by which increasing returns are secured and if accordingly we look too much at the individual firm or even, as I shall suggest presently, at the individual industry.

The second point is that the economies of roundabout methods, even more than the economies of other forms of the division of labor, depend upon the extent of the market — and that, of course, is why we discuss them under the head of increasing returns. It would hardly be necessary to stress this point, if it were not that the economies of large-scale operations and of "mass-production" are often referred to as though they could be had for the taking, by means of a "rational" reorganisation of industry. Now I grant that at any given time routine and inertia play a very large part in the organisation and conduct of industrial operations. Real leadership is no more common in industrial than in other pursuits. New catch-words or slogans like mass-production and rationalisation may operate as stimuli; they may rouse men from routine and lead them to scrutinise again the organisation and processes of industry and to try to discover particular ways in which they can be bettered. For example, no one can doubt that there are genuine economies to be achieved in the way of "simplification and standardisation", or that the securing of these economies requires that certain deeply rooted competitive wastes be extirpated. This last requires a definite concerted effort — precisely the kind of thing which ordinary competitive motives are often powerless to effect, but which might come more easily as the response to the dissemination of a new idea.

There is a danger, however, that we shall expect too much from these "rational" industrial reforms. Pressed beyond a certain point they become the reverse of rational. I have naturally been interested in British opinions respecting the reasons for the relatively high productivity (per laborer or per hour of labor) of representative American industries. The error of those who suggest that the explanation is to be found in the relatively high wages which prevail in America is not that they confuse cause and effect, but that they hold that what are really only two aspects of a single situation are, the one cause, and the other effect. Those who hold that American industry is managed better, that its leaders study its problems more intelligently and plan more courageously and more wisely can cite no facts in support of their opinion save the differences in the results achieved. Allowing for the circumstance that British industry, as a whole, has proved to be rather badly adjusted to the new post-war economic situation, I know of no facts which prove or even indicate that British industry, seen against the background of its own problems and its own possibilities, is less efficiently organised or less ably directed than American industry or the industry of any other country.

Sometimes the fact that the average American laborer works with the help of a larger supply of power-driven labor-saving machinery than the laborer of other countries is cited as evidence of the superior intelligence of the average American employer. But this will not do, for, as every economist knows, the greater the degree in which labor is productive or scarce — the words have the same meaning — the greater is the relative economy of using it in such indirect or roundabout ways as are technically advantageous, even though such procedure rolls for larger advances of capital than simpler methods do.

It is encouraging to find that a fairly large number of commentators upon the volume of the American industrial product and the scale of American industrial organisation have come to surmise that the extent of the American domestic market, unimpeded by tariff barriers, may have something to do with the matter. This opinion seems even to be forced upon thoughtful observers by the general character of the facts, whether or no the observers think in terms of the economists' conception of increasing returns. In certain industries, although by no means in all, productive methods are economical and profitable in America which would not be profitable elsewhere. The importance of coal and iron and other natural resources needs no comment. Taking a country's economic endowment as given, however, the most important single factor in determining the effectiveness of its industry appears to be the size of the market. But just what constitutes a large market? Not area or population alone, but buying power, the capacity to absorb a large annual output of goods. This trite observation, however, at once suggests another equally trite, namely, that capacity to buy depends upon capacity to produce. In an inclusive view, considering the market not as an outlet for the products of a particular industry, and therefore external to that industry, but as the outlet for goods in general, the size of the market is determined and defined by the volume of production. If this statement needs any qualification, it is that the conception of a market in this inclusive sense — an aggregate of productive activities, tied together by trade — carries with it the notion that there must be some sort of balance, that different productive activities must be proportioned one to another.

Modified, then, in the light of this broader conception of the market, Adam Smith's dictum amounts to the theorem that the division of labor depends in large part upon the division of labor. This is more than mere tautology. It means, if I read its significance rightly, that the counter forces which are continually defeating the forces which make for economic equilibrium are more pervasive and more deeply rooted in the constitution of the modem economic system than we commonly realise. Not only new or adventitious elements, coming in from the outside, but elements which are permanent characteristics of the ways in which goods are produced make continuously for change. Every important advance in the organisation of production, regardless of whether it is based upon anything which, in a narrow or technical sense, would be called a new "invention," or involves a fresh application of the fruits of scientific progress to industry, alters the conditions of industrial activity and initiates responses elsewhere in the industrial structure which in turn have a further unsettling effect. Thus change becomes progressive and propagates itself in a cumulative way.

The apparatus which economists have built up for the analysis of supply and demand in their relations to prices does not seem to be particularly helpful for the purposes of an inquiry into these broader aspects of increasing returns. In fact, as I have already suggested, reliance upon it may divert attention to incidental or partial aspects of a process which ought to be seen as a whole. If, nevertheless, one insists upon seeing just how far one can get into the problem by using the formulas of supply and demand, the simplest way, I suppose, is to begin by inquiring into the operations of reciprocal demand when the commodities exchanged are produced competitively under conditions of increasing returns and when the demand for each commodity is elastic, in the special sense that a small increase in its supply will be attended by an increase in the amounts of other commodities which can be had in exchange for it.[1] Under such conditions an increase in the supply of one commodity *is* an increase in the demand for other commodities, and it must be supposed that every increase in demand will evoke an increase in supply. The rate at which any one industry grows is conditioned by the rate at which other industries grow, but since the elasticities of demand and of supply will differ for different products, some industries will grow

[1] If the circumstance that commodity *a* is produced under conditions of increasing returns is taken into account as a factor in the elasticity of demand for *b* in terms of *a*, elasticity of demand and elasticity of supply may be looked upon as different ways of expressing a single functional relation.

faster than others. Even with a stationary population and in the absence of new discoveries[1] in pure or applied science there are no limits to the process of expansion except the limits beyond which demand is not elastic and returns do not increase.

If, under these hypothetical conditions, progress were unimpeded and frictionless, if it were not dependent in part upon a process of trial and error, if the organisation of industry were always such as, in relation to the immediate situation, is most economical, the realising of increasing returns might be progressive and continuous, although, for technical reasons, it could not always proceed at an even rate. But it would remain a process requiring time. An industrial dictator, with foresight and knowledge, could hasten the pace somewhat, but he could not achieve an Aladdin-like transformation of a country's industry, so as to reap the fruits of a half-century's ordinary progress in a few years. The obstacles are of two sorts. First, the human material which has to be used is resistant to change. New trades have to be learnt and new habits have to be acquired. There has to be a new geographical distribution of the population and established communal groups have to be broken up. Second, the accumulation of the necessary capital takes time, even though the process of accumulation is largely one of turning part of an increasing product into forms which will serve in securing a further increase of product. An acceleration of the rate of accumulation encounters increasing costs, into which both technical and psychological elements enter. One who likes to conceive of all economic processes in terms of tendencies towards an equilibrium might even maintain that increasing returns, so far as they depend upon the economies of indirect methods of production and the size of the market, are offset and negated by their costs, and that under such simplified conditions as I have dealt with the realising of increasing returns would be spread through time in such a way as to secure an equilibrium of costs and advantages. This would amount to saying that no real economic progress could come through the operation of forces engendered *within* the economic system

---

[1] As contrasted with such new ways of organising production and such new "inventions" as are merely adaptations of known ways of doing things, made practicable and economical by an enlarged scale of production.

— a conclusion repugnant to common sense. To deal with this point thoroughly would take us too far afield. I shall merely observe, first, that the appropriate conception is that of a *moving* equilibrium, and second, that the costs which (under increasing returns) grow less rapidly than the product are not the "costs" which figure in an "equilibrium of costs and advantages."

Moving away from these abstract considerations, so as to get closer to the complications of the real situation, account has to be taken, first, of various kinds of obstacles. The demand for some products is inelastic, or, with an increasing supply, soon becomes so. The producers of such commodities, however, often share in the advantages of the increase of the general scale of production in related industries, and so far as they do productive resources are released for other uses. Then there are natural scarcities, limitations or inelasticities of supply, such as effectively block the way to the securing of any important economies in the production of some commodities and which impair the effectiveness of the economies secured in the production of other commodities. In most fields, moreover, progress is not and cannot be continuous. The next important step forward is often initially costly, and cannot be taken until a certain quantum of prospective advantages has accumulated.

On the other side of the account are various factors which reinforce the influences which make for increasing returns. The discovery of new natural resources and of new uses for them and the growth of scientific knowledge are probably the most potent of such factors. The causal connections between the growth of industry and the progress of science run in both directions, but on which side the preponderant influence lies no one can say. At any rate, out of better knowledge of the materials and forces upon which men can lay their hands there come both new ways of producing familiar commodities and new products, and these last have a presumptive claim to be regarded as embodying more economical uses of productive resources than the uses which they displace. Some weight has to be given also to the way in which, with the advance of the scientific spirit, a new kind of interest — which might be described as a scientific interest conditioned by an economic interest — is beginning to infiltrate into industry. It is a point of controversy, but I venture to maintain that under most circumstances, though not in all, the growth of population still has to be counted a factor making for a larger *per capita* product — although even that cautious statement needs to be interpreted and qualified. But just as there may be population growth with no increase of the average *per capita* product, so also, as I have tried to suggest, markets may grow and increasing returns may be secured while the population remains stationary.

It is dangerous to assign to any single factor the leading role in that continuing economic revolution which has taken the modern world so far away from the world of a few hundred years ago. But is there any other factor which has a better claim to that role than the persisting search for markets? No other hypothesis so well unites economic history and economic theory. The Industrial Revolution of the eighteenth century has come to be generally regarded, not as a cataclysm brought about by certain inspired improvements in industrial technique, but as a series of changes related in an orderly way to prior changes in industrial organisation and to the enlargement of markets. It is sometimes said, however, that while in the Middle Ages and in the early modern period industry was the servant of commerce, since the rise of "industrial capitalism" the relation has been reversed, commerce being now merely an agent of industry. If this means that the finding of markets is one of the tasks of modern industry it is true. If it means that industry imposes its will upon the market, that whereas formerly the things which were produced were the things which could be sold, now the things which have to be sold are the things that are produced, it is not true.

The great change, I imagine, is in the new importance which the *potential market* has in the planning and management of large industries. The difference between the cost per unit of output in an industry or in an individual plant properly adapted to a given volume of output and in an industry or plant equally well adapted to an output five times as large is often much greater than one would infer from looking merely at the economics which may accrue as an existing establishment gradually extends the scale of its operations. Potential demand, then, in the planning of industrial undertakings, has to be balanced against potential economies, elasticity of demand against decreasing costs. The search for markets is not a matter of disposing of a "surplus product," in the Marxian sense, but of finding an outlet for a potential product. Nor is it wholly a matter of multiplying profits by multiplying sales; it is partly a matter of augmenting profits by reducing costs.

Although the initial displacement may be considerable and the repercussions upon particular industries unfavourable, the enlarging of the market for any one commodity, produced under conditions of increasing returns, generally has the net effect, as I have tried to show, of enlarging the market for other commodities. The businessman's mercantilistic emphasis upon markets may have a sounder basis than the economist who thinks mostly in terms of economic statics is prone to admit. How far "selling expenses," for example, are to be counted sheer economic waste depends upon their effects upon the aggregate product of industry, as distinguished from their effects upon the fortunes of particular undertakings.

Increasing returns are often spoken of as though they were attached always to the growth of "industries," and I have not tried to avoid that way of speaking of them, although I think that it may be a misleading way. The point which I have in mind is something more than a quibble about the proper definition of an industry, for it involves a particular thesis with respect to the way in which increasing returns are reflected in changes in the organisation of industrial activities. Much has been said about industrial integration as a concomitant or a natural result of an increasing industrial output. It obviously is, under particular conditions, though I know of no satisfactory statement of just what those particular conditions are. But the opposed process, industrial differentiation, has been and remains the type of change characteristically associated with the growth of production. Notable as has been the increase in the complexity of the apparatus of living, as shown by the increase in the variety of goods offered in consumers' markets, the increase in the diversification of intermediate products and of industries manufacturing special products or groups of products has gone even further.

The successors of the early printers, it has often been observed, are not only the printers of to-day, with their own specialised establishments, but also the producers of wood pulp, of various kinds of paper, of inks and their different ingredients, of type-metal and of type, the group of industries concerned with the technical parts of the producing of illustrations, and the manufacturers of specialised tools and machines for use in printing and in these various auxiliary industries. The list could be extended, both by enumerating other industries which are directly ancillary to the present printing trades and by going back to industries which, while supplying the industries which supply the printing trades, also supply other industries, concerned with preliminary stages in the making of final products other than printed books and newspapers. I do not think that the printing trades are an exceptional instance, but I shall not give other examples, for I do not want this paper to be too much like a primer of descriptive economics or an index to the reports of a census of production. It is sufficiently obvious, anyhow, that over a large part of the field of industry an increasingly intricate nexus of specialised undertakings has inserted itself between the producer of raw materials and the consumer of the final product.

With the extension of the division of labor among industries the representative firm, like the industry of which it is a part, loses its identity. Its internal economies dissolve into the internal and external economies of the more highly specialised undertakings which are its successors, and are supplemented by new economies. In so far as it is an adjustment to a new situation created by the growth of the market for the final products of industry the division of labor among industries is a vehicle of increasing returns. It is more than a change of form incidental to the full securing of the advantages of capitalistic methods of production — although it is largely that — for it has some advantages of its own which are independent of changes in productive technique. For example, it permits of a higher degree of specialisation in management, and the advantages of such specialisation are doubtless often real, though they may easily be given too much weight. Again, it lends itself to a better geographical distribution of industrial operations, and this advantage is unquestionably both real and important. Nearness to the source of supply of a particular raw material or to cheap power counts for most in one part of a series of industrial processes, nearness to other industries or to cheap transport in another part, and nearness to a larger centre of population in yet another. A better *combination* of advantages of location, with a smaller element of compromise, can be had by the more specialised industries. But the largest advantage secured by the division of labor among industries is the fuller realising of the economies of capitalistic or roundabout methods of production. This should be sufficiently obvious if we assume, as we must, that in most industries there are effective, though elastic, limits to the economical size of the individual firm. The output of the individual firm is generally a relatively small proportion of the aggregate output of an industry. The degree in which it can secure economies by making its own operations more roundabout is limited. But certain roundabout methods are fairly sure to become feasible and economical when their advantages can be spread over the output of the whole industry. These potential economies, then, are segregated and achieved by the operations of specialised undertakings which, taken together, constitute a new industry. It might conceivably be maintained that the *scale* upon which the firms in the new industry are able to operate is the secret of their ability to realise economies for industry as a whole, while presumably making profits for themselves. This is true in a way, but misleading. The scale of their operations (which is only incidentally or under special conditions a matter of the size of the individual firm) merely reflects the size of the market for the final products of the industry or industries to whose operations their own are ancillary. And the principal advantage of large-scale operation at this stage is that it again makes methods economical which would be uneconomical if their benefits could not be diffused over a large final product.

In recapitulation of these variations on a theme from Adam Smith there are three points to be stressed. First, the mechanism of increasing returns is not to be discerned adequately by observing the effects of variations in the size of an individual firm or of a particular industry, for the progressive division and specialisation of industries is an essential part of the process by which increasing returns are realised. What is required is that industrial operations be seen as an interrelated whole. Second, the securing of increasing returns depends upon the progressive division of labor, and the principal economies of the division of labor, in its modern forms, are the economies which are to be had by using labor in roundabout or indirect ways. Third, the division of labor depends upon the extent of the market, but the extent of the market also depends upon the division of labor. In this circumstance lies the possibility of economic progress, apart from the progress which comes as a result of the new knowledge which men are able to gain, whether in the pursuit of their economic or of their non-economic interests.

# Part V. The Austrian Insights

# Chapter 24*

# On the Origin of Money

**Carl Menger**

## I. Introduction

There is a phenomenon which has from of old and in a peculiar degree attracted the attention of social philosophers and practical economists, the fact of certain commodities (these being in advanced civilizations coined pieces of gold and silver, together subsequently with documents representing those coins) becoming universally acceptable media of exchange. It is obvious even to the most ordinary intelligence, that a commodity should be given up by its owner in exchange for another more useful to him. But that every economic unit in a nation should be ready to exchange his goods for little metal disks apparently useless as such, or for documents representing the latter, is a procedure so opposed to the ordinary course of things, that we cannot well wonder if even a distinguished thinker like Savigny finds it downright 'mysterious'.

It must not be supposed that the *form* of coin, or document, employed as current-money, constitutes the enigma in this phenomenon. We may look away from these forms and go back to earlier stages of economic development, or indeed to what still obtains in countries here and there, where we find the precious metals in an uncoined state serving as the medium of exchange., and even certain other commodities, cattle, skins,

* From *The Economic Journal* No.6 (Vol. II 1892), pp. 239–55.

cubes of tea,. slabs of salt, cowrie-shells, etc.; still we are confronted by this phenomenon, still we have to explain why it is that the economic man is ready to accept a certain kind of commodity, *even if he does not need it, or if his need of it is already supplied,* in exchange for all the goods he has brought to market, while it is none the less what he needs that he consults in the first instance, with respect to the goods he intends to acquire in the course of his transactions.

And hence there runs, from the first essays of reflective contemplation in social phenomena down to our own times, an uninterrupted chain of disquisitions upon the nature and specific qualities of money in its relation to all that constitutes traffic. Philosophers, jurists, and historians, as well as economists, and even naturalists and mathematicians, have dealt with this notable problem, and there is no civilized people that has not furnished its quota to the abundant literature thereon. What is the nature of those little disks or documents, which in themselves seem to serve no useful purpose, and which nevertheless, in contradiction to the rest of experience, pass from one hand to another in exchange for the most useful commodities, nay, for which every one is so eagerly bent on surrendering his wares? Is money an organic member in the world of commodities, or is it an economic anomaly? Are we to refer its commercial currency and its value in trade to the same causes conditioning those of other goods, or are they the distinct product of convention and authority?

## II. Attempts at Solution Hitherto

Thus far it can hardly be claimed for the results of investigation into the problem above stated, that they are commensurate either with the great development in historic research generally, or with the outlay of time and intellect expended in efforts at solution. The enigmatic phenomenon of money is even at this day without an explanation that satisfies; nor is there yet agreement on the most fundamental questions of its nature and functions. Even at this day we have no satisfactory theory of money.

The idea which lay first to hand for an explanation of the specific function of money as a universal current medium of exchange, was to refer it to a general convention, or a legal dispensation. The problem, which science has here to solve, consists in giving an explanation of a general, homogeneous course of action pursued by human beings when engaged in traffic, which, taken concretely, makes unquestionably for the common interest, and yet which seems to conflict with the nearest and immediate interests of contracting individuals. Under such circumstances what could lie more contiguous than the notion of referring the foregoing procedure to causes lying outside the sphere of individual considerations? To assume that certain commodities, the precious metals in particular, had been exalted into the medium of exchange by general convention or law, in the interest of the commonweal, solved the difficulty, and solved it apparently the more easily and naturally inasmuch as the shape of the coins seemed to be a token of state regulation. Such in fact is the opinion of Plato, Aristotle, and the Roman jurists, closely followed by the mediaeval writers. Even the more modern developments in the theory of money have not in substance got beyond this standpoint.[1]

Tested more closely, the assumption underlying this theory gave room to grave doubts. An event of such high and universal significance and of notoriety so inevitable, as the establishment by law or convention of a universal medium of exchange, would certainly have been retained in the memory of man, the more certainly inasmuch as it would have had to be performed in a great number of places. Yet no historical monument gives us trustworthy tidings of any transactions either conferring distinct recognition on media of exchange already in use, or referring to their adoption by peoples of comparatively recent culture, much less testifying to an initiation of the earliest ages of economic civilization in the use of money.

And in fact the majority of theorists on this subject do not stop at the explanation of money as stated above. The peculiar adaptability of the

---

[1] *Cf.* Roscher, *System der Volkswirthschaft,* I. § 116; my *Grundsätze der Volkswirtschaftslehre,* 1871, p. 255, *et seq.;* M. Block, *Les Progrès de la Science économique depuis* A. *Smith,* 1890, II., p. 59, *et seq.*

precious metals for purposes of currency and coining was noticed by Aristotle, Xenophon, and Pliny, and to a far greater extent by John Law, Adam Smith and his disciples, who all seek a further explanation of the choice made of them as media of exchange, in their special qualifications. Nevertheless it is clear that the choice of the precious metals by law and convention, even if made in consequence of their peculiar adaptability for monetary purposes, presupposes the pragmatic origin of money, and selection of those metals, and that presupposition is unhistorical. Nor do even the theorists above mentioned honestly face the problem that is to be solved, to wit, the explaining how it has come to pass that certain commodities (the precious metals at certain stages of culture) should be promoted amongst the mass of all other commodities, and accepted as the generally acknowledged media of exchange. It is a question concerning not only the origin but also the nature of money and its position in relation to all other commodities.

### III. The Problem of the Genesis of a Medium of Exchange

In primitive traffic the economic man is awaking but very gradually to an understanding of the economic advantages to be gained by exploitation of existing opportunities of exchange. His aims are directed first and foremost, in accordance with the simplicity of all primitive culture, only at what lies first to hand. And only in that proportion does the value in use of the commodities he seeks to acquire, come into account in his bargaining. Under such conditions each man is intent to get by way of exchange just such goods as he directly needs, and to reject those of which he has no need at all, or with which he is already sufficiently provided. It is clear then, that in these circumstances the number of bargains actually concluded must lie within very narrow limits. Consider how seldom it is the case, that a commodity owned by somebody is of less value in use than another commodity owned by somebody else! And for the latter just the opposite relation is the case. But how much more seldom does it happen that these two bodies meet! Think, indeed, of the peculiar difficulties obstructing the immediate barter of goods in those cases, where supply and demand do not quantitatively coincide; where, *e.g.*, an indivisible commodity is to be exchanged for a variety of goods in the possession of different persons, or indeed for such commodities as are only in demand at different times and can be supplied only by different persons! Even in the relatively simple and so often recurring case, where an economic unit, A, requires a commodity possessed by B, and B requires one possessed by C, while C wants one that is owned by A — even here, under a rule of mere barter, the exchange of the goods in question would as a rule be of necessity left undone.

These difficulties would have proved absolutely insurmountable obstacles to the progress of traffic, and at the same time to the production of goods not commanding a regular sale, had there not lain a remedy in the very nature of things, to wit, *the different degrees of saleableness (Absatzfähigkeit) of commodities.* The difference existing in this respect between articles of commerce is of the highest degree of significance for the theory of money, and of the market in general. And the failure to turn it adequately to account in explaining the phenomena of trade, constitutes not only as such a lamentable breach in our science, but also one of the essential causes of the backward state of monetary theory. *The theory of money necessarily presupposes a theory of the saleableness of goods.* If we grasp this, we shall be able to understand how the almost unlimited saleableness of money is only a special case, — presenting only a difference of degree — of a generic phenomenon of economic life — namely, the difference in the saleableness of commodities in general.

## IV. Commodities As More or Less Saleable

It is an error in economics, as prevalent as it is patent, that all commodities, at a definite point of time and in a given market, may be assumed to stand to each other in a definite relation of exchange, in other words, may be mutually exchanged in definite quantities at will. It is not true that in any given market 10 cwt. of one article = 2 cwt. of another = 3 lbs. of a third article, and so on. The most cursory observation of market-phenomena teaches us that it does not lie within our power, when we have bought an article for a certain price, to sell it again forthwith at that same price. If we but try to dispose of an article of clothing, a book, or a work of art, which we have just purchased, in the very same market, even though it be at once, before the same juncture of conditions has altered, we shall easily convince ourselves of the fallaciousness of such an assumption. The price at which anyone can at pleasure buy a commodity at a given market and a given point of time, and the price at which he can dispose of the same at pleasure, are two essentially different magnitudes.

This holds good of wholesale as well as retail prices. Even such marketable goods as corn, cotton, pig-iron, cannot be voluntarily disposed of for the price at which we have purchased them. Commerce and speculation would be the simplest things in the world, if the theory of the 'objective equivalent in goods' were correct, if it were actually true, that in a given market and at a given moment commodities could be mutually converted at will in definite quantitative relations — could, in short, at a certain price be as easily disposed of as acquired. At any rate there is no such thing as a general saleableness of wares in this sense. The truth is, that even in the best organized markets, while we may be able to purchase when and what we like at a definite price, viz.: the *purchasing price,* we can only dispose of it again when and as we like at a loss, viz.: at the *selling* situation, that is, at *economic* prices.[1]

The loss experienced by anyone who is compelled to dispose of an article at a definite moment, as compared with the current purchasing prices, is a highly variable quantity, as a glance at trade and at markets of specific commodities will show. If corn or cotton is to be disposed of at an organised market, the seller will be in a position to do so in practically any quantity, at any time he pleases, at the current price, or at most with a loss of only a few pence on the total sum. If it be a question of disposing, in larger quantities, of cloth or silk-stuffs at will, the seller will regularly have to content himself with a considerable percentage of diminution in the price. Far worse is the case of one who at a certain

---

[1] We must make a distinction between the higher purchasing prices for which the buyer is rendered liable through the wish to purchase at a definite point of time, and the (lower) selling prices, which he, who is obliged to get rid of goods within a definite period, must content himself withal. The smaller the difference between the buying and selling prices of an article, the more saleable it usually proves to be.

point of time has to get rid of astronomical instruments, anatomical preparations, Sanskrit writings, and such hardly marketable articles!

If we call any goods or wares *more or less saleable,* according to the greater or less facility with which they can be disposed of at a market at any convenient time at current purchasing prices: or with less or more diminution of the same, we can see by what has been said, that an obvious difference exists in this connection between commodities. Nevertheless, and in spite of its great practical significance, it cannot be said that this phenomenon has been much taken into account in economic science. The reason of this is in part the circumstance, that investigation into the phenomena of price has been directed almost exclusively to the *quantities* of the commodities exchanged, and not as well to the greater or less *facility* with which wares may be disposed of at normal prices. In part also the reason is the thorough-going abstract method by which the saleableness of goods has been treated, without due regard to all the circumstances of the case.

The man who goes to market with his wares intends as a rule to dispose of them, by no means at any price whatever, but at such as corresponds to the general economic situation. If we are going to inquire into the different degrees of saleableness in goods so as to show its bearing upon practical life, we can only do so by consulting the greater or less facility with which they may be disposed of at prices corresponding to the general economic situation, that is, at *economic* prices.[1] A commodity is more or less saleable according as we are able, with more or less prospect of success, to dispose of it at prices corresponding to the general economic situation, at *economic* prices.

---

[1] The height of saleableness in a commodity is not revealed by the fact that it may be disposed of at any price whatever, including such as result from distress or accident. In this sense all commodities are pretty well equally saleable. A high rate of saleableness in a commodity consists in the fact that it may at every moment be easily and surely disposed of at a price corresponding to, or at least not discrepant from, the general economic situation — at the economic, or approximately economic, price.

The price of a commodity may be denoted as *uneconomic* on two grounds: (1) in consequence of error, ignorance, caprice, and so forth; (2) in consequence of the circumstance that only a part of the supply is available to the demand, the rest for some reason or other being withheld, and the price in consequence not commensurate with the actually existing economic situation.

The *interval of time,* moreover, within which the disposal of a commodity at the economic price may be reckoned on, is of great significance in an inquiry into its degree of saleableness. It matters not whether the demand for a commodity be slight, or whether on other grounds its saleableness be small; if its owner can only bide his time, he will finally and in the long run be able to dispose of it at economic prices. Since, however, this condition is often absent in the actual course of business, there arises for practical purposes an important difference between those commodities, on the one hand, which we expect to dispose of at any given time at economic, or at least approximately economic, prices, and such goods, on the other hand, respecting which we have no such prospect, or at least not in the same degree, and to dispose of which at economic prices the owner foresees it will be necessary to wait for a longer or shorter period, or else to put up with a more or less sensible abatement in the price.

Again, account must be taken of the *quantitative* factor in the saleableness of commodities. Some commodities, in consequence of the development of markets and speculation, are able at any time to find a sale in practically any quantity at economic, or approximately economic, prices. Other commodities can only find a sale at economic prices in smaller quantities, commensurate with the gradual growth of an effective demand, fetching a relatively reduced price in the case of a greater supply.

## V. Concerning the Causes of the Different Degrees of Saleableness in Commodities

The degree to which a commodity is found by experience to command a sale, at a given market, at any time, at prices corresponding to the economic situation (economic prices), depends upon the following circumstances.

1. Upon the number of persons who are still in want of the commodity in question, and upon the extent and intensity of that want, which is unsupplied, or is constantly recurring.
2. Upon the purchasing power of those persons.

3. Upon the available quantity of the commodity in relation to the yet unsupplied (total) want of it.
4. Upon the divisibility of the commodity, and any other ways in which it may be adjusted to the needs of individual customers.
5. Upon the development of the market, and of speculation in particular. And finally,
6. Upon the number and nature of the limitations imposed politically and socially upon exchange and consumption with respect to the commodity in question.

We may proceed, in the same way in which we considered the degree of the saleableness in commodities at definite markets and definite points of time, to set out the *spatial and temporal limits* of their saleableness. In these respects also we observe in our markets some commodities, the saleableness of which is almost unlimited by place or time, and others the sale of which is more or less limited.

The *spatial* limits of the saleableness of commodities are mainly conditioned—

1. By the degree to which the want of the commodities is distributed in space.
2. By the degree to which the goods lend themselves to transport, and the cost of transport incurred in proportion to their value.
3. By the extent to which the means of transport and of commerce generally are developed with respect to different classes of commodities.
4. By the local extension of organised markets and their inter-communication by 'arbitrage'.
5. By the differences in the restrictions imposed upon commercial intercommunication with respect to different goods, in interlocal and, in particular, in international trade.

The time-limits to the saleableness of commodities are mainly conditioned—

1. By permanence in the need of them (their independence of fluctuation in the same).
2. Their durability, i.e. their suitableness for preservation.
3. The cost of preserving and storing them.
4. The rate of interest.

5. The periodicity of a market for the same.
6. The development of speculation and in particular of time- bargains in connection with the same.
7. The restrictions imposed politically and socially on their being transferred from one period of time to another.

All these circumstances, on which depend the different degrees of, and the different local and temporal limits to, the saleableness of commodities, explain why it is that certain commodities can be disposed of with ease and certainty in definite markets, i.e. within local and temporal limits, at any time and in practically any quantities, at prices corresponding to the general economic situation, while the saleableness of other commodities is confined within narrow spatial, and again, temporal, limits; and even within these the disposal of the commodities in question is difficult, and, in so far as the demand cannot be waited for, is not to be brought about without a more or less sensible diminution in price.

## VI. On the Genesis of Media of Exchange[1]

It has long been the subject of universal remark in centres of exchange, that for certain commodities there existed a greater, more constant, and more effective demand than for other commodities less desirable in certain respects, the former being such as correspond to a want on the part of those able and willing to traffic, which is at once universal and, by reason of the relative scarcity of the goods in question, always imperfectly satisfied. And further, that the person who wishes to acquire certain definite goods in exchange for his own is in a more favourable position, if he brings commodities of this kind to market, than if he visits the markets with goods which cannot display such advantages, or at least not in the same degree. Thus equipped he has the prospect of acquiring such goods as he finally wishes to obtain, not only with greater ease and security, but also, by reason of the steadier and more prevailing demand for his own commodities, at prices

---

[1] *Cf.* my article on 'Money' in *the Handwörterbuch der Staatswissenschaften* (Dictionary of Social Science), Jena, 1891, iii., p. 730 *et seq.*

corresponding to the general economic situation — at economic prices. Under these circumstances, when anyone has brought goods not highly saleable to market, the idea uppermost in his mind is to exchange them, not only for such as he happens to be in need of, but, if this cannot be effected directly, for other goods also, which, while he did not want them himself, were nevertheless more saleable than his own. By so doing he certainly does not attain at once the final object of his trafficking, to wit, the acquisition of goods needful to *himself*. Yet he draws nearer to that object. By the devious way of a mediate exchange, he gains the prospect of accomplishing his purpose more surely and economically than if he had confined himself to direct exchange. Now in point of fact this seems everywhere to have been the case. Men have been led, with increasing knowledge of their individual interests, each by his own economic interests, without convention, without legal compulsion, nay, even without any regard to the common interest, to exchange goods destined for exchange (their "wares") for other goods equally destined for exchange, but more saleable.

With the extension of traffic in space and with the expansion over ever longer intervals of time of prevision for satisfying material needs, each individual would learn, from his own economic interests, to take good heed that he bartered his less saleable goods for those special commodities which displayed, beside the attraction of being highly saleable in the particular locality, a wide range of saleableness both in time and place. These wares would be qualified by their costliness, easy transportability, and fitness for preservation (in connection with the circumstance of their corresponding to a steady and widely distributed demand), to ensure to the possessor a power, not only 'here' and 'now', but as nearly as possible unlimited in space and time generally, over all other market-goods at economic prices.

And so it has come to pass, that as man became increasingly conversant with these economic advantages, mainly by an insight become traditional, and by the habit of economic action, those commodities, which relatively to both space and time are most saleable, have in every market become the wares, which it is not only in the interest of everyone to accept in exchange for his own less saleable goods, but which also are those he actually does readily accept. And their superior saleableness depends only upon the relatively inferior saleableness of every other kind of commodity, by which alone they have been able to become *generally* acceptable media of exchange.

It is obvious how highly significant a factor is habit in the genesis of such generally serviceable means of exchange. It lies in the economic interests of each trafficking individual to exchange less saleable for more saleable commodities. But the willing acceptance of the medium of exchange presupposes already a knowledge of these interests on the part of those economic subjects who are expected to accept in exchange for their wares a commodity which in and by itself is perhaps entirely useless to them. It is certain that this knowledge never arises in every part of a nation at the same time. It is only in the first instance a limited number of economic subjects who will recognise the advantage in such procedure, an advantage which, in and by itself, is independent of the general recognition of a commodity as a medium of exchange, inasmuch as such an exchange, always and under all circumstances, brings the economic unit a good deal nearer to his goal, to the acquisition of useful things of which he really stands in need. But it is admitted, that there is no better method of enlightening anyone about his economic interests than that he perceive the economic success of those who use the right means to secure their own. Hence it is also clear that nothing may have been so favourable to the genesis of a medium of exchange as the acceptance, on the part of the most discerning and capable economic subjects, for their own economic gain, and over a considerable period of time, of eminently saleable goods in preference to all others. In this way practice and habit have certainly contributed not a little to cause goods, which were most saleable at any time, to be accepted not only by many, but finally by all, economic subjects in exchange for their less saleable goods: and not only so, but to be accepted from the first with the intention of exchanging them away again. Goods which had thus become generally acceptable media of exchange were called by the Germans *Geld,* from *gelten, i.e.* to pay, to perform, while other nations derived their designation for money mainly from the substance used,[1] the shape of the coin,[2] or even from certain kinds of coin.[3]

It is not impossible for media of exchange, serving as they do the commonweal in the most emphatic sense of the word, to be instituted also by way of legislation, like other social institutions. But this is neither the only, nor the primary mode in which money bas taken its origin. This is much more to be traced in the process depicted above, notwithstanding the nature of that process would be but very incompletely explained if we were to call it 'organic', or denote money as something 'primordial', of 'primeval growth', and so forth. Putting aside assumptions which are historically unsound, we can only come fully to understand the origin of money by learning to view the establishment of the social procedure, with which we are dealing, as the spontaneous outcome, the unpremeditated resultant, of particular, individual efforts of the members of a society, who have little by little worked their way to a discrimination of the different degrees of saleableness in commodities.[4]

## VII. The Process of Differentiation Between Commodities Which Have Become Media of Exchange and the Rest

When the relatively most saleable commodities have become 'money', the event has in the first place the effect of substantially increasing their originally high saleableness. Every economic subject bringing less saleable wares to market, to acquire goods of another sort, has thenceforth a stronger interest in converting what he has in the first instance into the wares which have become money. For such persons, by the exchange of their less saleable wares for those which as money are most saleable, attain not merely, as heretofore, a higher probability, but the certainty, of being able to acquire forthwith equivalent quantities of

---

[1] The Hebrew *Keseph*, the Greek *ἀργύριον*, the Latin *argentum*, the French *argent*, etc.

[2] The English *money*, the Spanish *moneda*, the portuguese *moeda*, the French *monnaie*, the Hebrew *maoth*, the Arabic *fulus*, the Greek *νόμισμα*, etc.

[3] The Italian *danaro*, the Russian *dengi*, the Polish *pienondze*, the Bohemian and Slavonian *penize*, the Danish *penge*, the Swedish *penningar*, the Magyar *penz*, &c. (*i.e. denare* = *Pfennige* = *penny*).

[4] *Cf.* on this point my *Grundsätze der Volkswirtshaftslehre*, 1871, p. 250 *et seq.*

every other kind of commodity to be had in the market. And their control over these depends simply upon their pleasure and their choice. *Pecuniam habens, habet omnem rem quem vult habere.*

On the other hand, he who brings other wares than money to market, finds himself at a disadvantage more or less. To gain the same command over what the market affords, he must first convert his exchangeable goods into money. The nature of his economic disability is shown by the fact of his being compelled to overcome a difficulty before he can attain his purpose, which difficulty does not exist for, *i.e.* has already been overcome by, the man who owns a stock of money.

This has all the greater significance for practical life, inasmuch as to overcome this difficulty does not lie unconditionally within reach of him who brings less saleable goods to market, but depends in part upon circumstances over which the individual bargainer has no control. The less saleable are his wares, the more certainly will he have either to suffer the penalty in the economic price, or to content himself with awaiting the moment, when it will be possible for him to effect a conversion at economic prices. He who is desirous, in an era of monetary economy, to exchange goods of any kind whatever, which are not money, for other goods supplied in the market, cannot be certain of attaining this result at once, or within any predetermined interval of time, at economic prices. And the less saleable are the goods brought by an economic subject to market, the more unfavourably, for his own purposes, will his economic position compare with the position of those who bring money to market. Consider, *e.g.*, the owner of a stock of surgical instruments, who is obliged through sudden distress, or through pressure from creditors, to convert it into money. The prices which it will fetch will be highly accidental, nay, the goods being of such limited saleable-ness, they will be fairly incalculable. And this holds good of all kinds of conversions which in respect of time are compulsory sales.[1] Other is his case who wants at a market to convert the commodity, which

---

[1] Herein lies the explanation of the circumstance why compulsory sales, and cases of distraint in particular, involve as a rule the economic ruin of the person upon whose estate they are carried out, and that in a greater degree the less the goods in question are saleable. Correct discernment of the uneconomic character of these processes will necessarily lead to a reform in the available legal mechanism.

has become *money,* forthwith into other goods supplied at that market. He will accomplish his purpose, not only with certainty, but usually also at a price corresponding to the general economic situation. Nay, the habit of economic action has made us so sure of being able to procure in return for money any goods on the market, whenever we wish, at prices corresponding to the economic situation, that we are for the most part unconscious of how many purchases we daily propose to make, which, with respect to our wants and the time of concluding them, are compulsory purchases. Compulsory sales, on the other hand, in consequence of the economic disadvantage which they commonly involve, force themselves upon the attention of the parties implicated in unmistakable fashion. What therefore constitutes the peculiarity of a commodity which has become money is, that the possession of it procures for us at any time, *i.e.* at any moment we think fit, assured control over every commodity to be had on the market, and this usually at prices adjusted to the economic situation of the moment: the control, on the other hand, conferred by other kinds of commodities over market goods is, in respect of time, and in part of price as well, uncertain, relatively if not absolutely.

Thus the effect produced by such goods as are relatively most saleable becoming money is an increasing differentiation between their degree of saleableness and that of all other goods. And this difference in saleableness ceases to be altogether gradual, and must be regarded in a certain aspect as something absolute. The practice of every-day life, as well as jurisprudence, which closely adheres for the most part to the notions prevalent in every-day life, distinguish two categories in the wherewithal of traffic — goods which have become money and goods which have not. And the ground of this distinction, we find, lies essentially in that difference in the saleableness of commodities set forth above — a difference so significant for practical life and which comes to be further emphasized by intervention of the state. This distinction, moreover, finds expression in language in the difference of meaning attaching to 'money' and' wares,' to 'purchase' and 'exchange.' But it also affords the chief explanation of that superiority of the buyer over the seller, which has found manifold consideration, yet has hitherto been left inadequately explained.

## VIII. How the Precious Metals Became Money

The commodities, which under given local and time relations are most saleable, have become money among the same nations at different times, and among different nations at the same time, and they are diverse in kind. The reason why the *precious metals* have become the generally current medium of exchange among here and there a nation prior to its appearance in history, and in the sequel among all peoples of advanced economic civilisation, is because their saleableness is far and away superior to that of all other commodities, and at the same time because they are found to be specially qualified for the concomitant and subsidiary functions of money.

There is no centre of population, which has not in the very beginnings of civilization come keenly to desire and eagerly to covet the precious metals, in primitive times for their utility and peculiar beauty as in themselves ornamental, subsequently as the choicest materials for plastic and architectural decoration, and especially for ornaments and vessels of every kind. In spite of their natural scarcity, they are well distributed geographically, and, in proportion to most other metals, are easy to extract and elaborate. Further, the ratio of the available quantity of the precious metals to the total requirement is so small, that the number of those whose need of them is unsupplied, or at least insufficiently supplied, together with the extent of this unsupplied need, is always relatively large — larger more or less than in the case of other more important, though more abundantly available, commodities. Again, the class of persons who wish to acquire the precious metals, is, by reason of the kind of wants which by these are satisfied, such as quite specially to include those members of the community who can most efficaciously barter; and thus the desire for the precious metals is as a rule more effective. Nevertheless the limits of the effective desire for the precious metals extend also to those strata of population who can less effectively barter, by reason of the great divisibility of the precious metals, and the enjoyment procured by the expenditure of even very small quantities of them in individual economy. Besides this there are the wide limits in time and space of the saleableness of the precious metals; a consequence, on the one hand, of the almost unlimited distribution in space of the need of them, together with their low cost of transport as compared with their value, and, on the other hand, of their unlimited durability and the relatively slight cost of hoarding them. In no national economy which has advanced beyond the first stages of development are there any commodities, the saleableness of which is so little restricted in such a number of respects — personally, quantitatively, spatially, and temporally — as the precious metals. It cannot be doubted that, long before they had become the generally acknowledged media of exchange, they were, amongst very many peoples, meeting a positive and effective demand at all times and places, and practically in any quantity that found its way to market.

Hence arose a circumstance, which necessarily became of special import for their becoming money. For any one under those conditions, having any of the precious metals at his disposal, there was not only the reasonable prospect of his being able to convert them in all markets at any time and practically in all quantities, but also — and this is after all the criterion of saleableness — the prospect of converting them at prices corresponding at any time to the general economic situation, *at economic prices.* The proportionately strong, persistent, and omnipresent desire on the part of the most effective bargainers has gone farther to exclude prices of the moment, of emergency, of accident, in the case of the precious metals, than in the case of any other goods whatever, especially since these, by reason of their costliness, durability, and easy preservation, had become the most popular vehicle for hoarding as well as the goods most highly favoured in commerce.

Under such circumstances it became the leading idea in the minds of the more intelligent bargainers, and then, as the situation came to be more generally understood, in the mind of every one, that the stock of goods destined to be exchanged for other goods must in the first instance be laid out in precious metals, or must be converted into them, even if the agent in question did not directly need them, or had already supplied his wants in that direction. But in and by this function, the precious metals are already constituted generally current media of exchange. In other words, they hereby function as commodities for which everyone seeks to exchange his market-goods, not, as a rule, in order to consumption but entirely because of their special saleableness, in the intention of exchanging them subsequently for other goods directly profitable to him. No accident, nor the consequence of state compulsion, nor voluntary convention of traders effected this. It was the just apprehending of their individual self-interest which brought it to pass, that all the more economically advanced nations accepted the precious metals as money as soon as a sufficient supply of them had been collected and introduced into commerce. The advance from less to more costly money-stuffs depends upon analogous causes.

This development was materially helped forward by the ratio of exchange between the precious metals and other commodities undergoing smaller fluctuations, more or less, than that existing between most other goods, — a stability which is due to the peculiar circumstances attending the production, consumption, and exchange of the precious metals, and is thus connected with the so-called intrinsic grounds determining their exchange value. It constitutes yet another reason why each man, in the first instance (*i.e.* till he invests in goods directly useful to him), should lay in his available exchange-stock in precious metals, or convert it into the latter. Moreover the *homogeneity* of the precious metals, and the consequent facility with which they can serve as *res fungibiles* in relations of obligation, have led to forms of contract by which traffic has been rendered more easy; this too has materially promoted the saleableness of the precious metals, and thereby their adoption as money. Finally the precious metals, in consequence of the peculiarity of their *colour,* their *ring,* and partly also of their *specific gravity,* are with some practice not difficult to recognise, and through their taking a durable stamp can be easily controlled as to quality and weight; this too has materially contributed to raise their saleableness and to forward the adoption and diffusion of them as money.

## IX. Influence of the Sovereign Power

Money has not been generated by law. In its origin it is a social, and not a state-institution. Sanction by the authority of the state is a notion alien to it. On the other hand, however, by sate recognition and state regulation, this social institution of money has been perfected and adjusted to the manifold and varying needs of an evolving commerce, just as customary rights have been perfected and adjusted by statute law. Treated originally by weight, like other commodities, the precious metals have by degrees attained as coins a shape by which their intrinsically high saleableness has experienced a material increase. The fixing of a coinage so as to include all grades of value *(Wertstufen)*, and the establishment and maintenance of coined pieces so as to win public confidence and, as far as is possible, to forestall risk concerning their genuineness, weight, and fineness, and above all the ensuring their circulation in general, have been everywhere recognised as important functions of state administration.

The difficulties experienced in the commerce and modes of payment of any country from the competing action of the several commodities serving as currency, and further the circumstance, that concurrent standards induce a manifold insecurity in trade, and render necessary various conversions of the circulating media, have led to the legal recognition of certain commodities as money (to legal standards). And where more than one commodity has been acquiesced in, or admitted, as the legal form of payment, law or some system of appraisement has fixed a definite ratio of value amongst them.

All these measures nevertheless have not first made money of the precious metals, but have only perfected them in their function as money.

(Translated by Caroline A. Foley)

# Chapter 25*

# The Use of Knowledge in Society

F. A. HAYEK†

## I

What is the problem we wish to solve when we try to construct a rational economic order?

On certain familiar assumptions the answer is simple enough. *If* we possess all the relevant information, *if* we can start out from a given system of preferences and *if* we command complete knowledge of available means, the problem which remains is purely one of logic. That is, the answer to the question of what is the best use of the available means is implicit in our assumptions. The conditions which the solution of this optimum problem must satisfy have been fully worked out and can be stated best in mathematical form: put at their briefest, they are that the marginal rates of substitution between any two commodities or factors must be the same in all their different uses.

This, however, is emphatically *not* the economic problem which society faces. And the economic calculus which we have developed to solve this logical problem, though an important step toward the solution of the economic problem of society, does not yet provide an answer to it. The reason for this is that the "data" from which the economic calculus

* From *The American Economic Review* No.4 (Vol. XXXV September 1945), pp.519–30.
† The author is Tooke professor of political economy and statistics at the University of London (London School of Economics and Political Science).

starts are never for the whole society "given" to a single mind which could work out the implications, and can never be so given.

The peculiar character of the problem of a rational economic order is determined precisely by the fact that the knowledge of the circumstances of which we must make use never exists in concentrated or integrated form, but solely as the dispersed bits of incomplete and frequently contradictory knowledge which all the separate individuals possess. The economic problem of society is thus not merely a problem of how to allocate "given" resources — if "given" is taken to mean given to a single mind which deliberately solves the problem set by these "data". It is rather a problem of how to secure the best use of resources known to any of the members of society, for ends whose relative importance only these individuals know. Or, to put it briefly, it is a problem of the utilization of knowledge not given to anyone in its totality.

This character of the fundamental problem has, I am afraid, been rather obscured than illuminated by many of the recent refinements of economic theory, particularly by many of the uses made of mathematics. Though the problem with which I want primarily to deal in this paper is the problem of a rational economic organization, I shall in its course be led again and again to point to its close connections with certain methodological questions. Many of the points I wish to make are indeed conclusions toward which diverse paths of reasoning have unexpectedly converged. But as I now see these problems, this is no accident. It seems to me that many of the current disputes with regard to both economic theory and economic policy have their common origin in a misconception about the nature of the economic problem of society. This misconception in turn is due to an erroneous transfer to social phenomena of the habits of thought we have developed in dealing with the phenomena of nature.

## II

In ordinary language we describe by the word "planning" the complex of interrelated decisions about the allocation of our available resources. All economic activity is in this sense planning; and in any society in which many people collaborate, this planning, whoever does it, will in some measure have to be based on knowledge which, in the first instance, is not given to the planner but to somebody else, which somehow will have to be conveyed to the planner. The various ways in which the knowledge on which people base their plans is communicated to them is the crucial problem for any theory explaining the economic process. And the problem of what is the best way of utilizing knowledge initially dispersed among all the people is at least one of the main problems of economic policy — or of designing an efficient economic system.

The answer to this question is closely connected with that other question which arises here, that of *who* is to do the planning. It is about this question that all the dispute about "economic planning" centers. This is not a dispute about whether planning is to be done or not. It is a dispute as to whether planning is to be done centrally, by one authority for the whole economic system, or is to be divided among many individuals. Planning in the specific sense in which the term is used in contemporary controversy necessarily means central planning — direction of the whole economic system according to one unified plan. Competition, on the other hand, means decentralized planning by many separate persons. The half-way house between the two, about which many people talk but which few like when they see it, is the delegation of planning to organized industries, or, in other words, monopoly.

Which of these systems is likely to be more efficient depends mainly on the question under which of them we can expect that fuller use will be made of the existing knowledge. And this, in turn, depends on whether we are more likely to succeed in putting at the disposal of a single central authority all the knowledge which ought to be used but which is initially dispersed among many different individuals, or in conveying to the individuals such additional knowledge as they need in order to enable them to fit their plans in with those of others.

## III

It will at once be evident that on this point the position will be different with respect to different kinds of knowledge; and the answer to our question will therefore largely turn on the relative importance of the different kinds of knowledge; those more likely to be at the disposal of particular individuals and those which we should with greater confidence expect to find in the possession of an authority made up of suitably chosen experts. If it is today so widely assumed that the latter will be in a better position, this is because one kind of knowledge, namely, scientific knowledge, occupies now so prominent a place in public imagination that we tend to forget that it is not the only kind that is relevant. It may be admitted that, so far as scientific knowledge is concerned, a body of suitably chosen experts may be in the best position to command all the best knowledge available — though this is of course merely shifting the difficulty to the problem of selecting the experts. What I wish to point out is that, even assuming that this problem can be readily solved, it is only a small part of the wider problem.

Today it is almost heresy to suggest that scientific knowledge is not the sum of all knowledge. But a little reflection will show that there is beyond question a body of very important but unorganized knowledge which cannot possibly be called scientific in the sense of knowledge of general rules: the knowledge of the particular circumstances of time and place. It is with respect to this that practically every individual has some advantage over all others in that he possesses unique information of which beneficial use might be made, but of which use can be made only if the decisions depending on it are left to him or are made with his active cooperation. We need to remember only how much we have to learn in any occupation after we have completed our theoretical training, how big a part of our working life we spend learning particular jobs, and how valuable an asset in all walks of life is knowledge of people, of local conditions, and special circumstances. To know of and put to use a machine not fully employed, or somebody's skill which could be better utilized, or to be aware of a surplus stock which can be drawn upon during an interruption of supplies, is socially quite as useful as the knowledge of better alternative techniques. And the shipper who earns his living from using otherwise empty or half-filled journeys of tramp-steamers, or the estate agent whose whole knowledge is almost exclusively one of temporary opportunities, or the *arbitrageur* who gains from local differences of commodity prices, are all performing eminently useful functions based on special knowledge of circumstances of the fleeting moment not known to others.

It is a curious fact that this sort of knowledge should today be generally regarded with a kind of contempt, and that anyone who by such knowledge gains an advantage over somebody better equipped with theoretical or technical knowledge is thought to have acted almost disreputably. To gain an advantage from better knowledge of facilities of communication or transport is sometimes regarded as almost dishonest, although it is quite as important that society make use of the best opportunities in this respect as in using the latest scientific discoveries. This prejudice has in a considerable measure affected the attitude toward commerce in general compared with that toward production. Even economists who regard themselves as definitely above the crude materialist fallacies of the past constantly commit the same mistake where activities directed toward the acquisition of such practical knowledge are concerned — apparently because in their scheme of things all such knowledge is supposed to be "given". The common idea now seems to be that all such knowledge should as a matter of course be readily at the command of everybody, and the reproach of irrationality leveled against the existing economic order is frequently based on the fact that it is not so available. This view disregards the fact that the method by which such knowledge can be made as widely available as possible is precisely the problem to which we have to find an answer.

## IV

If it is fashionable today to minimize the importance of the knowledge of the particular circumstances of time and place, this is closely connected with the smaller importance which is now attached to change as such. Indeed, there are few points on which the assumptions made (usually only implicitly) by the "planners" differ from those of their opponents as much as with regard to the significance and frequency of changes which will make substantial alterations of production plans necessary. Of course, if detailed economic plans could be laid down for fairly long periods in advance and then closely adhered to, so that no further economic decisions of importance would be required, the task of drawing up a comprehensive plan governing all economic activity would appear much less formidable.

It is, perhaps, worth stressing that economic problems arise always and only in consequence of change. So long as things continue as before, or at least as they were expected to, there arise no new problems requiring a decision, no need to form a new plan. The belief that changes, or at least day-to-day adjustments, have become less important in modern times implies the contention that economic problems also have become less important. This belief in the decreasing importance of change is, for that reason, usually held by the same people who argue that the importance of economic considerations has been driven into the background by the growing importance of technological knowledge.

Is it true that, with the elaborate apparatus of modern production, economic decisions are required only at long intervals, as when a new factory is to be erected or a new process to be introduced? Is it true that, once a plant has been built, the rest is all more or less mechanical, determined by the character of the plant, and leaving little to be changed in adapting to the ever-changing circumstances of the moment?

The fairly widespread belief in the affirmative is not, so far as I can ascertain, borne out by the practical experience of the business man. In a competitive industry at any rate — and such an industry alone can serve as a test — the task of keeping cost from rising requires constant struggle, absorbing a great part of the energy of the manager. How easy it is for an inefficient manager to dissipate the differentials on which profitability rests, and that it is possible, with the same technical facilities, to produce with a great variety of costs, are among the commonplaces of business experience which do not seem to be equally familiar in the study of the economist. The very strength of the desire, constantly voiced by producers and engineers, to be able to proceed untrammeled by considerations of money costs, is eloquent testimony to the extent to which these factors enter into their daily work.

One reason why economists are increasingly apt to forget about the constant small changes which make up the whole economic picture is probably their growing preoccupation with statistical aggregates, which show a very much greater stability than the movements of the detail. The comparative stability of the aggregates cannot, however, be accounted for — as the statisticians seem occasionally to be inclined to do — by the "law of large numbers" or the mutual compensation of random changes. The number of elements with which we have to deal is not large enough for such accidental forces to produce stability. The continuous flow of goods and services is maintained by constant deliberate adjustments, by new dispositions made every day in the light of circumstances not known the day before, by *B* stepping in at once when *A* fails to deliver. Even the large and highly mechanized plant keeps going largely because of an environment upon which it can draw for all sorts of unexpected needs; tiles for its roof, stationery for its forms, and all the thousand and one kinds of equipment in which it cannot be self-contained and which the plans for the operation of the plant require to be readily available in the market.

This is, perhaps, also the point where I should briefly mention the fact that the sort of knowledge with which I have been concerned is knowledge of the kind which by its nature cannot enter into statistics and therefore cannot be conveyed to any central authority in statistical form. The statistics which such a central authority would have to use would have to be arrived at precisely by abstracting from minor differences between the things, by lumping together, as resources of one kind, items which differ as regards location, quality, and other particulars, in a way which may be very significant for the specific decision. It follows from this that central planning based on statistical information by its nature cannot take direct account of these circumstances of time and place, and that the central planner will have to find some way or other in which the decisions depending on them can be left to the "man on the spot".

## V

If we can agree that the economic problem of society is mainly one of rapid adaptation to changes in the particular circumstances of time and place, it would seem to follow that the ultimate decisions must be left to the people who are familiar with these circumstances, who know directly of the relevant changes and of the resources immediately available to meet them. We cannot expect that this problem will be solved by first communicating all this knowledge to a central board which, after integrating *all* knowledge, issues its orders. We must solve it by some form of decentralization. But this answers only part of our problem. We need decentralization because only thus can we ensure that the knowledge of the particular circumstances of time and place will be promptly used. But the "man on the spot" cannot decide solely on the basis of his limited but intimate knowledge of the facts of his immediate surroundings. There still remains the problem of communicating to him such further information as he needs to fit his decisions into the whole pattern of changes of the larger economic system.

How much knowledge does he need to do so successfully? Which of the events which happen beyond the horizon of his immediate knowledge are of relevance to his immediate decision, and how much of them need he know?

There is hardly anything that happens anywhere in the world that *might* not have an effect on the decision he ought to make. But he need not know of these events as such, nor of *all* their effects. It does not matter for him *why* at the particular moment more screws of one size than of another are wanted, *why* paper bags are more readily available than canvas bags, or *why* skilled labor, or particular machine tools, have for the moment become more difficult to acquire. All that is significant for him is *how much more or less* difficult to procure they have become compared with other things with which he is also concerned, or how much more or less urgently wanted are the alternative things he produces or uses. It is always a question of the relative importance of the particular things with which he is concerned, and the causes which alter their relative importance are of no interest to him beyond the effect on those concrete things of his own environment.

It is in this connection that what I have called the economic calculus proper helps us, at least by analogy, to see how this problem can be solved, and in fact is being solved, by the price system. Even the single controlling mind, in possession of all the data for some small, self-contained economic system, would not — every time some small adjustment in the allocation of resources had to be made — go explicitly through all the relations between ends and means which might possibly be affected. It is indeed the great contribution of the pure logic of choice that it has demonstrated conclusively that even such a single mind could solve this kind of problem only by constructing and constantly using rates of equivalence (or "values," or "marginal rates of substitution"), *i.e.*, by attaching to each kind of scarce resource a numerical index which cannot be derived from any property possessed by that particular thing, but which reflects, or in which is condensed, its significance in view of the whole means-end structure. In any small change he will have to consider only these quantitative indices (or "values") in which all the relevant information is concentrated; and by adjusting the quantities one by one, he can appropriately rearrange his dispositions without having to solve the whole puzzle *ab initio,* or without needing at any stage to survey it at once in all its ramifications.

Fundamentally, in a system where the knowledge of the relevant facts is dispersed among many people, prices can act to coordinate the separate actions of different people in the same way as subjective values help the individual to coordinate the parts of his plan. It is worth contemplating for a moment a very simple and commonplace instance of the action of the price system to see what precisely it accomplishes. Assume that somewhere in the world a new opportunity for the use of some raw material, say tin, has arisen, or that one of the sources of supply of tin has been eliminated. It does not matter for our purpose — and it is very significant that it does not matter — which of these two causes has made tin more scarce. All that the users of tin need to know is that some of the tin they used to consume is now more profitably employed elsewhere, and that in consequence they must economize tin. There is no need for the great majority of them even to know where the more urgent need has arisen, or in favour of what other needs they ought to husband the supply. If only some of them know directly of the new demand, and switch resources over to it, and if the people who are aware of the new gap thus created in turn fill it from still other sources, the effect will rapidly spread throughout the whole economic system and influence not only all the uses of tin, but also those of its substitutes and the substitutes of these substitutes, the supply of all the things made of tin, and their substitutes, and so on; and all this without the great majority of those instrumental in bringing about these substitutions knowing anything at all about the original cause of these changes. The whole acts as one market, not because any of its members survey the whole field, but because their limited individual fields of vision sufficiently overlap so that through many intermediaries the relevant information is communicated to all. The mere fact that there is one price for any commodity — or rather that local prices are connected in a manner determined by the cost of transport, etc. — brings about the solution which (it is just conceptually possible) might have been arrived at by one single mind possessing all the information which is in fact dispersed among all the people involved in the process.

## VI

We must look at the price system as such a mechanism for communicating information if we want to understand its real function — a function which, of course, it fulfils less perfectly as prices grow more rigid. (Even when quoted prices have become quite rigid, however, the forces which would operate through changes in price still operate to a considerable extent through changes in the other terms of the contract.) The most significant fact about this system is the economy of knowledge with which it operates, or how little the individual participants need to know in order to be able to take the right action. In abbreviated form, by a kind of symbol, only the most essential information is passed on, and passed on only to those concerned. It is more than a metaphor to describe the price system as a kind of machinery for registering change, or a system of telecommunications which enables individual producers to watch merely the movement of a few pointers, as an engineer might watch the hands of a few dials, in order to adjust their activities to changes of which they may never know more than is reflected in the price movement.

Of course, these adjustments are probably never "perfect" in the sense in which the economist conceives of them in his equilibrium analysis. But I fear that our theoretical habits of approaching the problem with the assumption of more or less perfect knowledge on the part of almost everyone has made us somewhat blind to the true function of the price mechanism and led us to apply rather misleading standards in judging its efficiency. The marvel is that in a case like that of a scarcity of one raw material, without an order being issued, without more than perhaps a handful of people knowing the cause, tens of thousands of people whose identity could not be ascertained by months of investigation, are made to use the material or its products more sparingly; *i.e.,* they move in the right direction. This is enough of a marvel even if, in a constantly changing world, not all will hit it off so perfectly that their profit rates will always be maintained at the same constant or "normal" level.

I have deliberately used the word "marvel" to shock the reader out of the complacency with which we often take the working of this mechanism for granted. I am convinced that if it were the result of deliberate human design, and if the people guided by the price changes understood that their decisions have significance far beyond their immediate aim, this mechanism would have been acclaimed as one of the greatest triumphs of the human mind. Its misfortune is the double one that it is not the product of human design and that the people guided by it usually do not know why they are made to do what they do. But those who clamour for "conscious direction" — and who cannot believe that anything which has evolved without design (and even without our understanding it) should solve problems which we should not be able to solve consciously — should remember this: The problem is precisely how to extend the span of our utilization of resources beyond the span of the control of any one mind; and, therefore, how to dispense with the need of conscious control and how to provide inducements which will make the individuals do the desirable things without anyone having to tell them what to do.

The problem which we meet here is by no means peculiar to economics but arises in connection with nearly all truly social phenomena, with language and most of our cultural inheritance, and constitutes really the central theoretical problem of all social science. As Alfred Whitehead has said in another connection, "It is a profoundly erroneous truism, repeated by all copy-books and by eminent people when they are making speeches, that we should cultivate the habit of thinking what we are doing. The precise opposite is the case. Civilization advances by extending the number of important operations which we can perform without thinking about them." This is of profound significance in the social field. We make constant use of formulas, symbols and rules whose meaning we do not understand and through the use of which we avail ourselves of the assistance of knowledge which individually we do not possess. We have developed these practices and institutions by building upon habits and institutions which have proved successful in their own sphere and which have in turn become the foundation of the civilization we have built up.

The price system is just one of those formations which man has learned to use (though he is still very far from having learned to make the best use of it) after he had stumbled upon it without understanding it. Through it not only a division of labor but also a coordinated utilization of resources based on an equally divided knowledge has become possible. The people who like to deride any suggestion that this may be so usually distort the argument by insinuating that it asserts that by some miracle just that sort of system has spontaneously grown up which is best suited to modern civilization. It is the other way round: man has been able to develop that division of labor on which our civilization is based because he happened to stumble upon a method which made it possible. Had he not done so he might still have developed some other, altogether different, type of civilization, something like the "state" of the termite ants, or some other altogether unimaginable type. All that we can say is that nobody has yet succeeded in designing an alternative system in which certain features of the existing one can be preserved which are dear even to those who most violently assail it — such as particularly the extent to which the individual can choose his pursuits and consequently freely use his own knowledge and skill.

## VII

It is in many ways fortunate that the dispute about the indispensability of the price system for any rational calculation in a complex society is now no longer conducted entirely between camps holding different political views. The thesis that without the price system we could not preserve a society based on such extensive division of labor as ours was greeted with a howl of derision when it was first advanced by von Mises twenty-five years ago. Today the difficulties which some still find in accepting it are no longer mainly political, and this makes for an atmosphere much more conducive to reasonable discussion. When we find Leon Trotsky arguing that "economic accounting is unthinkable without market relations"; when Professor Oscar Lange promises Professor von Mises a statue in the marble halls of the future Central Planning Board; and when Professor Abba P. Lerner rediscovers Adam Smith and emphasizes that the essential utility of the price system consists in inducing the individual, while seeking his own interest, to do what is in the general interest, the differences can indeed no longer be ascribed to political prejudice. The remaining dissent seems clearly to be due to purely intellectual, and more particularly methodological, differences.

A recent statement by Professor Joseph Schumpeter in his *Capitalism, Socialism and Democracy* provides a clear illustration of one of the methodological differences which I have in mind. Its author is pre-eminent among those economists who approach economic phenomena in the light of a certain branch of positivism. To him these phenomena accordingly appear as objectively given quantities of commodities impinging directly upon each other, almost, it would seem, without any intervention of human minds. Only against this background can I account for the following (to me startling) pronouncement. Professor Schumpeter argues that the possibility of a rational calculation in the absence of markets for the factors of production follows for the theorist "from the elementary proposition that consumers in evaluating ('demanding') consumers' goods *ipso facto* also evaluate the means of production which enter into the production of these goods."[1]

Taken literally, this statement is simply untrue. The consumers do nothing of the kind. What Professor Schumpeter's *"ipso facto"* presumably means is that the valuation of the factors of production is implied in, or follows necessarily from, the valuation of consumers' goods. But this, too, is not correct. Implication is a logical relationship which can be meaningfully asserted only of propositions simultaneously present to one and the same mind. It is evident, however, that the values of the factors of production do not depend solely on the valuation of the consumers' goods but also on the conditions of supply of the various factors of production. Only to a mind to which all these facts were simultaneously known would the answer necessarily follow from the facts given to it. The practical problem, however, arises precisely because these facts are never so given to a single mind, and because, in consequence, it is necessary that in the solution of the problem knowledge should be used that is dispersed among many people.

The problem is thus in no way solved if we can show that all the facts, *if* they were known to a single mind (as we hypothetically assume them to be given to the observing economist), would uniquely determine the solution; instead we must show how a solution is produced by the interactions of people each of whom possesses only partial knowledge. To assume all the knowledge to be given to a single mind in the same manner in which we assume it to be given to us as the explaining

---

[1] J. Schumpeter, *Capitalism, Socialism, and Democracy* (New York, Harper, 1942), p. 175. Professor Schumpeter is, I believe, also the original author of the myth that Pareto and Barone have "solved" the problem of socialist calculation. What they, and many others, did was merely to state the conditions which a rational allocation of resources would have to satisfy, and to point out that these were essentially the same as the conditions of equilibrium of a competitive market. This is something altogether different from showing how the allocation of resources satisfying these conditions can be found in practice. Pareto himself (from whom Barone has taken practically everything he has to say), far from claiming to have solved the practical problem, in fact explicitly denies that it can be solved without the help of the market. See his *Manuel d'économie pure* (2nd ed., 1.927), pp. 233-34. The relevant passage is quoted in an English translation at the beginning of my article on "Socialist Calculation: The Competitive 'Solution,'" in *Economica,* New Series, Vol. VIII, No. 26 (May, 1940), p. 125.

economists is to assume the problem away and to disregard everything that is important and significant in the real world.

That an economist of Professor Schumpeter's standing should thus have fallen into a trap which the ambiguity of the term "datum" sets to the unwary can hardly be explained as a simple error. It suggests rather than there is something fundamentally wrong with an approach which habitually disregards an essential part of the phenomena with which we have to deal: the unavoidable imperfection of man's knowledge and the consequent need for a process by which knowledge is constantly communicated and acquired. Any approach, such as that of much of mathematical economics with its simultaneous equations, which in effect starts from the assumption that people's *knowledge* corresponds with the objective *facts* of the situation, systematically leaves out what is our main task to explain. I am far from denying that in our system equilibrium analysis has a useful function to perform. But when it comes to the point where it misleads some of our leading thinkers into believing that the situation which it describes has direct relevance to the solution of practical problems, it is time that we remember that it does not deal with the social process at all and that it is no more than a useful preliminary to the study of the main problem.

# Name Index

# Subject Index